After t
The Francophone World and
Postcolonial France

Series Editor
Valérie Orlando, Illinois Wesleyan University

Advisory Board
Robert Bernasconi, Memphis University
Alec Hargreaves, Florida State University
Chima Korieh, Central Michigan University
Françoise Lionnet, UCLA
Obioma Nnaemeka, Indiana University
Kamal Salhi, University of Leeds
Tracy D. Sharpley-Whiting, Hamilton College
Frank Ukadike, Tulane University

Dedicated to the promotion of intellectual thought on and about the Francophone world, *After the Empire* publishes original works that explore the arts, politics, history, and culture that have developed in complex negotiations with the French colonial influence. The series also looks at the Hexagon and its borders, and at the transgressions of those borders that problematize notions of French identity and expression.

Of Suffocated Hearts and Tortured Souls: Seeking Subjecthood through Madness in Francophone Women's Writing of Africa and the Caribbean, by Valérie Orlando

Francophone Post-Colonial Cultures: Critical Essays, edited by Kamal Salhi

In Search of Shelter: Subjectivity and Spaces of Loss in the Fiction of Paule Constant, by Margot Miller

French Civilization and Its Discontents: Nationalism, Colonialism, Race, edited by Tyler Stovall and Georges Van Den Abbeele

After the Deluge: New Perspectives on Postwar French Intellectual and Cultural History, edited by Julian Bourg with an Afterword by François Dosse

Remnants of Empire in Algeria and Vietnam: Women, Words, and War, by Pamela A. Pears

Packaging Post/Coloniality: The Manufacture of Literary Identity in the Francophone World, by Richard Watts

The Production of the Muslim Woman: Negotiating Text, History, and Ideology, by Lamia Ben Youssef Zayzafoon

France and "Indochina": Cultural Representations, edited by Kathryn Robson and Jennifer Yee

Against the Postcolonial: 'Francophone' Writers at the Ends of French Empire, by Richard Serrano

Youth Mobilization in Vichy Indochina and Its Legacies, 1940 to 1970, by Anne Raffin

Afrique sur Seine: A New Generation of African Writers in Paris, by Odile Cazenave

France and "Indochina"

Cultural Representations

Edited by
Kathryn Robson and Jennifer Yee

LEXINGTON BOOKS
Lanham • Boulder • New York • Toronto • Oxford

LEXINGTON BOOKS

Published in the United States of America
by Lexington Books
An imprint of The Rowman & Littlefield Publishing Group, Inc.
4501 Forbes Boulevard, Suite 200, Lanham, Maryland 20706

PO Box 317
Oxford
OX2 9RU, UK

British Library Cataloguing in Publication Information Available

Library of Congress Cataloging-in-Publication Data

France and Indochina : cultural representations / edited by
Kathryn Robson and Jennifer Yee.
     p. cm. — (After the empire)
  Includes bibliographical references and index.
  ISBN 0-7391-0839-5 (cloth : alk. paper) — ISBN 0-7391-
0840-9 (pbk. : alk. paper)
  1. Indochina—Foreign public opinion, French. 2.
Indochina—Civilization. 3. Indochina—Relations—France. 4.
France—Relations—Indochina. 5. Public opinion—France. I.
Robson, Kathryn. II. Yee, Jennifer. III. Series.
DS546.5.F8F73 2005
959.7'03—dc22   2005006746

Printed in the United States of America

♾™ The paper used in this publication meets the minimum requirements of American
National Standard for Information Sciences—Permanence of Paper for Printed Library
Materials, ANSI/NISO Z39.48–1992.

Contents

Transport Networks

Tropical angst?

Women in and against Empire

Screening Indochina

      Carrie Tarr

Writing Indochina

11.   From Incest to Exile: Linda Lê and the Incestuous   165
      Vietnamese Immigrants
      Tess Do

12.   "Cholen, la capitale chinoise de l'Indochine française":   179
      Rereading Marguerite Duras's (Indo)Chinese Novels
      Julia Waters

13.   Playing Hardball: Linda Lê's *Les Trois Parques*   193
      Jane Bradley Winston

14.   Jean Hougron's Indochina: Fantasy and Disillusionment   207
      Jack A. Yeager

      Selected Bibliography   219

      Name Index   229

      Contributors' Details   235

Illustrations

Acknowledgments

The individual chapters of this volume are considerably revised and extended versions of papers presented at the conference "'Indochina,' India and France: Cultural Representations," held at the University of Newcastle (GB) in September 2003. It was not possible to include all the papers, but the editors would like to thank all the participants in what was a very exciting conference.

We would also like to thank the Institut français, the Society for French Studies, the Society for Francophone Postcolonial Studies, and the Arts and Humanities Research Fund of Newcastle University, for their financial assistance in organizing the conference. We are also grateful to Professor Brian Stimpson of Newcastle University for his contributions to the organization of the conference; and to the conference advisory committee, Nicola Cooper, Rachel Edwards and Panivong Norinder.

Our thanks, finally, to Serena Krombach of Lexington Books for her advice and support in preparing this volume.

Foreword

Panivong Norindr

Fifty years after the defeat of French forces at Dien Bien Phu, it might be thought that relations between France and its ex-colonies in Indochina belong to a past all the more distant and relegated to history that it has been followed by what was, for the French, the greater trauma of the Algerian war, and for the Vietnamese the anguish of their war of resistance against American imperialism. But the chapter is far from closed.

The work of francophone writers of Vietnamese descent such as Linda Lê and Anna Moï complicates in a challenging and imaginative fashion our understanding of French colonialism and American imperialism in the Indochinese peninsula. Their dark and vibrant work takes the unequal relation of power that characterized French or American hegemony over Cambodia, Laos, and Vietnam in new and unexpected directions. The traumatic experience of war and the resilience of the Vietnamese people during their struggle to liberate themselves from foreign hegemony continue to be vividly examined in their short stories and novels, but the literary representation of this entanglement in and with history takes us on a less trodden path, quite remote from the sentimentalizing impulse pervasive in the fiction and novels of acculturation of the previous generation of writers. Their protagonists find themselves in uncharted and dangerous territories. In Anna Moï's first novel *Riz noir* (2004), for instance, the Suong sisters, French-educated young *lycéennes* who chose to fight the oppressive South Vietnamese regime of Ngô Đình Diệm, are emblematic figures of colonized subjects who have chosen to be historical agents of change rather than passive and acculturated victims, even if it means detention, physical torture and mental persecution in the infamous Poulo-Condor penal colony. Like the widely disseminated photographs of the abuse of Abu Ghraib prisoners in our own time, the graphic depiction of the tortured bodies of these adolescent modern-day Trung Sisters should not simply make us recoil in horror, but elicit the type of probing reflection that aims to uncover the historical circumstances that produced these young and courageous resistance fighters. Linda Lê's protagonists also undermine the colonial and postcolonial order of things but on a different register. By narrating the desire and experience of dislocated subjects who reject the normative discourse on exile and diaspora, she explores, in an impressive corpus of texts, the aesthetic and political stakes in being at home in the in-between space of culture and nation.

The vibrant work of these Francophone Vietnamese writers is matched by the equally exciting filmic production of directors like Lâm Lê, Trần Anh Hùn, and Rithy Panh, a new wave of diasporic Francophone filmmakers from Vietnam and Cambodia currently living and working in France. Their work not only functions in dialogue with productions by French filmmakers like Régis Wargnier and Jean-Jacques Annaud, it also challenges the accepted boundaries of national and cultural identity. In short, they provide not so much a corrective to the stereotypical image of the native Indochinese women fetichized by French writers and filmmakers alike, but an alternative and more nuanced view of the ambivalent relation linking France and Indochina. These demanding works that also reflect on key issues such as the notion of testimonial, eyewitnessing, individual and collective memory as well as the inscription of the subject in a transnational world, constitute the leading edge of textual and filmic experimentation, which has inspired many of the innovative scholarly essays collected in this volume. This rewriting of colonial history and undermining of imperialist dichotomies, so striking in the cinematic and literary productions of the ex-Indochinese diaspora today, suggest the importance of turning a renewed critical gaze on the historic entanglement between France and Indochina. With its sophisticated new critical analyses of that encounter from a number of disciplinary and theoretical locations, this volume is indeed a timely and important contribution to the scholarly corpus on Francophone South East Asia.

Introduction

Kathryn Robson and Jennifer Yee

"Indochina" was a French invention. A political and administrative tool used in the management of a large area of Southeast Asia, the "Union indochinoise" was created by the French Third Republic in 1887, bringing together Cambodia, Laos (from 1893 onwards), and the three *ky* or regions of what is now modern Vietnam—Annam, Cochin-China and Tonkin. Yet the term "Indochina" also evokes an imagined land that had—and has—a particular significance in "l'imaginaire français."

As its name suggests, the area was defined first and foremost as the point of contact between the Indian and Chinese civilizations. Invented almost simultaneously by a Danish geographer working for Napoleon, Conrad Malte-Brun (1775-1826) and a Scottish linguist, John Leyden (1775-1811), the term "Indo-Chine" arose naturally in response to this concept of a frontier zone (the hyphen was to disappear in the following decades).

"Indochina" is now often seen by cultural historians as an "artificial construction," an "elaborate fiction."[1] More traditional historians such as Pierre Brocheux and Daniel Hémery, however, react against this idea: "French Indochina, far from being artificial, was the result not only of the process of events and the shock of opposing initiatives but the application of a program mapped out in advance." From this point of view French Indochina was a logical result of the reorganization of Far-Eastern political space after the weakening of the Chinese civilization/State and the rival aggressions of British and French imperialism.[2] The argument appears to depend on a linguistic nuance concerning the meaning of the word "artificial:" there seems to be general agreement that the unity of Indochina (which we will refer to from now onward without scare quotes) was the product of French imperialism, but the process behind this im-

1

perialism was more complex than might at first be thought, as Brocheux and Hémery very capably demonstrate.

The motivations for France's imperial domination of Indochina were partly economic.[3] France's territories in the area were effectively, if not all in name, *colonies d'exploitation* rather than settler colonies like Algeria, although there were (not particularly successful) attempts to attract more French settlers to Vietnam, as Marie-Paule Ha's chapter in this volume attests. The number of French inhabitants of Indochina reached a peak of around 34,000 in 1940. Economic motivations also included the tantalizing possibility of opening up a trade route to South China. But France's ambitions were perhaps more immediately inspired by the desire to affirm its status as one of the "Great Powers," in particular in rivalry with Britain. Having lost most of its Indian imperial possessions to Britain, France's hopes of remaining a Power in Asia were pinned to its domination of Indochina. The key symbolic role of Angkor as a response to Britain's domination of India is analyzed in Penny Edward's contribution here.

This volume concerns the representations or frames through which Franco-Indochinese relations were understood in the modern period, from the late nineteenth century to the present day, a period which includes the heyday of colonialism, decolonization, and the new post-colonial relations that have fallen into place since then. It is arranged thematically rather than chronologically, in order to establish links across disciplines and periods. This last part of this introduction gives a succinct historical overview of representations which will help the less expert reader to situate the individual chapters within a chronology.

Cultural Representations, Intercultural Frames

The chapters collected here approach strikingly different sources and materials (archival, literary, cinematic and visual, amongst others) from a wide range of critical perspectives. If they can be grouped under the tentative heading of "cultural studies," this is only insofar as the term allows approaches through a variety of academic disciplines including history, literary studies and film studies. What links these chapters is a common focus on cultural representations of Indochina within their specific social, historical and political context. An emphasis akin to that of Pierre Nora's project in *Les Lieux de mémoire* (*Realms of Memory*), where he calls for a history "not of actions as they are committed to memory or even commemorated, but of the trace of these actions and the play of commemorations; not of events in themselves, but of their construction over time, the obliteration and resurgence of their meanings; not of the past as it happened, but of its constant reinvestments, its uses and misuses, its potentiality in successive presents."[4]

The representations looked at here run parallel to a history of events (*histoire événementielle*), yet arguably the latter can only be perceived through the former, since what we know of the past is so often only glimpsed through a textual residue or a series of frames that are necessarily "representational" rather than directly "representative." The post-colonial critic Gayatri Chakravorty Spivak identifies two types of representation, *Vertretung* (meaning "proxy," or "stepping in someone's place") and *Darstellung*, meaning "portrait" or "placing there," yet she goes on to emphasize that the two are inextricably interwoven.[5] Speaking for another person, or a designated group, also inevitably means constructing a portrait of that individual or collective, whilst the act of naming or defining a group necessarily implies speaking on its behalf. Spivak thus distinguishes between these two modes of "representation" only to warn us that they are ultimately both at play in any attempt to portray or speak for cultures, peoples, nationalities, and so on; "unless the complicity between these two things is kept in mind, there can be a great deal of political harm."[6] This volume deliberately does not claim to offer a "representative" portrait of any "real" or originary Indochina nor to speak on behalf of any "authentic" "native" voice; instead, it seeks to explore how various (literary, cinematic, archival, visual) representations of Indochina have been negotiated and framed.

Inevitably these chapters therefore tell us more about France and French attitudes than they do about Indochina or Indochinese points of view. As the title of the volume suggests, cultural representations are (at the least) double: not only implying French views on Indochina, but also the ways in which France has been portrayed within Indochina itself and by those people from Indochina who lived in or visited France. Both the spiritual and political leader Hồ Chí Minh and the infamous Pol Pot spent some of their formative years living in Paris. Judith Henchy's contribution to this volume suggests the complex ways in which French culture provided modernizing "frames" for women in 1930s Vietnam. The majority of contributions to this volume, however, analyze representations that offer most insight into the culture, history and politics of France. French imperialism in Indochina was the product of a particular mindset that must be located historically as well as culturally: scientific imperialism, the "mission civilisatrice" and industrialization went hand in hand with France's Republican ideology and ambitions as a "Great Power" on the global stage.

To situate the individual contributions of this volume within a broader view of these cultural representations, a brief (and necessarily incomplete) chronological survey is offered below.

Towards a Chronology of "Representations": Beginnings

The first direct contacts between France and the countries that she was one day to call Indochina date back to the seventeenth century, and were primarily due to missionaries who established Christian communities there. A modern reflection of early contacts in the eighteenth century is the short tale *Annam*, by Christophe Bataille (1996), in which Dominican monks live and die as missionaries in Vietnam while Revolution shakes their homeland.[7]

No doubt the most important cultural inheritance of these early contacts was the introduction of *quốc ngữ*, which transcribed Vietnamese using Latin characters, thus providing an alternative to the use of Chinese characters. First invented by Portuguese missionaries, *quốc ngữ* was perfected in the seventeenth century by the French Jesuit Alexandre de Rhodes (1591-1660) and although initially intended as a tool for evangelization, it was to play a major role in Vietnamese modernization and in the affirmation of Vietnam's identity as an independent modern state.

The protection of French missionaries provided the pretext for military intervention from 1858 onwards.[8] From the beginning these contacts generated textual representations, often first-person *témoignages* written by missionaries such as Charles-Emile Bouilleveaux (*Voyages dans l'Indochine, 1848-1856*, 1858) or explorers such as the botanist and entomologist Henri Mouhot (1826-1861) who spent three weeks in Angkor in 1860 and described it in his journal which was published posthumously in 1863.[9] Many of the major actors of the colonial conquest staked territorial claims not only through exploration and military prowess but also through textual representation: Jean Dupuis (1829-1912), the arms trader whose attempt to open a trade route along the Red River and resulting conflicts with Vietnamese mandarins triggered outright hostilities in 1873, published books and articles on his travels; Francis Garnier (1839-1873), the military commander sent to support him, wrote a *Voyage d'exploration en Indochine,* in which he recounts his exploration of the Mekong; it was published in 1873, the year he was killed at the citadel of Hanoi.[10]

Colonization of Indochina thus began more or less without a concerted plan. A protectorate was established in Cambodia, and Cochin-China (South Vietnam) was conquered in the early period 1858-1867; a further period of military conquest and intense resistance, in 1883, was to be the subject of a novel by Albert de Pouvourville, in which he adopts the point of view of one of the leaders of the resistance against the French (*L'Annam sanglant,* 1898). In these early years French political opinion was split between the colonial party that sought to maintain France's rank as a "Great Power" through expansion abroad, and those who feared the expenses of such expansion, or would prefer *la Revanche* (revenge) against Prussia for the loss of Alsace and Lorraine in 1870. Indochina was central to debates on colonial issues in this period of hesitation at the beginning of the Third Republic. Jules Ferry (1832-1893) backed a policy of colonial expansion and decided on the conquest of Tonkin, but defeat and the evacuation of Lang Son caused the fall of his Ministry on March 30, 1885 (the "crise de Tonkin"); by June 9, however, a French protectorate had been established over all of Indochina.

The Colonial Heyday

Imperialism in general, and Indochina along with it, became an integral part of the political and popular culture of the Third Republic.[11] The conquest of Indochina was officially complete in 1896, though some "pacification" continued until after the first World War. Symptomatic of this new wave of popular interest and enthusiasm was the arrival in Indochina of journalists whose articles appeared in the newspapers that had financed their travels, and were often then published in separate volumes. Paul Bonnetain (1858-1899), for example, worked as a reporter for *Le Figaro*, and subsequently published his collected articles (*Au Tonkin*, 1885), as well as a novel (*L'Opium*, 1886) and some short stories (*Amours nomades*, 1888). Travel writing of all kinds remained an important textual "frame" for metropolitan experiences of Indochina, and descriptions of the ruins of Angkor in Cambodia, and in particular of the temple Angkor Wat, were a recurrent theme (notably *Un pèlerin d'Angkor* by Pierre Loti, 1911[12]). But the last decades of the nineteenth century and the first thirty years of the twentieth also saw the publication of a considerable number of novels concerning Indochina, often written by officers or civil servants in the colonies themselves.

Various "genres" can be distinguished in this flourishing production of fiction. The archeologist and literary critic Louis Malleret (1901-1970) distinguishes between what he calls "le cycle européen" ("the European cycle") and the "cycle asiatique" ("the Asian cycle"): the former tells the tale of the conquest, and of the life of Europeans in Indochina, while the latter analyses "l'âme indigène" ("the native soul").[13] Novels dealing with the European cycle told of heroic exploration or conquest or, in a more or less satirical vein, examined expatriate society itself. As for those which claimed to analyze "l'âme indigène"—native society and psychology—one can cite as an example *La Barque annamite* (1910), by Emile Nolly (a.k.a. Emile Détanger, 1880-1914). Many novels, however, combine these two approaches, attempting to describe the relationship between the "Whites" and the "natives," often looking primarily at the mixed couple in which a white man took a native mistress, called a *congaie* (or sometimes a "petite épouse," as is suggested by the title of a novel by Myriam Harry: *Petites épouses*, 1901). In many writings the city of Saigon itself emerges as a topos of corruption, a citadel of turn-of-the century decadence denounced (and celebrated) in *Les Civilisés* by Claude Farrère (1876-1957), which won the Prix Goncourt in 1905. Indochina is a literary pretext for the exploration of easy relationships with sometimes extremely young native girls, but also homosexuality and the ambiguities of androgyny.[14] Another important "decadent" theme of the Indochinese colonial novel was opium (see in particular Jules Boissière (1863-1897), *Fumeurs d'opium*, 1896); around the same time, with more hardheaded realism, the fiscal reforms of governor-general Paul Doumer (1857-1932) instituted a state monopoly on sales of opium (as well as alcohol and salt), and encouraged its use by the native population. A minority of texts reveal a fascination with Buddhism or Taoism and the character of the mandarin/sage who has renounced the follies of the world (see for example Albert de Pouvourville, *L'Heure silencieuse*, 1923).

Somewhat paradoxically, much colonial writing appears, almost in spite of itself, to analyze the failure of the French imperial ideal of assimilation. Many colonial textual and graphic representations reflect a deep underlying unease with the role of the French colonists, as shown in the chapters by Nicola Cooper

and Michael Vann in this volume. Further undermining the image of a successful French colonialism, texts that set out to analyze the psychology of the natives often present them as being *impénétrables*, impossible to understand; other
recurrent clichés are their treachery and the cupidity of women and "boys"
(male servants) alike. From the 1920s onward, a series of novels analyze the
shame and difficulties of the *métis*, the mixed-race child born to a white man
and a native woman (for example Herbert Wild, *L'Autre race*, 1920; Clotilde
Chivas-Baron (*Confidences de métisse*, 1927); Jehan Cendrieux, *François
Phuoc, métis*, 1929). Among the many other novelists writing on Indochinese
themes in the 1920s and 1930s are Jean Marquet (*La Jaune et le Blanc*, 1926),
and several female writers such as Jeanne Leuba (*L'Aile du feu*, 1920) and
Yvonne Schultz (*Le Sampanier de la Baie d'Along*, 1931).[15]

The best known French novel of Indochina from this period is of course
André Malraux's novel of jungle exploration and danger, *La Voie royale*, which
revisits the Khmer ruins in Cambodia as the site of a phantasmatic masculinity
(1930).[16] Yet the colonial imaginary more often depicted Cambodia, like Laos,
as docile, peaceful, and rural; less developed than Annam, Tonkin or Cochin-
China (modern Vietnam), but inhabited by a gentler people with whom the
colonizer lived in harmony.

Another surprising (and largely forgotten) characteristic of French textual
production during the height of the colonial period (1880s-1930s) is the preva-
lence of poetry. The early poets were inspired in particular by the poetry of
Baudelaire and Parnassus: Maurice Olivaint (*Les Fleurs du Mékong*, 1894);
Alfred Droin (*La Jonque victorieuse*, 1907); Stéphane Moreau (*Les Jardins de
l'Orient*, 1904); or continuing into the 1930s, Raphaël Barquissau (*Poèmes
d'Asie et des Îles*, 1930). The first work published in French by an Indochinese
writer was a volume of poetry (Nguyễn Văn Nho, *Mes heures perdues*, 1913);
other poets later adapted local poetry into French: Makhali Phal (*Cambodge*,
1933; *Le Chant de paix*, 1937), Phạm Văn Ky (*Fleurs de jade*, 1943) and Trần
Văn Tùng (*Poésies d'Extrême-Orient*, 1945). This was a period of intense literary production in French by Vietnamese writers, continuing even after 1954.[17]

The 1920s and 1930s saw an increased resistance to colonialism, notably
with the insurrection at Yen Bay in 1929. The 1930s were however marked by
the rise of a more celebratory "colonial" ideology; in reactionary mode, the expatriate community sought to celebrate its own colonial literature with several
works of literary criticism, and the introduction of literary prizes. The new literature, it was claimed, reflected the exemplary quality of Indochina which was
a model of harmonious colonization, where East met West at last.[18] Much of the
textual and graphic production of colonial Indochina sought in various ways to
celebrate the industrial and economic development of the region under French
domination. Many early postcards emphasize European-style colonial buildings,
and also bridges, hospitals, and schools. As well as introducing major im-
provements in health care (which were to result in a demographic explosion
whose effects are still felt in Vietnam today), the French did indeed construct
schools, which replaced the system of training for the mandarins who had run

the bureaucracy in the past; in 1942, 731,000 children were in schooling (from a total population of 24.6 million), and there were over a thousand students at the Université indochinoise in Hanoi. A major part of the *mise en valeur* of the region depended on the construction of transportation networks—roads, bridges, railways—and this laborious "opening up" of the more remote areas was explored by literary and nonliterary texts alike, as David del Testa and Christopher Robinson's contributions to this volume attest. French Indochina was celebrated in various colonial exhibitions, culminating in the Colonial Exhibition of 1931, held in the Bois de Vincennes, whose centerpiece was a full-scale model of Angkor Wat.[19]

For Indochina to be seen as a model colony, it was necessary for colonial textual representation to maintain a conscious or subconscious denial of resistance to imperialism, and as early as the 1880s one finds the theme of "la piraterie" (pirates) as a way of dismissing an underground struggle that can be seen as foreshadowing General Võ Nguyên Giáp's (1911-) development of guerilla warfare in the twentieth century. The *Cần Vương* ("Support for the King") movement in Vietnam was, though fragmented, a national uprising against the occupying power. Annam, like Cambodia, technically remained a protectorate rather than a colony, with France maintaining a native monarch who was deprived of any real power (interestingly, both the emperor of Annam, Bảo Đại (1913-1997), and the King of Cambodia, Norodom Sihanouk (1922-), were to publish their memoirs, contributing their own strands to the web of textual representations). With the ruling dynasty of Vietnam largely discredited by collaboration, it was succeeded, from the late nineteenth-century onward, by one of the earliest nationalist movements in the history of decolonization. The very existence of these resistance movements—nationalist-traditionalist, revolutionary, or mystical and millenarian in their inspiration—was frequently denied by colonialist discourse. In fact, various groups of Marxist-Leninist inspiration were active from the 1920s onward, and in 1930 they were united in the Parti communiste indochinois under the guidance of Nguyễn Ái Quốc, who was to be known under the name of Hồ Chí Minh (1890-1969).

French Defeat and Decolonization

The rise of communist and nationalist resistance in Vietnam was helped by the effects of the depression, and French psychological, as well as political domination was profoundly shaken by France's defeat in the Second World War and Japan's occupation of Vietnam. When the Japanese surrendered in 1945, the puppet emperor, Bảo Đại, abdicated and Hồ Chí Minh proclaimed the Democratic Republic of Vietnam. An attempt to negotiate an agreement between the Viet Minh and the French failed, and "la guerre d'Indochine," or from the Vietnamese point of view the First War of Resistance,[20] began. There is clearly no space within this introduction to recount this war, which remains today the most frequently studied and narrated period of Vietnamese history in France. The war

was to last for seven and a half years, during which it was increasingly unpopular in metropolitan France. General Giáp's combination of guerilla and conventional warfare, along with the aid, after 1949, of communist China, were too
much for the French despite the financial support of the United States (which
paid more than half of their war budget from 1952 onward), and the war culmi-
nated in the Viet Minh victory at Dien Bien Phu in 1954. This victory over the
elite of the French army was to signal the possibility of independence to all of
France's colonies. The Geneva agreement concluded with the withdrawal of the
French from all of Indochina (the last troops left South Vietnam in 1956), ending a century of French colonization in Southeast Asia. It also divided Vietnam
along the seventeenth parallel, leaving the Viet Minh in control north of that
line and to the South a regime supported by the United States, a situation that
would lead to the second Vietnamese war of independence, that the English-
speaking world knows as the Vietnam war. Although it is outside the scope of
this volume, it is interesting to note that a search for Vietnamese subjects in
English-language bookshops reveals an enormous majority of publications on
the American-Vietnamese war (1964-1973), while a similar search in France
unearths volumes on France's own "guerre d'Indochine" (1946-1954); a double
perspective on the wars that dominated Vietnamese history in the twentieth century that is a salutary reminder of the relativism of cultural perspectives.

The 1940s saw a much reduced Franco-Indochinese literary production, but
in the 1950s new writers with a journalistic style emerged: Jean Hougron, discussed in Jack Yeager's chapter in this volume, as well as Jean Lartéguy and
Lucien Bodard.[21] Graham Greene's *The Quiet American* (1955) also put Indochina on the literary map in the English-speaking world for the first time. Marguerite Duras (1914-1996) published her first work set in Indochina, *Un Barrage contre le Pacifique* (*Sea wall*) (1950); she was to return to the themes and
places of *Un Barrage* again and again, in *L'Amant* (1984) and *L'Amant de la
Chine du Nord* (1991).[22] These later texts are both analyzed by Julia Waters'
chapter here.

Postcolonialism and Colonial Nostalgia

The Guerre d'Indochine and decolonization were the subject of troubled reac-
tions in France from the 1950s onward, since the war had generally been fairly
unpopular and some activists, of anticolonial or communist affiliation, had actively supported decolonization and sometimes even the Viet Minh; the amnesty
of 1966, for crimes committed in Algeria, was extended to Indochina. Yet as
recently as 1991 the "cas Boudarel" saw accusations of torture against Georges
Boudarel, an anticolonialist who had joined the Viet Minh.[23] The commemoration of France's dead in a war that had little popular support in some cases
waited until the 1980s, with the inauguration of the Monument aux morts
d'Indochine in Fréjus (in 1983; Prime Minister Jacques Chirac inaugurated a
collective tomb there in 1988), and the appropriation of the Indochinese *monu-*

ment aux morts of Nogent-sur-Marne, as explored by Eric Jennings' contribution to this volume; the 1980s also saw the publication of several books on the French prisoners of the Viet Minh.

In 1975 the Viet Minh forces took Saigon, thus unifying the country once again for the first time in over a century. The years 1975-1979 also saw the domination of Cambodia by the Khmer rouge under Pol Pot (1925-1998). Throughout the late 1970s hundreds of thousands of people fled Laos, Cambodia and Vietnam in fear of political persecution; they became known as "Boat people," and many of them were accepted in France. French imaginings of Indochina are now being rewritten by these Vietnamese, Cambodian and Laotian immigrants in France itself.

With the fall of the Berlin wall, and new critiques of communism as a totalitarian ideology even in France (where the left had traditionally had much sympathy for communism), the memory of French imperialism in Indochina appears to have been rehabilitated and the word "Indochine" has regained a certain power to evoke past colonial grandeur to French ears. Thus the 1990s saw the development of a new mythic, cinematographic Indochina: in 1992 alone appeared Jean-Jacques Annaud's adaption of Marguerite Duras's novel *L'Amant*; Régis Warnier's *Indochine* (discussed in Lily Chiu's chapter in this volume), and Pierre Schoendoerffer's *Dien Bien Phu*. This cinema of the 1990s can be seen as renewing many of the "phantasms that have sustained the myths of the legitimacy of the French colonial presence in Indochina—founding myths of this 'geographical romance.'"[24] This is not, of course, the whole story: as Carrie Tarr argues in her chapter in this volume, Trần Anh Hùng, one of the most globally acclaimed directors of Vietnamese descent, has produced quite different representations of France and of Vietnam.

From the early twentieth century onward a certain number of Vietnamese writers chose to write in French, but Vietnamese literature in French has been completely rejuvenated by the descendants of the Vietnamese refugees of the 1970s living in France. This new "post-colonial," migrant literature includes the Eurasian Kim Lefèvre, a translator of Vietnamese texts who has also published autofictional texts (*Métisse Blanche*, 1989; *Retour à la saison des pluies*, 1990). And much more stylistically innovative, Linda Lê's writings are now attracting a growing respect in France and elsewhere (in particular *Les Trois Parques*, 1997; *Lettre morte*, 1999). Lê, born in Vietnam but now living in France, refuses any kind of ethnic labeling, insisting, for example, that she does not consider herself to be a Vietnamese francophone writer.[25] Responding to the implicit challenges of situating Lê's writing, the chapters by Jane Winston and Tess Do in this volume both reframe Lê's texts and analyze the framing devices within the texts themselves to consider how they fit into and reshape different literary traditions within this "post-colonial" context.

The revival of representations of Indochina over the last decade or so in films and in literary texts written in French highlights that Indochina is far from forgotten in French cultural productions. Yet what is at stake in these representations of Indochina and of France? This is the question that this volume seeks to address, underlining once more that "colonization is not completely over to-day, that it continues in the obscurity of the collective unconscious."[26] Re-writing colonialism is still of immediate relevance to the twenty-first century, and even as this book is being prepared, new cultural representations through which France contemplates its Indochinese past are emerging. Jean-Jacques Annaud's most recent film, *Deux frères* (2004) offers a satirical vision of colo-nialism through the adventures of two tigers in Indochina in the 1920s; Linda Lê's *Kriss* (2004) uses Greek myth and Shakespeare as part of a meditation on a chain of bloodshed inherited from the Vietnam War. These very recent produc-tions implicitly return to and rewrite earlier representations of France and of Indochina while paving the way for new and different forms and modes of rep-resentation in the twenty-first century.

Notes

1. Nicola Cooper, *France in Indochina: Colonial Encounters* (Oxford/New York: Berg, 2001), 5; Panivong Norindr, *Phantasmatic Indochina: French Colonial Ideology in Architecture, Film, and Literature* (Durham/London: Duke University Press, 1996), 1.

2. Pierre Brocheux and Daniel Hémery, *Indochine, la colonisation ambiguë 1858-1954* (Paris: La Découverte, 2001), 72, 13. This and subsequent translations are the authors' own.

3. Although the results were initially disappointing, by 1897 colonization of Annam and Tonkin were running at a profit and would in general continue to do so. Brocheux and Hémery, *Indochine*, 83-84, 99.

4. Pierre Nora, ed. *Les Lieux de mémoire* (Paris: Gallimard, 1997), vol. 2, 2229.

5. Gayatri Chakravorty Spivak, "Practical Politics of the Open End," in *The Post-Colonial Critic: Interviews, Strategies, Dialogues* (New York and London: Routledge, 1990), 95-112, 108.

6. Spivak, "Practical Politics of the Open End," 109.

7. English translation as *Annam*, by Richard Howard (New York: New Directions, 1996).

8. For more details of the impact of Christianity and the early French contacts in Viet-nam, see "Vietnam, 1802-1867," in *In Search of Southeast Asia: A Modern History*, ed. David Joel Steinberg (University of Hawai'i Press, 1987 (First edition 1971)), 128-38.

9. His journal was published in English as early as 1864, and the same translation has been reedited more recently by Oxford University Press.

10. English translations of Garnier's travel writing by Walter E. J. Tips are published by White Lotus (Bangkok, 1996).

11. On the rise of colonial ideology in France, see Raoul Girardet, *L'Idée coloniale en France* (Paris: La Table Ronde, 1972).

12. English translation by W. P. Baines and Michael Smithies (Chiang Mai: Silkworm Books, 1996/99).

13. Louis Malleret, *L'Exotisme indochinois dans la littérature française depuis 1860* (Paris: Larose, 1934).

14. For more on this subject, see Jennifer Yee, "'L'Indochine androgyne': the Curious Theme of Androgyny in Turn-of-the-century French Writing on 'Indochina,'" in *Textual Practice*, 15: 2 (Summer 2001): 269-82.

15. Useful re-editions of colonial literary works have been published recently by the Editions Kailash (Paris/Pondicherry); some are available in Alain Quella-Villéger's anthology *Indochine: un rêve d'Asie* (Paris: Omnibus, 1995).

16. English translation published by Stuart Gilbert as *The Royal Way* (New York: Vintage, 1961). For further analysis of *La Voie royale* see, among others, Panivong Norindr, *Phantasmatic Indochina*, ch. 4.

17. See Jack Yeager, *The Vietnamese Novel in French: A Literary Response to Colonialism* (Hanover/London: University Press of New England, 1987), particularly 46-60.

18. Raphaël Barquisseau, *Les Poètes de l'Indochine et l'Indochine des Poètes* (Saigon: Imprimerie moderne J. Testelin, 1932), 33.

19. For an analysis of the 1931 exhibition in particular see Nicola Cooper, *France in Indochina*, chapter 4; Panivong Norindr, *Phantasmatic Indochina*, chapter 1; Pascal Blanchard and Sandrine Lemaire, *Culture coloniale: La France conquise par son Empire 1871-1931* (Paris: Autrement, 2003), 201-31.

20. See for example Nguyễn Khắc Viện, *Vietnam: A Long History* (Hanoi: Thế Giới Publishers, 1999).

21. Many different titles by Hougron, Lartéguy and Bodard are available in English translation.

22. English translations are available for most of Duras's work: *The Sea Wall*, trans. Herma Briffault (1952; several re-editions), *The Lover*, trans. Barbara Bray (London: Bloomsbury Publishing, 1993); *The North China Lover*, trans. Leigh Hafrey (London: Flamingo, 1994).

23. Pierre Brocheux, "Le Cas Boudarel," in *Indochine/Vietnam: Colonisation, Guerres et Communisme* (Numéro spécial, *L'Histoire*, 23, April-June 2004), 62-63.

24. Panivong Norindr, *Phantasmatic Indochina*, 132.

25. See Jack Yeager, "Culture, Citizenship, Nation: The Narrative Texts of Linda Lê," in *Postcolonial Cultures in France*, eds. Alec G Hargreaves and Mark McKinney (London: Routledge, 1997), 255-67, 257.

26. Brocheux and Hémery, *Indochine*, 8.

1

Taj Angkor:
Enshrining *l'Inde* in *le Cambodge*

Penny Edwards

Writing in 1951, France's longest-serving curator at Angkor, Henri Marchal, declared that for both the Hindus and the Khmers "who received their civilization and their religions from India, the material world . . . [is] nothing but appearances, illusions."[1] Turning Marchal's statement on its head, this essay examines how the twelfth-century temple complex of Angkor Vat operated as a theatre of illusions in *l'imaginaire français*, and locates France's fascination for Angkor in another, more nebulous detritus: the ruins of French rule in India. Through on-site renovations and Metropolitan representations, Angkor is both a site of memory and a staging ground for fantasies of what *l'Inde* could have become under French rule.

France's early descriptions of Angkor emphasized its aesthetic and historic value as a trophy of a specifically Indian history and culture. From the establishment of the Ecole Française d'Extrême Orient (EFEO) in 1901, to the founding of the Buddhist Institute in Cambodia in 1930, France's cultural projects in Cambodia were dominated by Indologists. Within the broader theatre of French colonial consciousness, Angkor acted as a monument to *l'Inde perdue*, and was frequently compared to the Taj Mahal, a seventeenth-century monument in what was now British India, built by the Mughul Emperor Shah Jahan as a mausoleum for his wife. Such comparisons lent weight to one colonial commentator's reading of French expansion into Indochina as an attempt to compensate for the "lamentable loss of India."[2] By the time of Pierre

Loti's visit to "le Taje" in 1903, this Muslim monument had emerged as a metonym for India, securing its place on an elite list of architectural wonders of the world whose members were the monumental equivalent of colonized natives. Where colonialism's civilizing mission offered a menu of *relèvement* (uplift) for its human charges, colonial archaeology lent a twist to this theme. As part of the *patrimoine* (heritage) of diverse colonies, such historic tombs and temples signaled a reservoir of ancient knowledge capable of embellishing France's colonial *patrimoine* and enriching French arts and scholarship through the introduction of new knowledge and aesthetic models. Angkor's location in a stretch of territory annexed by Siam, known in colonial patois as "Indochina's Alsace-Lorraine," and comprising a corridor between British India and French Indochina, enhanced its potency as a site associated with loss, longing, and the possibility of recovery.

Excavating and Exhibiting Angkor

When the naturalist and diarist Henri Mouhot discovered Angkor for Europe's growing reading public in 1860, he urged France to add this "jewel" to her crown before Britain snatched it.[3] Three years later, France established the Protectorate of Cambodia, prompting the Saigon Courrier first to gloat at the British "Snobbs" [*sic*] discomfort at the sight of the French navy threatening India from the East now that the Tricolor flew over Cambodia, and then to call for the dispatch of a team of French scholars and artists to Angkor.[4] Captain Doudart de Lagrée, France's representative in Cambodia, led one such mission as Head of the newly established Mekong Exploration Commission.[5] Its leading artist was a young naval officer named Louis Delaporte,[6] who was so inspired by what he saw that he persuaded the Ministry of Education to send him on a return expedition to Cambodia to make acquisitions for the Louvre, and to finance a subsequent field trip to India to study the relationship between Hindu and Cambodian art.[7] In a lavish account of his missions, Delaporte compared the Khmer Kingdom's glory days with those of the "brilliant Indian empires."[8] Forums for the substantiation of such comparisons were growing in Europe with the expansion of public museums and the emergence of international exhibitions. In 1851, the East Indian Pavilion at London's Great Exhibition set a precedent for the erection of fabulous facsimiles of Indian monuments in England, and was followed by the great gateway of Sanchi at South Kensington's International Exhibition of 1871.[9]

By 1878, Delaporte had amassed a collection of Khmer sculptures and bas-reliefs which were displayed at that year's Exposition Universelle in Paris, where one observer compared the "inscriptions on the mysterious monuments of Cambodia" to the Egyptian hieroglyphs on the Rosetta Stone, which had been deciphered by the young French scholar Jean-François Champollion (1790-1832).[10] Champollion had worked from copies and casts. Discovered by a French naval officer at Alexandria, the original Rosetta Stone now lay in the

British Musuem, symbolizing the quandary of a colonizing power which had at once made the greatest investment in the cultivation of Orientalist knowledge and had lost two of its primary archaeological terrains—Egypt and India—to Britain.[11] Edward Said has traced the French "Orient of memories, suggestive ruins, [and] forgotten secrets" to this archaeological angst.[12] Both the growing international climate of imperial competition to collect and flaunt rival colonial *patrimoines*, and the historic fascination of the eighteenth-century romantic movement for Indian and Egyptian cultures, honed this anxiety.

The following decades saw the establishment of a Musée Khmer in Paris, where relics and casts from Angkor and other Cambodian sites accumulated under Delaporte's care, providing a material repository and image bank for a series of increasingly extravagant representations of Cambodia. In 1889, a replica of the innermost sanctuary of the temple was constructed on the *rue des Invalides* for the Exposition Universelle, and in 1900, pastiches of Angkor appeared inside and outside a Cambodia pavilion which one journalist described as Indochina's "Indian face."[13]

But it took Governor General of Indochina Paul Doumer (1897-1902) to galvanize the creation of facilities for the study and display of Khmer and other artifacts *within* Indochina by issuing the first official conservation order on historic monuments in Indochina and forming a Permanent Archaeological Mission at Angkor in 1900.[14] In 1901, the Mission became the Ecole Française d'Extrême-Orient (EFEO).[15] Its first President, Louis Finot, was France's premier Indologist.[16] In his inaugural address, Finot warned that France's scholarly neglect of Indochina had made this territory easy prey for Orientalists from rival empires, and declared that the School would study that part of Indochina which owed "its monuments, its customs and its culture to India"— that is, Cambodia.[17] Even as he spoke, French access to the Angkorean temples was restricted by Sikh and Gurkha detachments from the British army, who patrolled Siem Reap province, with the occasional intervention of British military officers.[18] While French Indochina feared Siam as a hive of British influence, British India eyed Pondicherry, that lasting fragment of France's seventeenth-century hold on India, with similar consternation. In 1902, mindful of the potential of Pondicherry as a sanctuary for anti-British Indian nationalists, the Governor General of India Lord Curzon oversaw the suppression of French language education in universities and schools in British India.[19]

It was in this climate that Finot's deputy, the Indologist Alfred Foucher— who had recently completed a two-year archaeological mission to India—wrote to the Governor General of Indochina stressing the EFEO's determination to take over the conservation of Angkor.[20] As one visitor to Angkor remarked in 1903, the EFEO was exploring the temples in order to ascertain "whether Cambodia represents, and to what extent it could represent, the part of India in Indochina."[21] This view was corroborated by C-E. Maître, a Japan specialist who became Director of the EFEO in 1907, and who held that Cambodia had received "all [its] religion and civilization from India" and as such, did not merit study by itself.[22] The presumed disappearing act of Angkor's builders allowed for competing myths of the Hindu presence in the past. One version held that Angkor's builders were "the naked savages who welcomed the first Hindu colonists . . . [and] speedily revealed themselves great artists" who mastered techniques passed on by the Hindus and then "suddenly vanished"; another that Angkor was the creation of "Hindus, uprooted from their native soil" who, in Cambodia, had developed artistic talents 'that their mother country stifled under the weight of traditions and rites.'[23] Such narratives simultaneously situated Angkor in India and asserted Cambodia's superiority—both as a contemporary colony, and an ancient society—to the structure and legacies of British India. "Everyone has seen the Taje, everyone has described the Taje," wrote Pierre Loti in 1903. But despite Loti's assertion that le Taje was "incomparable," and the obvious distinctions between this Muslim monument and Angkor's purported Hindu genesis, Angkor was frequently described in relation to the Taj. France might have lost India, but it had at least gained, in Angkor, an "authentic" Hindu monument.[24]

In 1906, references to Angkor Vat appeared in the Exposition Coloniale at Marseille, which was attended by the Cambodian monarch King Norodom I and a cortège of royal dancers who attracted the attention of the sculptor Auguste Rodin. The following year, Siam relinquished the province of Siem Reap and with it the temples of Angkor, to the French Protectorate, prompting Finot, Delaporte, Doumer and others to found the Société d'Angkor pour la conservation des monuments anciens d'Indochine (Angkor Society for the Conservation of Ancient Monuments of Indochina) in Paris.[25] Patronized by Emile Guimet and Prince Roland Bonaparte among a hundred others, the society was committed to "the conservation and study of monuments in Indochina," but above all to Angkor. Comparing Angkor to "the Parthenon, Luxor and the Taj Mahal"—all of which now stood in British empires or British zones of influence—the Society stressed France's duty to conserve these archaeological "treasures" which had suffered long enough from the "wounds of time and past depredations."[26] As we will see, colonial conservation and the onus of "ownership" entailed its own depredations.

Re-Indianizing Angkor

In 1866, three years after the establishment of the protectorate, the pioneer of conservation of France's national monuments, Eugène Viollet-le-Duc, declared: "To restore a building is not to maintain it, to repair it, or remake it, but to re-establish it in a state of completeness which can never have existed at a given moment."[27] It was in the search for such an impossibly pristine moment that French savants set about dismantling the dynamic site of worship that Angkor had become. The attendant compression of Cambodia's past and present into a triptych of Angkorean glory, post-Angkorean decay, and colonial redemption tallied with Orientalist paradigms purveyed in British India. As a "runic reality" and "the ruin of time," Cambodia occupied a similar position in the French colonial imaginary to that of India in British colonial thought-worlds.[28]

Within the context of imperial conservation agendas, Angkor did indeed comprise France's India. The Archaeological Survey of India, established in 1861, decided what were the great monuments of India and which were "fit for preservation or description as part of the Indian 'heritage.'"[29] In London and Calcutta, museum curators streamlined images and artifacts into a linear narrative of nation which subsequently informed Nehru's notion of a palimpsest of India.[30] In its first decades, the Archaeological Survey did little to stymie the desecralization, vandalism and looting of monuments in British India, culminating in plans to auction off the Taj Mahal.[31] In the late 1890s and early 1900s, outraged by this devaluation of British India's cultural heritage, Doumer's rough contemporary, the Viceroy of India Lord Curzon, translated the letter and spirit of the Archaeological survey into a robust series of heritage conventions embracing India and Burma. In Burma, the ensuing colonial intervention in active religious sites led to monastic protests, bringing some projects of the Burma Archaeological Survey to a temporary halt. Although conservation in Cambodia never invited this level of protest, French attempts to acquire sacred relics and to "cleanse" old sites, provoked similar anxieties.

These anxieties came into sharp focus in 1891, when a French sculptor named Raffegaud asked to remove pieces of sacred statuary from temples of the Angkor era for transport to Paris. In response, King Norodom I expressly forbid "the abduction of pieces of religious sculpture," explaining that "the removal of statues of monumental stone from the Cambodians, would be tantamount to destroying the Cambodian religion."[32] In its nineteenth-century usage, the Khmer term for religion, *sāsanā* embraced a range of the sacred, without regard for denominational divides. Most Cambodians were Theravadan Buddhists, but animist practices and ancestral beliefs coexisted with Buddhist precepts, as did a veneration for such Hindu figures as Vishnu and Shiva. Conversely, the presence of Buddhist statues and the practice of Buddhist worship at Angkor presented unwelcome challenges to colonial desires to compartmentalize Cambodia both vertically, through time, and horizontally, through the categorization of religion. On site, the Hindu framing of Cambodia encouraged Angkor's new guardians not only to relocate members of the Cambodian monkhood, or *sangha*, but also to take down and remove Buddhist statues that had been erected in positions of central prominence and sacred significance during the temple's centuries-long conversion to a site of Buddhist worship.[33] During the following decade, colonial attempts to re-Indianise Angkor would see the quarantining of scores of such Buddhist icons in a designated space which became known as the *Mille Bouddha* (thousand Buddha) gallery.[34] Those monks who had been the chief curators of the temple complex long before the EFEO was founded, were also cleared off the land in 1909 as their presence in front of the temple was considered an eyesore.[35] This was not only because their "Buddhist" identities spoiled the "Hindu" template presented to tourists, but because their 'contemporary' status disturbed the colonial presentation of

Angkor as both monument *and* frozen moment, a material archive to the "golden" era of Khmer greatness and glory from which, colonial propaganda repeatedly maintained, the Khmers had fallen. In the place of Cambodian monks, a hotel was built, in the style of an Anglo-Indian bungalow, to cater to growing numbers of tourists.[36] In a similar treatment of sacred space in British India, the mosques on either side of the Taj Mahal were rented out to honeymooners, while the Taj itself became a favored locale for open-air balls and picnic parties.[37]

Following the success of the Indochina pavilions at the Exposition Coloniale at Marseille in 1906, the Geography Society of Marseille and the Department of Colonies co-convened a conference on tourism to Indochina in 1914. Keynote speaker Alfred Meynard spoke of the "unrivalled monuments of Angkor, the world's loftiest architectural wonders" which allowed visitors to "capture a feeling of Indian history, monuments and customs."[38] The same year, the French travel writer Marcel Genlis lambasted the government buildings of British India as the "monstrous product of fornication between gothic art and Hindu architecture," likening them to "the sons of prostitutes" who could claim many fathers.[39] In a bid to stop such cross-pollination across eras as well as genres, Louis Finot had banned the practice of using materials from Angkorean temples to repair contemporary Buddhist monasteries.[40] Colonialism's push to segregate Hinduism and Buddhism was not restricted to questions of monumental and monastic architecture, but also informed policies on religious practice in the French Protectorate.

Showcasing Buddha: Indology

The school of Buddhist studies which emerged in Europe during the early nineteenth century remained dominated by Indologists well into the 1900s. Influenced by late eighteenth and early nineteenth-century attempts to reconstruct a "classical period" for India, these scholars constructed Buddhism as "an historical projection, derived exclusively from manuscripts and blockprints." In France, this textual reification of Buddhism was exemplified by the work of Eugène Burnouf (1801-1852), a Parisian philologist who "systematiz[ed] the increasing amount of information on Buddhist text and concepts" in his *L'Introduction à l'histoire du buddhisme indien* (Paris: Imprimerie Royal 1844). This in turn focused Buddhist studies on the pursuit of master texts for deposit in European libraries.[41]

The rise of heritage committees and public museums in the late nineteenth century expanded this reification of Buddhism from a purely textual bias to a museological one. This material dimension was signaled in France by the appearance of a hall dedicated to the "Religions of the Far East" at the 1878 Exposition Universelle in Paris, not far from Louis Delaporte's Angkor display. The wealthy Lyonnais industrialist and amateur antiquarian Emile Guimet (1836-1918) was so impressed by this exhibit that he established his own *Musée des religions* (Museum of Religions) in Lyon the following year.[42] This was the genesis of the Musée Guimet, opened in Paris in 1889, and dedicated primarily to "religious objects of Asian origin, and especially from India and Indochina."[43]

An avid supporter of the Guimet museum, Louis Finot initiated and supported a number of projects to partition contemporary Buddhism from Siam through the establishment of facilities for religious study in Cambodia.[44] The Ecole de Pali was founded in Phnom Penh in 1914 to provide Cambodia's clerical elite with the religious education which they had habitually sought in Bangkok,[45] and to further the Indianist ambitions of the EFEO, which hoped that the school would succeed in fostering the "methods and results of French Indology."[46]

In an inversion of Pierre Loti's fantasy of *L'Inde sans les anglais*, but in line with both a broader global "yellow peril" discourse and colonial views of Chinese as exploiters of the French, one colonial commentator conjured up *l'Indochine avec les Hindous et sans les Chinois*.[47] From the first decades of the Protectorate of Cambodia, French and Indian entrepreneurs had eyed each other as stiff competitors.[48] By the 1920s, Cambodia possessed a vibrant Indian population—Catholic, Hindu and Muslim—including several thousand "of French nationality," from Pondicherry and elsewhere, who acted as civil servants, and as teachers in the Franco-Cambodian school system. Lesser numbers of "British subjects" from Madras, Bombay, Gujerat and Bengal, engaged in commerce and credit, textile trade, banking and money-lending.[49] In 1912, one of this community, an Indian peddler who sold peanuts at a Buddhist monastery in the capital, taught Sanskrit to two Cambodian monks—Chuon Nath (1883-1969) and Huot Tath (1891-1975)—who later went on to study with Louis Finot at the EFEO in Hanoi. Here they became acquainted with France's first female Indologist. Born in Paris, Suzanne Karpelès (1890-1968) had spent much of her preschool childhood in Pondicherry, where her father had business interests. Apparently motivated by nostalgia for these early encounters, she later specialized in Indian religions, Sanskrit and Pâli. In 1922, she became the first woman to graduate from l'Ecole des Langues Orientales.[50] Shortly after, she joined the EFEO, whose activities had found a major showcase earlier that year in Angkor's largest ever reconstruction, at the Exposition Coloniale in Marseille.

Karpelès was posted to Hanoi in early 1923, and then to Phnom Penh. Her first project was to collate a Pâli text published in Ceylon with a Cambodian manuscript, and she subsequently expanded her focus to a broader conservatory mission to trace and rehabilitate the scriptural integrity of Khmer Buddhist manuscripts. Chuon Nath and Huot Tath later emerged as Karpelès' key partners in the "regeneration" of Khmer Buddhism.[51]

During the 1920s, the EFEO began to turn away from India and toward Southeast Asia, through a series of exchanges with the Archaeologische Dienst (archaeological service) in Java, then in the Dutch East Indies. Increasingly, Cambodia's ties with India were emphasized less, and its place in Indochina

more. Expanded excavations, new scholarship and tighter collaboration with
Dutch archaeologists in Java brought fresh revelations, while curator Henri
Marchal further elaborated the multiple foreign cultural influences in Khmer
art.[52] Links with Siamese scholarship were also tightened.[53] In 1931, under
Coedès' new directorship, the EFEO officially adopted anastylosis, a technique
developed in the Dutch East Indies, which involved the dismantling and
subsequent reconstruction of ancient sites.[54] The same year, another opportunity
presented itself for Angkor's rebuilding, at the Exposition Coloniale
Internationale in Paris.

Issued in Hanoi, the General Directives for Indochina's participation in the
1931 Exposition conceived a general exhibit to demonstrate the scope and
potential of colonial activity in Indochina, and local displays which would
communicate to the public the "Indochinese reality" by broadcasting "real"
images of France in Asia.[55] The apotheosis of this window on the "real" was the
largest ever recreation of Angkor Vat. Costing 12.5 million francs, it was built
to disappear.

Angkor in Paris: The 1931 Exhibition

This reconstruction was symbolic of the belief, now firmly established in
French academic and administrative circles, that colonial intervention in
Cambodian culture had led to the country's "reincarnation."[56] It also reflected
the place of architecture as a major metronome of the sophistication of an
indigenous civilization.[57] In this vein, French discourses on India extolled the
"unsurpassed" architectural beauty of the Taj Mahal, while the display of
"pseudo Taj Mahals" at the Wembley British Empire Exhibition in 1924 led one
editor to conclude that "building in its finest aspects reflects the character of a
nation as a community."[58] By contrast, British ignorance of Angkor was still
commonplace. Although novelist Claude Farrère (1876-1957) could safely
assume, in 1923, that his French readership had all seen "images, or paintings,
or casts, or evocations of Angkor, at colonial exhibitions . . . or in . . .
photographs," the travel writer Rachel Wheatcroft remained aghast in 1928, at
how few English people had even heard of Angkor.[59]

Two eminent Parisian architects, Charles and Gabriel Blanche were
assigned to reproduce Angkor. During the 1920s, the Blanches had supervised
the cleaning and recording of over eight hundred temple sites at Angkor, and
made numerous casts for future replication.[60] On their return to France, the
Blanches mapped out the entire Indochina section of the Exposition to
reproduce the spatial arrangement of Angkor (see figure 1.1). The temple's
transplantation to metropolitan soil, and its integration into a larger historical
and geographical theme park, were nothing new. But Angkor's exaggerated
presence in the Métropole's political and cultural heartland in 1931, represented
an unequivocal assertion of Angkor's place in France's *patrimoine*, and
France's place as the rightful guardian of this colonial heirloom. Most

importantly, it presented the French, and not Cambodians, as the only people capable of rebuilding Angkor here and now, in the present. While contemporary dwellings had been removed from Angkor in Cambodia, the 1931 exposition deployed Cambodian wooden houses as a powerful architectural foil to the Angkor extravaganza, precisely to emphasize the contemporary Cambodian's designated place as "timid debris."[61] In this context, as Farrère put it in 1931, Angkor symbolized a "dead civilization," and France became the "legitimate heir of this ancient Khmer civilization."[62]

Figure 1.1: *Exposition coloniale internationale de Paris 1931, album hors série*, Paris: L'Illustration, 1931, "Le Temple d'Angkor Vat (C. et G. Blanche, archit.—Auberlet, sculpt.)—La grande chaussée conduisant au temple. Au premier plan, nagas (serpents à sept têtes) servant de motifs décoratifs.—Phot. Pacific and Atlantic."

Within the Angkor pavilion, a larger waxwork tableau depicted Cambodians at worship in the inner hall of a Buddhist temple. This projection of elite prescriptions for the desired shape of "Khmer religion," cordoned off from Annam, Tonkin, Laos and Cochin-China, belied a far more complex reality, but cohered with the vision of a newly established institute in Phnom Penh. Where the EFEO had determined to "Hinduize" Angkor, the Buddhist Institute, founded by Karpelès in 1930, was devoted to the reification, conservation and delineation of a "Khmer Buddhism." Karpelès' aim was to insulate Buddhism in Cambodia from "superstition" and "degeneration," and most particularly from the dangers of cross-border movements, whether by Khmer monks to Siam, or by Khmer laity to the centre of the new and popular pantheistic Caodai sect, established in Cochin-China in the 1920s.

With a similar aim in mind, the 1931 Exhibition depicted each of the five separate constituents of Indochina as crystalline, discrete structures designed to emphasize their intrinsic difference and lack of cultural commonality. Farrère warned that Indochina's independence would result in the "massacre or enslavement of all Cambodians," describing communist chants of "Indochina for the Indochinese" as a Soviet plot to extinguish the Khmer nation.[63] Accompanying literature trumpeted the theme of the Khmer's spiritual, moral and "artistic" superiority vis-à-vis the Vietnamese, locating this difference in an "Aryan" heritage. Stressing the complete dissimilarity of the Khmers and Annamites—who differ in "skin color, features, religion, morals, character and language"—one writer (1925) notes that the Khmers belong to a group "on which shines the rays of Hindu civilization, to the great Aryan family which sprang from the cradle of India."[64] Another (1930) lamented the terrible invasion of "yellows" suffered by the poor Khmers who have "Aryan blood coursing in their veins."[65] A 1931 publication funded by the Society of Indochinese Studies noted that the "Cambodians or Khmers" were "absolutely different" to their neighbors and were "attached to that great Aryan family one of whose sources was India."[66]

Four years after Angkor appeared, and disappeared, at Vincennes, Farrère published his *L'Inde perdue*, a history of France's conquests and losses in India, in which he compared India, "immense and complex" with "simple Indo-Chine," and turned loss to gain in his conclusion that France had seen "success" in Indochina while in India, it was the Indians who had won everything, and England who had lost.[67] India had long fascinated Farrère, who subscribed to Loti's notion that India was the cradle and ancestor of Europe.[68] While speculation about Europe's Aryan roots became fashionable among reactionary intellectuals in interwar France, as demonstrated by Louis Jacolliot's theorization of the Aryan race, a similar line was adopted by Cambodian nationalists to stress the Khmer "race's" superiority to the "yellow" races of Vietnam, China and Japan. Writing for the nationalist newspaper *Nagaravatta* (Angkor Wat), "Son of the Khmers" declared that Khmers had Indian blood, and that the Indians and French shared the same bloodlines, which explained why Khmers were big and strong.[69] This conflation of Khmers and Indians also offered Cambodians another avenue of identity, with Mahatma Gandhi, whose positioning as an adversary of "British" Empire meant that many French people reserved for him feelings of admiration rather than the disdain and fear with which they viewed Indochina's anti-colonial activists.

During the 1930s, scholars discerned that the temples of Angkor "were not public spaces, like the temples of classical antiquity or our cathedrals," but were—like the Taj Mahal—"mausoleums" and "funerary temples."[70] Ironically this discovery coincided with the irreversible assimilation of the notion of Angkor as national monument in Cambodian nationalist imaginings. While the Blanche brothers were erecting their Angkor palladium in Paris, a 1931 article in *Kampuchea Bodemien* preached the virtues of national revival through scholarly application. Like their counterparts in India, Cambodia's first nationalists juxtaposed the golden age of Angkor and the contemporary world of colony, nation and progress, justifying their demands for social reform as a quest to revive past glory.[71]

The establishment of Vichy France in 1940, and Pondicherry's declaration of allegiance to General de Gaulle's Free France meant the literal rewriting of myth and history in Vichy Indochina. In July 1941, the Phnom Penh policechief stretched the Vichy censor's ban to the British film *Gunga Din*, for "exalting the courage and esprit de corps of the British Army in India."[72] From 1941 to 1943, several French and Khmer newspapers and journals published rewrites of Cambodian legend which cast India and Hindu figures of myth as rapacious captors and eternal enemies.[73] In this climate, but specifically under the Vichy Statute for the Jews which stripped her of her government post, Karpelès left Cambodia for Pondicherry. There she joined the Sri Aurobindo Ashram, whose first foreign visitor had been her former teacher, the celebrated Indologist Sylvain Lévi.[74]

Conclusion

The colonial drive to return Angkor to a state of past perfection ensured that what was billed as a rehabilitation was in fact a recreation. In film, literature, art, architecture and archaeology, Angkor was remade as both the embodiment of Khmer national essence and an irretrievable, unachievable and impossible moment of cultural perfection. The flipside to the colonial propagandists' constant chorus of Cambodia's "need" for French protection, was that France "needed" Cambodia to assert its own stakes in the global hegemony of colonial scholarship. While France boasted the success of its policies of *relèvement* in Indochina, Angkor, as a symbol of borrowed glory, provided its own uplift to the French national psyche, providing an antidote to fears of national decline and cultural decadence. In their myriad incarnations, the temples stood as enduring testimony to France's imperial power and cultural prowess. Where architecture and landscaping helped to create and sustain Taj Angkor, maps, literature, museology and exhibitions displayed and entrenched this mythology in the Métropole, embroidering Angkor onto the French consciousness as a peripheral emblem of empire which demarcated France's geographic and scholastic reach in the Orient, and, through its transplantation to Paris, whether as plaster cast, cinema or purloined relics, inlaid the temple into the national mosaic. Suspended in space and time as *une idée fixe*, the fiction of Angkor-as-national-icon played a critical role in nationalist mythmaking. In *l'imaginaire français*, Taj Angkor was fraught with anxiety and promise. A locus of nostalgia for lost empire, Taj Angkor had served as a site for the resurrection of the fantasy of India's return to France, and a symbol of the hoped for immortality of French rule in Indochina. By 1954, when both Pondicherry and Cambodia gained full independence, and the Vietminh defeated France at Dien Bien Phu, such yearnings were both anachronistic and unrealistic. Although the ghosts of colonialism and its fantasies of immortality were not easily laid to rest, the trope of Taj Angkor had served its course. Writing as an archaeologist and art historian, but reflecting these seismic shifts in the colonial landscape as well as the emergence of a strong Cambodian nationalism, Henri Marchal declared in 1955 that "The Cambodian is not of the Hindu race," but is the result of many crossings with Malays, Indonesians and others, and "differs totally" from the inhabitants of India.[75] From now on, Angkor in *l'imaginaire français* would increasingly come to symbolize not the decline and fall of an ancient Khmer civilization, but the glory and vanishing of French power in Cambodia and beyond. Once an altar to memories of a French India that never was, it was fast becoming a funerary monument to *l'Indochine perdue*.

Notes

1. Henri Marchal, *Le Décor et la Sculpture Khmers* (Paris: Vanoest, 1951), 54. All translations are the author's own unless otherwise stated.

2. Marcel Dubois, Preface, in *Empire Colonial de la France: L'Indochine* (Paris: Librairie Coloniale Augustin Challamel, u.d.), ix.

3. Henri Mouhot, *Travels in Siam, Cambodge and Laos 1858-1860* (Singapore: Oxford University Press, 1989).

4. "Comment Angkor fut révélé au grand public" in *Courrier de Saïgon* (February 10, 1864); *Courrier de Saïgon* (August 5, 1865).

5. Léon Garnier, *Notice sur Francis Garnier* (Paris: Imprimerie Emile Martinet, 1882), ix-xiii.

6. Roger Vercel, *Le Fleuve: les grandes heures de la vie de Francis Garnier* (Paris: Les Editions de la nouvelle France, 1946), 29-30.

7. Louis Delaporte, "Rapport fait au Ministre de la Marine et des colonies et au Minstre de l'Instruction Publique, des cultes et des beaux arts, par M. Louis Delaporte, sur la mission scientifique aux ruines des monuments khmers de l'ancien Cambodge," *Journal Officiel de la Republique Française* 6: 90, 2511; Centre d'Acceuil et de Recherche des Archives Nationales (hereafter CARAN) F21 4489 3a Arrêt, Ministry of Public Education, Religion and Fine Arts (Paris November 10, 1876).

8. Louis Delaporte, *Voyage au Cambodge: L'architecture Khmer* (Paris: Librairie Ch. Delagrave, 1880), 159, 337-38.

9. Peter Hoffenberg, *An Empire on Display: English, Indian and Australian Exhibitions from the Crystal Palace to the Great War* (Berkeley and Los Angeles: University of California Press, 2001), 276.

10. Col. Duhousset, "Exposition ethnographique des missions scientifiques au Palais de l'Industrie," *L'Illustration* (January 19, 1878), 39.

11. Anthony Barnett, "Cambodia Will Never Disappear" in *New Left Review* 180 (Mar/Apr 1990), 101-25. See also Jeannette Greenfield, *The Return of Cultural Treasures* (Cambridge University Press: Second Edition, 1996), 108-9 and Jean Vercoutter, *The Search for Ancient Egypt* (New York: Thames and Hudson, 1992), 3-9, 90-95.

12. Edward Said, *Orientalism* (New York: Pantheon, 1978), 169.

13. "L'Exposition de L'Indochine" in *L'Illustration* (September 1, 1900), 134-35.

14. "Le dégagement de Sambor Prei-Kuk" in *Extrême-Asie*, 36 (June 1929), 536.

15. *Les Colonies françaises: Petite encyclopédie coloniale*, edited by Maxime Petit (Paris: Larousse, 1903), 456.

16. Paul Levy, "L'École Française d'Extrême-Orient" *France-Asie* 15 (June 15, 1947), 523.

17. Doumer, *L'Indochine française (Souvenirs): Nouvelle Edition* (Paris : Librairie Vuibert, 1930), 270-74.

18. Albert Pouvourville "Chasses du Siam," *Revue Indo-Chinoise* 6, no. 209 (October 20, 1902), 971-79: 972.

19. Emmanuelle Ortoli, "Le Temps du Rapprochement" in *L'Aventure des Français en Inde XVIIe – Xxe siècles*, edited by Rose Vincent (All India Press: Pondicherry, 1998) 207-35, 208.

20. AOM INDO GGI 23789 Foucher, Directeur Adjoint, EFEO, to GGI 10 August 1902; MS2966, Cœdès Collection, National Library of Australia Curriculum vitae of Alfred Foucher (b. 1865). Foucher, who arrived in Indochina in 1901, published two volumes on the Buddhist iconography of India in 1902 and 1905, and succeeded Finot as director of the EFEO from 1905 to 1907.

21. Louis Salaun, *L'Indochine* (Paris: Imprimerie Nationale, 1903), 100.

22. Georges Maspéro, ed. *Un Empire Colonial Français: L'Indochine* (Paris: Les Editions G.Van Oest, 1930), 113; "EFEO" in *Bulletin du Comité de l'Asie-Française* 7, no. 70 (January 1907), 30.

23. Pierre Dieulefils, *Ruins of Angkor: Cambodia in 1909* (Bangkok: River Books, 2001), 6.

24. Pierre Loti, *L'Inde (sans les Anglais)* (Paris/Pondicherry: Kailash Editions, 1992), 234.

25. "Cambodge" *Bulletin de l'EFEO* (hereafter *BEFEO*) 7 (1907), 422.

26. Article 2 of "Statutes of Society of Angkor" and "Programme of Society of Angkor" *BEFEO* Vol. 7 (1907), 209-10; "Société d'Angkor pour la conservation des monuments anciens de l'Indochine: Statuts" in *Bulletin du Comité de l'Asie-Française* 8, no. 88 (July 1908), 284-85; "Programme of Society of Angkor" *BEFEO* 7 (1907), 210.

27. Eugène-Emmanuel Viollet-le-Duc, "Restauration" *Dictionnaire raisonné* Tome VIII (Paris, 1866) cited in Bruno Foucart "Viollet-le-Duc et la Restauration," in *Les Lieux de mémoire: Tome II: La Nation*, edited by Pierre Nora (Paris: Gallimard, 1986), 618-49, 622.

28. Homi Bhabha, *The Location of Culture* (London: Routledge, 1994), 130; Marinalini Sinha *Colonial Masculinity: The "manly" Englishman and the "effeminate Bengali" in the late nineteenth-century* (Manchester: Manchester University Press), 22.

29. Bernard Cohn, "Representing Authority in Victorian India," in *The Invention of Tradition*, edited by Eric Hobsbawm and Terence Ranger (Cambridge: Cambridge University Press), 182-83.

30. Bernard Cohn, *Colonialism and its Forms of Knowledge: the British in India* (Princeton University Press, 1996), 77, 80 (his emphasis); Michael M. Ames *Cannibal Tours and Glass Boxes: The Anthropology of Museums* (Vancouver: University of British Columbia), 144; K. N. Momin and Ajay Pratrap "Indian museums and the public" in Peter G. Stone and Brian L. Molyneaux *The Presented Past: Heritage, Museums, and Education* (London: Routledge, 1994), 291.

31. David Caroll, *The Taj Mahal* (New York: Newsweek, 1972); see "Ancient Monuments" in <http://members.tripod. com/~INDIARESOURCE/colonial.html> (September 1, 2003).

32. Archives d'Outre Mer (hereafter AOM) INDO GGI 23794 S.M. le Roi du Cambodge Norodom to RSC 2 February 1891; AOM INDO GGI 23794 RSC to GGI February 6, 1891.

33. C-E Bouillevaux, *L'Annam et le Cambodge: Voyages et Notices Historiques* (Paris: Victor Palmé, 1874).

34. Bruno Dagens, *Angkor: la forêt de pierre* (Paris: Gallimard, 1994), 173.

35. "Cambodge" in *BEFEO* 9 (1909): 828; *BEFEO* 10 (1910): 268.

36. "Cambodge" *BEFEO* 8 (1908): 420.

37. Carroll, *Taj Mahal*.

38. "Le grand tourisme en Extrême-Orient: Une promenade à travers l'Indochine" *in Bulletin de la Société de Géographie de Marseille* 38 (1914), 83-85.

39. Marcel Genlis, *Dans l'Incendie Tropicale: Angkor-Java-Burma-India (octobre 1912-mars 1913)* (Paris: Librairie Plon, 1914), 131-32.

40. Ingrid Muan, "Citing Angkor: The Cambodian Arts in the Age of Restoration, 1918-2000," PhD thesis, Columbia University School of Arts and Sciences, 2001, 22-23.

41. Donald S. Lopez Jr., *Curators of the Buddha: The Study of Buddhism under Colonialism* (Chicago: University of Chicago Press, 1995), 7-12.

42. Emile Guimet, *Le Jubilé du Musée Guimet: 25eme anniversaire de sa fondation 1879-1904* (Paris: Ernest Leroux: 1904), i, xvii.

43. CARAN File 214471 "Projet d'installation à Paris du Musée Guimet" in *Bulletin Municipal Officiel de la Ville de Paris* 4, no. 76 (March 17, 1885), 574-77; CARAN F214470 3 E. Guimet, Directeur, Musée Guimet, to Minister of Public Education, November 12, 1889.

44. "Cambodge" *BEFEO* 3 (1903), 368.

45. "Ecole supérieure de pâli" *BEFEO* 35 (1935), 463.

46. "Ecole de pâli (Phnom Penh)" *BEFEO* 14 (1914), 95.

47. Albert Foulaz, "Etude de colonisation de l'Indo-Chine Française par les Japonais et la race Malaise" in *Bulletin de la Societe des Etudes Indo-Chinoises de Saigon*, 1896 (Saigon: Imprimerie Commerciale Rey, Curiol & Co. 1897), 21-31: 23-24.

48. Gregor Muller, "Visions of Grandeur, Tales of Failure: The Establishment of French Colonial Rule in Cambodia and the Life Story of Thomas Caraman 1840-1887" (Doctoral dissertation, University of Zurich, 2002).

49. Pierre Dreyfus, *Le Cambodge Economique* (Giard & Brière: Paris, 1910), 21; Jean Loubet and Georges Taboulet *L'Indochine française* 38; "Monographie of Kompong Chhnang" *Bulletin de Société des Etudes Indochinoises* April 1914 (Saigon, 1915), 114-20: 120.

50. Dr Germaine Montreuil-Strauss, "Suzanne Karpelès (1890-1968)" in *Femmes médecins* (juin 1969). I am grateful to Marie Paule-Ha for sharing this article with me.

51. For a more detailed treatment of Chuon Nath, Huot Tath and Karpelès' projects to revive and purify Khmer Buddhism, see Penny Edwards "Making a Religion of the Nation and its Language: The French Protectorate (1863-1954) and the Dhammakāy" in John Marston and Elizabeth Guthrie (Eds), *History, Buddhism and New Religious Movements in Cambodia* (Honolulu: Hawai'i University Press, 2004), 63-85.

52. Henri Marchal, "Des influences étrangères dans l'art et la civilisation khmères" *BSEIS* 11, no. 2 (1936): 9-10.

53. Georges Cœdès, "L'EFEO: Méthodes modernes et orientation nouvelle": 2.

54. Georges Cœdès, "Angkor: Les Travaux de l'EFEO," *Indochine Hebdomadaire Illustrée* October 3, 1940, II; Anthony Reid "Who Made Southeast Asia," *The Asia-Pacific Magazine* 9/10 (1998): 62-67.

55. Commissariat de l'Indo-Chine *Directives Générales* (Hanoi: Imprimerie d'Extrême Orient, 1929), 2.

56. Georges Maspéro, *Un Empire Colonial Français: L'Indochine Volume II* (Paris: Van Oest, 1930), 442.

57. Panivong Norindr, *Phantasmatic Indochina: French Colonial Ideology in Architecture, Film and Literature* (Durham: Duke University Press, 1996), 24-25, 27.

58. Carra de Vaux, *The Philosophers of Islam* (Paris, 1921); Hoffenberg *Empire on Display*, 276.

59. Claude Farrère, *Mes voyages: la promenade d'Extrême-Orient* (Paris: Flammarion, 1923), 41. Farrère's Indochina novel *Les Civilisés* won the Prix Goncourt in 1905. Rachel Wheatcroft *Siam and Cambodia in Pen and Pastel with excursions in China and Burmah* (London: Constable, 1928), 51.

60. Gwendolen Wright, *The Politics of Design in French Colonial Urbanism* (Chicago: University of Chicago Press, 1988), 194.

61. "Les Pavillons de la Chasse et de la Pêche Indochinoise" *L'Illustration* (June 27, 1931), 313.

62. Claude Farrère, "Angkor et l'Indochine," *Exposition Coloniale Internationale de Paris 1931* (Paris: L'Illustration, 1931).

63. Farrère, "Angkor et l'Indochine."

64. Paul Collard, *Cambodge et Cambodgiens: Metamorphose du royaume Khmer par une méthode française de protectorat* (Paris: Société d'Editions géographiques, maritimes et coloniales, 1925), 4-6.

65. Luc Durtain, *Dieux Blancs, Hommes Jaunes* (Paris: Ernest Flammarion, 1930), 256.

66. P. Gastaldy, *La Cochinchine* (Saigon: Société des études indochinoises, 1931), 14.

67. Claude Farrère, *L'Inde perdue* (Paris/Pondicherry: Kailash Editions, 1998), 212.

68. Alain Quella-Villéger, "Postface: Farrère-Kipling: Même Combat" in Claude Farrère, *L'Inde Perdue* (Paris/Pondicherry: Kailash Editions, 1998), 213-16.

69. Keemorah Botraa (Son of the Khmers), "The Fearfulness of the Khmer Nation" *Nagaravatta* 19 March 1938.

70. Cœdès, "Angkor," VI.

71. Partha Chatterjee, *The Nation and its Fragments: Colonial and Postcolonial Histories* (Princeton: Princeton University Press, 1993) 95-99; *"Secday romluk dal ah kounchiw aoy uusaa rien sout"* (A Reminder to all grandchildren to study hard) *Kampuchea Bodemien* (Cambodia News) May 2, 1931, 1.

72. AOM RSC 655 Brocheton, local chief of police, to the President of CICIP, Phnom Penh July 31, 1941.

73. Penny Edwards, "'Propagender': Marianne, Joan of Arc and the Export of French Gender Ideology to Colonial Cambodia (1863-1954)" in *Promoting the Colonial Idea: Propaganda and Visions of Empire in France*, edited by Tony Chafer and Amanda Sackur (London: Palgrave, 2002), 116-30: 125.

74. Ortoli, "Le temps du rapprochement," 209.

75. Henri Marchal, "Le symbolisme des temples Hindous et Khmers," *France Asie: Revue Mensuelle de culture Franco-Asiatique,* 114-15 (Nov.-Dec., 1955): 339-344: 340.

2

Representing Indochinese Sacrifice:
The Temple du Souvenir Indochinois of Nogent-sur-Marne

Eric T. Jennings

On April 21, 1984, a fire[1] gutted and destroyed a singular building in the East-ernmost part of the Bois de Vincennes, in the Parisian suburb of Nogent-sur-Marne. The wooden edifice had seen its share of peregrinations and reinven-tions before then. Commissioned in 1905, it had first been transported overland, then by ship from the province of Thudaumôt,[2] Northwest of Saigon, to France, where it had served as the "Cochin-China pavilion" at the Colonial exhibition of Marseille in 1906. A year later, this communal village house or *dinh*, variously labeled by the French a "Cochin-Chinese house," or "Sculpted house of Thu-daumôt,"[3] was moved to the outskirts of Paris for the 1907 colonial exhibition at the Jardin Colonial of Nogent-sur-Marne. In 1920, the displaced structure saw its function change drastically, when it was officially converted into a Bud-dhist temple dedicated to the memory of the 1,548 Indochinese soldiers who had "died for France" in the Great War (see figure 2.1). Losing its nominal tie to Thudaumôt, it then became the Temple du Souvenir Indochinois, itself the centerpiece of a vaster site of commemoration. Its final resting place was no accident: it was moved to the heart of the Jardin Colonial of Nogent-sur-Marne, a laboratory of tropical agronomy akin to Kew Gardens, whose buildings—which once included a Mosque—had served between 1914 and 1918 as a make-shift hospital for colonial soldiers.

29

Today, on the other side of the Bois de Vincennes from the few remaining vestiges of the grand 1931 colonial exhibition, one can still visit this curious site, littered with the statuaries of empire. A new, smaller Temple was erected in 1992, with an eye to maintaining its "Oriental" qualities.[4] Sifting through these layers of colonial memories, it is the shifting commemoration of Indochinese soldiers of the Great War that is the most striking function of this "site of memory" in the suburbs of Paris.

Figure 2.1: Indochinese veterans assembled before the Thudaumôt *dinh*. Date unknown, but presumably around the time of the *dinh*'s 1920 transformation into the *Temple du Souvenir Indochinois*. Courtesy CAOM, Aix-en-Provence 8 Fi 112/67. Tous droits réservés (All rights reserved) Indochine GGI 33416.

Representing the *Tirailleurs Indochinois*

Bertrand Tavernier's 1989 film *La Vie et rien d'autre* (*"Life and nothing but"*) depicts recurrent, almost comical debates amongst French military leaders over the race and appearance of the unknown soldier to be entombed under the Arc de Triomphe. A sideshow to these wranglings, a unit of Indochinese men led by a French officer, are charged with the task of actually finding this elusively anonymous and prototypical white *poilu*. The Indochinese *tirailleurs* resist undertaking this macabre task, refusing on religious and cultural grounds to touch a corpse with their own hands. This filmic representation is revealing indeed. First of all, Indochinese recruits are shown conducting largely menial tasks—

reflecting very real and widespread earlier prejudices against the valor of Indochinese soldiers, considered to be less martial in the popular French imagination
than the "fierce" *Tirailleurs Sénégalais*.[5] This stereotype explains in part why
most Indochinese recruits were sent to toil on road construction, fortifications,
or in munitions factories, rather than fight on the front lines.[6] But such representations risk obfuscating the substantial sacrifice of Indochinese recruits in
World War I: some 48,922 Indochinese served in the French military during the
war; of these 30,425 were sent to France, the Eastern theater, and 1,548 per-
ished.[7] Secondly, Tavernier's film betrays the recurring notion that Indochinese
rites and beliefs differed so significantly from those of the French, that cultural
conflicts emerged over the handling of the dead. And this, in turn, perpetuates
the founding logic for the Temple du Souvenir Indochinois itself: a belief that
Indochinese commemoration was so radically "other" from that of the Souvenir
Français, that the unknown soldier of the Arc de Triomphe could not even begin
to represent Indochinese losses, and that a separate fund, memorial, and agency
need be set up to commemorate them. Ironically, as we shall see, this would
leave out entire segments of the Indochinese population, like Indochinese
Catholics, whose place in this scheme was not readily evident.

Pagoda, Dinh, or Tea Palace?

The clusters of war memorials which one still witnesses at Nogent today were
the result of a long, complex set of negotiations over the plurality and politics of
commemoration. An underlying concern for authenticity was ultimately reflected in the style of monuments chosen: a genuine wooden sculpted house
from Cochin-China to commemorate "Annamite" (read Vietnamese) Buddhist
losses, a war memorial in faux Stupa style for Cambodians and Laotians, and a
"Europeanized" stele bearing gilded mosaic inlay for Indochinese Christians.
    The Temple du Souvenir Indochinois calls to mind several parallels. In its
final configuration, the site fused the functions of tropical laboratory, war memorial for colonial soldiers, with a landscape dotted with the remains of the
1907 colonial exhibition. In this sense, the Temple du Souvenir Indochinois can
be seen as a precursor to the gargantuan replica temple of Angkor erected on the
other end of the Bois de Vincennes, for the 1931 colonial exposition.[8] Indeed,
the two exhibitions share some common points of design, landscape, and aesthetic—down to the motifs on Khmer bridges. Panivong Norindr's description
of the Indochina section at the 1931 colonial exhibition could easily be trans-
posed to the Temple du Souvenir Indochinois: "The Exposition Coloniale Internationale de Paris homogenizes and consolidates the heterogeneity of Indochina's history and geography through a variety of representations."[9] Fantasies
of Indochinese diversity and otherness were enshrined in very similar ways at
the expositions of 1907 and 1931.
    At Nogent, the war memorials themselves were surrounded by a pastiche of
Indochinese stylistic elements designed to take the visitor on a mental voyage

from the Bois de Vincennes to Southeast Asia. The elaborate wooden gate was drawn by the French architect Lichtenfelder, and carved by a team of Indochinese artists—likely former "war laborers" who had been brought to France during the Great War. The large funerary urn at the center of the ensemble was itself a replica of a dynastic urn in the Imperial palace at Hue (see figure 2.2).[10]

Of course, neither the Jardin Colonial of Nogent-sur-Marne, nor the sculpted house/*dinh* of Thudaumôt, had been in any sense predisposed to become the cornerstones of Indochinese commemoration to the Great War. Here, the construction of memory was at once negotiated and rooted in Nogent's previous colonial connection. The Jardin Colonial had been established in Nogent-sur-Marne in 1899.[11] Its founder, colonial "explorer" cum agronomist Jean Dybowski,[12] described the garden as an experimental tropical laboratory—transforming suburban Nogent-sur-Marne into something of an imperial hub.

Figure 2.2: The Hue dynastic urn.

Figure 2.3: The monument to Christian Indochinese war dead.

The colonial exhibition of 1907 would further cement Nogent's colonial ties. The event was organized by the Société française de colonisation, the same organization which had been responsible for the Marseille exhibition the previous year—explaining in part how and why the Thudaumôt house made its way to Nogent. Jean Dybowski, who presided over the Nogent exhibition, overlooked none of the exotic tropes that were fast becoming formulaic hallmarks of colonial exhibitions: hundreds of "natives" were brought from West Africa,

New Caledonia, Laos etc., ten Indian elephants and their handlers were transported from Pondichéry, and two "giants," one from New Caledonia, the other from Timbuktu, were put on display.[13] The Parisian press described with racist wonder how "a Laotian village offers the curious display of Asian swarms [*grouillement asiatique*]."[14] The star of the show, however, seems to have been the sculpted "notable's house" from Thudaumôt. Its interior was used for official tea receptions over the course of the exhibition. Passers by marveled at its architecture, of course, but more specifically at its lavish interior, including a golden Tan Taï throne.[15] Eleven years later, plans would be drawn up to convert this *dinh* into a "temple of memory," dedicated to Indochinese World War I casualties.

The fact that this *dinh* from the town of Phu-Cuong in Thudaumôt province, was variously described by colonial sources as either a notable's house or a temple, and either Cochin-Chinese, Cambodian, or even Chinese in inspiration, might be seen as a measure of how little of a grasp the public had over the precise nature of this "exotica." In her paper on the history of the building, Isabelle Aragon shows that the structure was actually originally commissioned by the prominent politician from Cochin-China Ernest Outrey, for specific use at the 1906 colonial exhibition in Marseille. So as to endow the project with greater authenticity, it was initially agreed that the building would be "returned"[16] to its village of origin after the closing of the Marseille exhibition. The construction was undertaken with great urgency in 1905, and in March of that year, Outrey even requested from the Governor of Cochin-China permission to use some twenty prisoners from Saigon's Central jail, in a bid to accelerate the project's completion.[17]

It is of course remarkable to what extent this commissioned product of forced labor was later reinvented as an authentic piece of ancestral village architecture. It is interesting to note as well that although the building had clearly been ordered for a colonial exhibition, its precise designation had been that of a typical *dinh*, rather than positing any sort of uniqueness. The *dinh*, as the French were certainly aware, is a temple dedicated to a village's tutelary deity. But because the *dinh* fulfilled multiple roles in colonial Vietnam, from the role of communal house, to that of repository of sacred tablets protecting the village, to a center of social, cultural, governmental and even judicial activity, colonial authorities soon came to consider it an especially malleable artifact. French authorities no doubt read this functional polyvalence as license to reconfigure the *dinh* into a "mandarin's house" at the Marseille exhibition, a "tea palace" at the 1907 exhibition,[18] a "sculpted house," a "pagoda," and in due course, a temple. Over the course of its reinvention into the Temple du Souvenir Indochinois, the religious dimension of the building was of course privileged, in an effort to derive legitimacy for its new role as a sacred site sheltering tablets listing the names of the Vietnamese dead in the Great War. According to Isabelle Aragon, the final 1918 decision to convert the *dinh* into the temple part of the Temple du Souvenir Indochinois, essentially metamorphosed the *dinh* into a *dên*, a regional or "imperial" temple.[19] But one wonders whether the French colonial authorities at the helm of the Souvenir Indochinois were sufficiently versed in Vietnamese culture fully to grasp the transformation they had undertaken; contemporaneous sources suggest instead that they saw themselves enacting a fusion of commemorative genres, superimposing the model of the Parisian Panthéon onto the Vietnamese cult of family ancestors, enshrined in the village *dinh*.

An "authentic" Indochinese *Panthéon*

In January 1918, when the blueprints for Indochinese memorials were still being considered, the founder of the Souvenir Indochinois cited as his organization's goal: "to establish in France, and if possible in Indochina, one or several pagodas of memory, sorts of Indochinese *Panthéons*, where tablets would be kept registering the names of natives who died for France, and where the funerary cult would be celebrated each year . . . with the help of Annamites themselves."[20] This glimpse into the founding logic of the Temple du Souvenir Indochinois is revealing indeed. It shows an effort at establishing a centralized site of memory, akin to the Panthéon in Paris, where, rather than being entombed, "great men" would be remembered on tablets. The Vietnamese use of tablets to pay tribute to ancestors is well documented. Already in the colonial era, these tablets had fascinated French missionaries and anthropologists. They noted the belief that the soul of the deceased entered into a tablet bearing a series of specifications, which was itself worshiped on the anniversary of death, when offerings were made before it.[21]

A few days before the Armistice of November 11, 1918, French Colonial authorities concluded the first phase in the sensitive debate over memorializing Indochinese losses. Daniel Sherman has shown how considerations of cost on the one hand, and emotional imperatives of remembrance on the other hand, made for strange bedfellows in the construction of war monuments; various layers of local and national government usually ended up combining to foot the bill for local war monuments.[22] But this memorial was more than local; it was designed to represent a vast and heterogeneous colonial federation, comprising Tonkin, Cochin-China, Annam, Cambodia and Laos—rooting all of these "provinces" and kingdoms in the soil of France. The task of balancing the local, the colonial, the national and the Indochinese, not to mention diverse Indochinese constituencies, would prove a considerable challenge at Nogent.

Funding the Memorial

From the outset, commemoration at Nogent was articulated as an Indochinese *geste*. In December 1917, the Souvenir Indochinois—a smaller associational equivalent to the much vaster Commonwealth grave commission, was established to maintain the grounds at Nogent. Later, its jurisdiction would further extend to smaller memorials soon planned for Toulouse, Marseille and Aix-en-

Provence. The organization would accept both Indochinese and French dona-tions. Its mandate was to "maintain the upkeep of the graves of our Indochinese subjects and protégés, who died outside of their homeland, in the service of France, and to accomplish this in keeping with their rites." Thus the uniqueness of Indochinese commemoration was expressed already in 1918. Indeed, the very raison d'être of the Souvenir Indochinois centered around "the importance which the Indochinese attach to the accomplishment of duties to be paid to the dead."[23] The otherness and exoticism which the French ascribed to Indochinese cults of the dead thus explain in large part the effort to establish a separate site of commemoration in the first place.

However, already in 1918, French authorities were careful to insist that the Indochinese themselves had first desired this memorial. The founding president of the Souvenir Indochinois, a former director of education in Indochina, Henri Gourdon,[24] declared in January 1918:

> On several occasions, our indigenous auxiliaries, *tirailleurs*, or workers in war factories, currently in France, expressed their desire that we tend to the graves of their comrades who perished in France or in the Eastern Theater. In some areas, they themselves pooled their resources to achieve this pious duty; but they prefer that this task be entrusted more generally to an association placed under the authority of the Administration, offering guarantees that funds will be justly spent, and that after their departure from France, their scheme will be followed to fruition. It is of this thought that was born the Souvenir Indochinois.[25]

Though official ownership rested with France, Paris, and the Museum d'Histoire naturelle (proprietor of the Jardin colonial), original impetus was ascribed to the Indochinese, thereby justifying the campaign to ask Indochinese peoples to fund "their own" memorials. In June 1918, the then Governor General of Indochina Albert Sarraut launched this campaign, writing to the ministry of the colonies in Paris that "all will be done to create local committees to en-sure a propaganda campaign all across Indochina for the memorial, and to raise subscriptions for it."[26] This was achieved on a grand scale. The 1920 inaugura-tion ceremony of the Temple du Souvenir was even filmed by a Gaumont crew, and screened in early public showings in Indochina.[27]

In her dissertation on everyday practices in French colonial Indochina, Er-ica Peters has shown how contributions to the Temple du Souvenir Indochinois surpassed all expectations. She attributes this success in part to the fact that Vietnamese relatives and friends of fallen *tirailleurs* wished "to alleviate the danger of untended, unvisited graves, a motive that made sense to communities and individuals in Vietnam."[28] Peters argues more generally that Vietnamese donations under colonial rule served to subvert the colonial order of things. Giving to "European" causes, she contends, provided the empowering role-reversing spectacle of Indochinese giving to *French* charity, thereby upsetting the power relations between colonizer and colonized.[29] But what renders the case of the Temple du Souvenir Indochinois so significant, is that it was strictly speaking neither a French nor a uniquely Vietnamese cause, but rather a pan-Indochinese and imperial one. And in this sense, perhaps refusing to give to such a cause would be more subversive than contributing to it.

Not surprisingly, the French colonial archives contain message after message trumpeting the generosity of donations in specific Indochinese regions, districts, and municipalities. By November 30, 1920, the region of Tonkin alone had raised 543,893 Francs for the cause, sending installments by cheque to Jean Gourdon, president of the Souvenir Indochinois. For its part, the entire colony of Laos contributed some 5,123 Francs to the cause in August and September 1920 alone.[30] Not to be outdone, the economically vital and populous Southern colony of Cochin-China reported in September 1920 that it had raised some 619,996 Francs in subscriptions alone for the Souvenir Indochinois. The Governor of Cochin-China noted in his letter accompanying the September cheque:

> As you will judge from the importance of the sums collected, Cochin-China has made it a point of honor to give an important percentage of the resources which will allow the Souvenir Indochinois to achieve its goals. The indigenous population has given the majority of these donations, but the French population too has made a most notable participation, if one considers the smallness of the French community . . . You will find enclosed the list of all donors French and native, having pledged a sum of 200 Francs or more. No doubt you will wish to inscribe . . . these names as benefactors of the Souvenir Indochinois.[31]

Here, the individualized act of giving was of course memorialized itself. Of these high-end donors, one finds a number of banks, corporations and associations, ranging from a Masonic lodge[32] to a Saigon real estate company. But among individual donors, one does count forty-seven Indochinese individuals having made such donations, to be contrasted with a mere seventeen French personal donations (and yet, predictably the local committee or Conseil d'administration overseeing the Souvenir Indochinois did not include a single Indochinese representative).[33] Naturally, the promise of prestige constituted an important motivation for giving; a 1920 article by Lê-Quang-Liêm in the Saigon-based *Echo Annamite* called upon "generous notables" from all Indochina to give to the Temple du Souvenir, guaranteeing that there would still be time to engrave a tardy donor's name on the temple's lacquered inner wall.[34] Giving a large sum to the Souvenir Indochinois thus ipso facto procured the label of "notable," and a measure of recognition if not immortalization.

More importantly for our purposes, in his statement above, the Governor of Cochin-China went to great lengths at once to underscore that most of the giving had been done by "natives," and, without the slightest contradiction, argued that the French too had been tremendously generous, given the smallness of the French community. In this instance, a delicate balance needed to be struck: the Indochinese need appear enthusiastic, but not exploited, and the French must seem to support the project, while neither dominating nor steering it. The Résident Supérieur du Tonkin seems to have walked this same tightrope. He reported in May 1920:

> Our fundraising results are all the more impressive because the campaign was launched after Têt, before the harvest, and after taxes, in other words in rather unfavorable conditions. I had given very firm instructions that no pressure be applied, but Annamites wished spontaneously to testify their sentiments for those who gave their lives to France.[35]

In this case, a high-ranking colonial official emphasized that no pressure had been brought to bear on indigenous populations, and that this purely voluntary élan coincided with the worst possible time of year, rendering it all the more remarkable.

However, not all segments of Indochinese society approved the goals of the Souvenir Indochinois. Many undoubtedly held the French responsible for the 1,548 Indochinese casualties in Europe, and, closer to home, for the simultaneous ironfisted crackdown on the Thai Nguyen rebellion in 1917.[36] Several voices of opposition specifically contested the forms of First World War memorialization and remembrance that the French seemed to be imposing on the Indochinese. None other than Hồ Chí Minh lampooned the French for the way in which moneys were raised to fund a monument to Vietnamese war dead from the province of Bien-Hoa. In one of his early writings, the budding Vietnamese revolutionary noted first that traditional Vietnamese etiquette required a village to mourn its dead by maintaining silence; thus farmers in charge of sheathing rice would refrain from singing near the village of the deceased. In contrast, noted Hồ Chí Minh, Bien Hoa was now celebrating its war dead with a lavish buffet and Western garden-party, attended by the crème de la crème of French colonial society.[37] No doubt the lack of sobriety of these French fundraising campaigns shocked the sensitivities of more than merely young Vietnamese revolutionaries.

More sardonically still, the Saigon journalist Đỗ-Biệt lambasted both the proliferation of fundraising campaigns for war memorials, and French politicians' view of Indochina as a playground. Under the straight-faced title: "a project for a war monument to the dead of Indochina," a dialogue between two fictitious characters concludes with cynicism: "Who will pay for the monument? The taxpayer of course. . . . At least he will be able to admire a masterpiece of art . . . or another horror of sculpture and architecture. . . . Besides, a monument to the war dead makes all the living happy!" Worse yet, it soon becomes apparent from the article that the fictitious war monument in question is dedicated not to Indochinese soldiers as the title leads one to believe, but instead to two tigers which the Parisian politician Valude boasted of having shot on his recent hunting escapade in Dalat. The column imagines a war monument featuring one or more tigers: "the tiger will be the unknown soldier, anonymous, arbitrarily chosen from amongst all other soldier-tigers."[38] Here Đỗ-Biệt took aim at what he saw as several of the trappings of French commemoration, confusing a variety of commemorative forms in the process: from the selection of a prototypical, anonymous victim for a national cenotaph, to the motifs represented on local and national war memorials. To be sure, he was concerned more with the projected local war monument for Saigon, than he was with the pan-Indochinese Nogent memorial. Still, Đỗ-Biệt, like Hồ Chí Minh, clearly considered such memorials an imposition, a hybrid, or worse yet, something of a farce. In this sense, not contributing to such a memorial—and indeed actively opposing it—became far more of an oppositional endeavor than endorsing it.

Identity, Marginality, and Commemoration

Discontent soon emerged over Indochinese victims who had seemingly been left out in the original plan, which had called for the Thudaumôt house to serve as a Buddhist shrine—an odd interpretation of the *dinh*, which in Vietnam centered more on the cult of ancestors than on Buddhist religion.[39] In any event, in May 1920, the apostolic vicar of Western Tonkin, Msgr. Gendreau, expressed his shock to the Résident Supérieur of Tonkin that the Souvenir Indochinois had planned a temple for Buddhist losses, and not for Catholic ones. From his parish in Késo, this cleric proposed that the Church of Nogent be designated as a commemorative temple to Indochinese Catholics—an exact parallel designation to that of the Thudaumôt "temple." In a compromise measure, a stele to all Indochinese Christians was erected in the alley of war monuments in the Jardin Colonial, at a right angle from the Thudaumôt "temple." In this way, Indochinese Christians were fully integrated into the commemorative ensemble of Nogent (see figure 2.3).

Concerns that there be a plurality of memorials, reflecting the diversity of Indochina, had emerged from the very inception of the Souvenir Indochinois. Arduous discussions soon ensued as to whether such monuments should be secular or religious, and whether each of Indochina's quite distinct *"pays"*—Laos, Cambodia, Tonkin, Annam and Cochin-China, ought to be represented. In 1919, Gourdon had already entertained the possibility of a separate monument to Cambodian fatalities, given Cambodia's cultural specificity. In Gourdon's words: "next to the pagoda there would be a Buddhist Stupa in memory of Cambodians who died for France."[40] A later source described the Stupa as follows (see figure 2.4): "A Phnom was erected for Cambodians and Laotians, on the model of the most beautiful specimens of religious architecture from Phnom-Penh, so as to ensure that their funerary cult be practiced exactly as if they had died in their land of origin."[41] The emphasis here resided in absolute authenticity, in rerooting "native" soldiers into their original culture by paying a nativist tribute to them. But a very important shift had occurred between Gourdon's initial blueprint and the Stupa's eventual construction: the monument as it now stands is dedicated to *both* Cambodian and Laotian losses. Clearly, in this instance, Laotian memorialization was utterly subsumed into that of Cambodia.

Figure 2.4: The Stupa, whose inscription reads "To Cambodians and Laotians who died for France." Author's photograph, all rights reserved.

Whereas Laotian and Christian casualties were eventually included, other categories were not. The Saigon press noted with some bitterness: "we regret that Cochin-China was not represented at this inauguration in Nogent. We regret even more that our own temple, the *Panthéon* of our national glory . . . has not even gotten off the ground."[42] This must have seemed all the more vexing because the keystone of the Souvenir Indochinois, the *dinh* from Thudaumôt, was of course Cochin-Chinese, and had moreover been constructed and shipped to France at the colony of Cochin-China's expense. More broadly then, tensions emerged between local and imperial commemoration, but also over the exclusion of Cochin-China as a viable commemorable entity. Indeed, the Souvenir Indochinois had evidently privileged ethnic taxonomies over the more conventionally recognized *Ky* or *pays*. Thus, instead of featuring memorials to the dead of Tonkin, Cochin-China, Annam, Cambodia and Laos, which would have reflected the official administrative division of Indochina, the Souvenir Indochinois selected a classification along religious and ethnic lines.[43]

The Moment of Dedication

Furnishings were still trickling into Nogent as final preparations were undertaken to inaugurate the Temple du Souvenir Indochinois. As late as mid-December 1919, Parisian authorities bemoaned that neither incense sticks nor genuine Indochinese firecrackers had arrived, thereby potentially jeopardizing the authenticity of the dedication ceremony.[44] After several postponements, the ceremony finally took place on June 9, 1920, and was attended by such notables as Marshal Joffre, Alexandre Millerand, and Đặng Ngọc Oanh, a personal representative of the Emperor of Annam.

The press in both France and Indochina widely reported the inauguration ceremony of June 1920, reading various exotic fantasies into the event, and telling the sacrifice of "little Asian men" with the utmost paternalism. Interestingly, the Saigon press simply lifted from its Parisian colleagues. *L'Echo an-*

namite reprinted an article from *Le Journal*, describing the abrupt transition between the ceremony's first and second act: "Then, suddenly, the ceremony became Oriental: strange music came from the end of the park: gongs and drums . . . were slowly resonating. When, suddenly, a bizarre and magnificent cortege appeared."[45] *Le Petit Parisien* described "a decor which could very well be set in Indochina, on the edge of a calm pond with inclined reeds."[46] Others eschewed images of luxuriance in favor of "exotic" sights and sounds. *L'Echo de Paris* reported: "The cortege stops; only the priests have entered so as to accomplish the rites of dedication. Gong sounds mingle with melancholy music, sung in high notes. Flames go to and fro; one can spot them deep inside the sanctuary. Clouds of blue incense billow from the open doors, rising to the azure of the heavens."[47] Nearly all French accounts employed patronizing and racist epithets to describe Indochinese combatants. To some, they were "little soldiers born under a warmer sun."[48] To *Le Figaro*, more tellingly, these "little Asiatic soldiers" need be remembered at Nogent for the simple reason that "Each one of them, by dying, had saved the life of a Frenchman."[49] The logic of relying on colonial troops would continue unabated during the inter-war period.

Memory and Meanings since 1920

A journalist contemplating the Temple du Souvenir during the trying months of the Phony War in 1939, painted the following portrait:

> This temple, in true Annamite style . . . is representative of the religious architecture of Annam. It recalls Chinese buildings with its low roofs, its vast peristyle and its long wooden colonnade. As we enter . . . we see three altars in a grand central nave: in the center, the imperial altar, dedicated by Emperor Khaï-Dinh and devoted to the souls of the heroes; on the right that of the tirailleurs who fell at the hands of the enemy. On the left, that of the workers who died serving the metropole. . . . Quoting Georges Mandel, this devotion [from natives] may surprise those who ignore the humane spirit which underlies our colonial actions. . . . And this is why grateful peoples come to fight side by side with France's sons. That is why the enemy will find in front of the Maginot line wills and hearts that we know to be invincible . . . that is why the empire will rise glorious out of our common victory.[50]

This passage is notable first for its gross errors and distortions: the Thudaumôt house, of course, had not been designed as a strictly religious structure, and was representative of Southern, not Central Vietnamese, let alone Chinese architecture. But accuracy was manifestly not the prime objective here. The transparent attempt to reinscribe the Temple du Souvenir Indochinois with presentist concerns over Hitlerian expansionism shows to what extent this shrine was instrumentalized and reinvented in the aftermath of the Great War.

The Souvenir Indochinois' records of deliberations show that the association and temple's functions would continue to be rearticulated and reinvented after 1939. In 1941, the Souvenir Indochinois set about establishing the number of Indochinese casualties in the most recent conflict, so as to add name tablets in the postwar period—thereby grafting the memory of the Second World War onto that of the First—a common phenomenon amongst French war memorials.[51] Final 1945 calculations would reveal some 500 Indochinese dead in action, roughly 30 FFI (Resistance forces), and some 900 worker fatalities, for a total falling just shy of the 1548 Indochinese dead of the First World War.[52]

A Dissident Voice

At the May 1945 meeting of the administrative council of the Souvenir Indochinois, Mr. Lanh, representing the Amicale des Annamites de Paris, seized the stage, using it as a platform to preach for liberal reform and equality of opportunity in the emerging French postwar society. Although his voice is partly muted in the minutes, the outraged reaction of the other members of the Souvenir Indochinois reveals the gist of Lanh's grievances. Lanh underscored the sacrifices of Indochinese workers and soldiers in the two world wars, commenting on the unexpectedly high totals for the latest conflict, before arguing that the Indochinese should be allowed to gain access to public sector positions in both France and Indochina. An indignant Souvenir Indochinois president retorted that ever since 1926, Indochinese and French candidates had been afforded equal opportunity for public posts. Nowhere is the Souvenir Indochinois' position as the archimedian point of imperial tension more clearly evidenced. In this instance, a representative of Indochinese voices attempted to invoke a memory of sacrifice while speaking for a larger community, in a bid to extract concessions from an intransigent colonial institution.

Authenticity or Pastiche?

The records of the Souvenir Indochinois for the second half of the twentieth century reveal a determined effort to earn the site's recognition by the Caisse nationale des monuments historiques (CNMH)—a manner of conferring legitimacy to this landscape of commemoration of course, but also of obtaining funds from the French government, and of protecting the site from erosion or decay. This goal was achieved on May 6, 1965, when an architect for the CNMH, familiar with the jardin d'agronomie tropicale, lobbied his superiors to confer this status on the Temple du Souvenir Indochinois. Although delighted by this turn of events, the Souvenir Indochinois' leadership nonetheless bemoaned that only the "temple" proper—that is the sculpted house of Thudaumôt—had gained this recognition. In the words of the Association's president, André Angladette:

> What is regrettable is that only the "temple" has been listed, when
> there are within this area where ceremonies are performed, a number
> of other monuments, like the Khmer one, the one dedicated to Chris-
> tians, etc. which have been considered by the Inspector General to be
> pastiches which do not deserve to be registered with the *Monuments
> historiques*. This is especially regrettable in the case of the portal at
> the garden's entrance, which is authentic. But unfortunately, we have
> no proof that this portal was delivered with the pagoda, or that it
> constitutes an integral part of it.[53]

Here the triumph of recognition was tempered by allegations of inauthenticity,
or even kitsch. My analysis shows that only two factors seem to set the temple
apart from the rest of the ensemble at Nogent: first that it was built in Indochina
itself, albeit for direct export to Marseille; and second that it was constructed by
Vietnamese people, albeit partly by prisoners under duress. Thus, the portal was
ruled out, simply because its appellation or origin seemed questionable. Here,
place of construction trumped ethnicity, function, and considerations of overall
harmony, in ascribing historical legitimacy.

A Secular Temple

The year 1965 also brought a fundamental reappraisal of the sacred nature of
the Temple du Souvenir Indochinois. The new president of the Souvenir Indochinois, André Angladette decided to break with the Temple's religious function altogether, refusing to renew its Buddhist ties—hence the later creation of a
separate Indochinese Buddhist shrine (Tibetan today) on the other end of the
Bois de Vincennes. Angladette's new line was simple: "no religious ceremony
of any sort at the monument du Souvenir Indochinois."[54] Official republican
secularism had finally caught up with these explicitly religiously plural sites of
commemoration—a change crystallized in Angladette's use of the term
"Monument du Souvenir Indochinois." Another member of the administrative
council, Mr. Auger, concurred that the building could be termed neither a "temple" nor a "pagoda," but should be designated instead as a communal house or
dinh. By reversing the site's religious conversion of 1918-1920, and returning
to a lay reading of the structure, Angladette and his companions were no doubt
reflecting ambient sentiments concerning republican secular commemoration.
But in many ways, they were also stripping one of the Temple du Souvenir Indochinois' identifying features, and reducing it to either a piece of exotica, or a
mirror of the tomb of the unknown soldier.

Conflating the Indochinese and the *Parachutistes*

Perhaps the most unexpected shift in the politics of commemoration came after
the Souvenir Indochinois was dissolved in 1980 (the association had suffered

financial troubles, and could no longer claim any viable "friendly" Southeast Asian institutional connection, given the defeat of South Vietnam). The commemoration ceremony of November 2, 1980 was dominated not by elderly Indochinese veterans of the world wars, but by French veterans of the Vietnamese war of Independence, members of the "Fédération Nationale des Anciens d'outre-mer."[55] A year later, Angladette orchestrated the integration of the former Souvenir Indochinois into the ANAI, a hybrid association whose acronym stands for "Association Nationale des Anciens Amis de l'Indochine et du Souvenir Indochinois."[56] This organization brought together former settlers (the *"amis"*), French veterans of campaigns like Dien Ben Phu, and some Vietnamese, Laotians, and Cambodians living in France. Two striking points emerge here: first the illusory and anachronistic use of the very term "Indochine," more evocative by 1981 of a nostalgic imperial fantasy, than of any geographical reality; secondly, the remarkable subsuming of Indochinese casualties of the two world wars into the commemoration of colonizers fallen during the wars of decolonization. Angladette appears to have been conscious of the political stakes involved in this merger. In his November 2, 1981 speech at the newly renamed "Monument du Souvenir Indochinois," he declared:

> Over the years, we have found it logical to extend the cult of [First World War Indochinese victims] to those of the Second World War who fought alongside French troops. . . . Then, taking one more step, we have deemed that it would be right no longer to separate in our memory those brothers in arms be they French or Indochinese. That is why we have decided to merge the Association du Souvenir Indochinois with the much larger Anciens d'Indochine.[57]

Thus conflated under the guise of egalitarianism, Indochinese soldiers of the First World War could be comfortably seen as having fought a precocious struggle to keep Indochina French.

Nor was Angladette alone in taking the gamble of conflating the memories of French paratroopers with those of *tirailleurs indochinois*. General Simon wrote in October 1981 of needing to "go on the offensive and practice indoctrination" on this very issue. He "dreamed of a single, common invitation to former colonials and the ANAI, intelligently addressed. . . . There is nothing to lose . . . and everything to gain: many people will learn something about the history of France and Indochina."[58] This meta-narrative presented a single history for France and Indochina, perceived in this way as eternally bound by colonial ties. Here, colonial nostalgia, settler fantasies of indissoluble links between France and its former colonial empire, were reflected in the commemorative configuration of Nogent-sur-Marne. By the 1980s November remembrance ceremonies at Nogent featured more French "colonial" units, than they did Vietnamese, Laotian or Cambodian mourners or veterans.

Conclusion

In his 1992 inauguration of the new "temple" built to replace the original Thu-daumôt house, General Simon underscored the continuity of Indochinese sacri-fice for France, charting a long line of Indochinese casualties, from the First World War to the most recent: a Franco-Vietnamese former "boat-person," who died on the coalition side during the Gulf War. General Simon further alluded to a reciprocity of sacrifice, constructing an image of a France that had supposedly protected Indochina, even positing that Dien Ben Phu had been fought to save Laos from communism.[59]

In the final analysis, the Temple du Souvenir Indochinois, and the sur-rounding memorial landscape, provide a fruitful prism through which to view issues of colonial power relations, Indochinese identities, the seduction of the exotic in France, imperial tensions, and the shifting meanings of colonial com-memoration. The difference embedded into this site dedicated to specifically Indochinese sacrifice was subjected to a variety of readings. The French press seized it as an emblem of orientalist exotica. Some Vietnamese utilized the memorialization of Nogent to expose a gulf between commemorative cultures. Later, French sources would rearticulate commemorative genres in a bid to root Indochinese soldiers into a broader colonial matrix, and finally to evoke in the same breath the memory of both colonial conscripts and crack metropolitan troops sent to suppress colonial revolt. In a very interesting way, the "site of memory" that had been fairly uncharacteristically set aside by the French as both "alien" and "national"[60]—and simultaneously rooted in the suburbs of Paris, was finally reinvented into a space of fantasy where French colonial In-dochina could live on. This was achieved by merging the cult of Indochinese losses in France, with the memory of French losses in Southeast Asia.

Notes

An earlier version of this chapter was published in the journal *History and Memory* under the title "Remembering 'Other' Losses: The Temple du Souvenir Indochinois of Nogent-sur-Marne" (15, no. 1, 5-48). Thank you to Indiana University Press for permis-sion to reproduce this article.

1. There have been persistent rumors that arson was responsible. See "Discours du Gé-néral Simon," *Bulletin de l'ANAI* (April-June 1992): 3.

2. Throughout this chapter, I will use former colonial-era names to designate sites in modern-day Laos, Cambodia and Vietnam.

3. The many misnomers used to describe the house are listed by Isabelle Aragon in her paper: "Le Temple du Souvenir Indochinois de Nogent-sur-Marne" (Mémoire du D.E.A. de Vietnamien, Université de Paris III, 1983), 10-12.

4. Robert Aldrich, "Vestiges of the Colonial Empire: The Jardin Colonial in Paris" in *The Sphinx in the Tuileries,* eds Robert Aldrich and Martyn Lyons (Sydney: Department of Economic History, 1999), 203.

5. See Duong Van Giao, "L'Indochine pendant la Guerre de 1914-1918" (Ph.D. thesis, Université de Paris, Faculté de droit, 1925), 39.

6. Most Indochinese recruits were assigned to *"bataillons d'étape"* where they built and maintained military infrastructures. See Giao, "L'Indochine pendant la Guerre," 35. On racism behind the lines in World War I, see Tyler Stovall, "The Color Line behind the Lines: Racial Violence in France during the Great War," *American Historical Review* 103, no. 3 (1998): 737-69.

7. On Indochinese laborers and soldiers in the Great War, see Mireille Le Van Ho, "L'Indochine" in *Mémoires d'outre-mer: les colonies et la Première Guerre mondiale,* edited by Marc Michel and Thomas Compère-Morel (Catalogue de l'exposition au Mémorial de Peronne, 1996), 80-90. In 1925, Duong Van Giao gave slightly different figures. Although he shared the total of 48,922 recruited between 1914 and the Armistice, he had 43,430 Indochinese coming to Europe, and 1,123 dying. Giao, "L'Indochine pendant la Guerre," 38.

8. On the 1931 colonial exhibit, see Charles-Robert Ageron, "L'Exposition coloniale de 1931: Mythe républicain ou mythe impérial," in *Les Lieux de Mémoire.* Vol. 1: *La République,* ed. Pierre Nora (Paris: Gallimard, 1984); Patricia Morton, *Hybrid Modernities: Architecture and Representation at the 1931 Colonial Exposition, Paris* (Cambridge: MIT Press, 2000); Panivong Norindr, *Phantasmatic Indochina: French Colonial Ideology in Architecture, Film and Literature* (Durham/London: Duke University Press, 1996), 14-33; Herman Lebovics, *True France: The Wars over Cultural Identity, 1900-1945* (Ithaca: Cornell University Press, 1992), 51-97; Catherine Hodeir and Michel Pierre, *L'Exposition coloniale, 1931* (Brussels: Editions Complexe, 1991).

9. Norindr, *Phantasmatic Indochina,* 20.

10. "Le Souvenir Indochinois," undated commemorative book found in the CIRAD's library. The Bibliothèque historique du CIRAD will be referred to henceforward as BHC.

11. On the Jardin colonial, and its *ancien régime* antecedents, see Aldrich, "Vestiges of the Colonial Empire," 196-98.

12. On Dybowski, see C. Vidal, "Une exposition au Jardin Colonial de Nogent-sur-Marne," *Bulletin de la société historique et archéologique de Nogent-sur-Marne* 7 (1953), 98.

13. Vidal, "Une exposition au Jardin Colonial."

14. Aragon, "Le Temple du Souvenir Indochinois de Nogent-sur-Marne," 30.

15. On the 1907 Nogent exhibit, see Vidal, "Une exposition au Jardin Colonial."

16. On the projected "return" to Phu-Cuong, see Aragon, "Le Temple du Souvenir Indochinois de Nogent-sur-Marne," 28.

17. Aragon, "Le Temple du Souvenir Indochinois de Nogent-sur-Marne," 16.

18. Aragon, "Le Temple du Souvenir Indochinois de Nogent-sur-Marne," 30, describes the *dinh's* designation as the "Palais du thé" at the 1907 Nogent exhibit, and a as "la Maison des Mandarins" at the Marseille exhibit.

19. Aragon, "Le Temple du Souvenir Indochinois de Nogent-sur-Marne," 40.

20. Archives d'outre-mer, Aix-en-Provence (hereafter CAOM), GGI 33413.

21. Leopold Cadière, *Croyances et pratiques religieuses des Vietnamiens* (Ecole française d'Extrême Orient, reprinted 1992), pp. 36-39. For a more recent discussion of tablets, see Shawn Kingsley Malarney, *Culture, Ritual and Revolution in Vietnam* (New York, 2002), 110.

22. Daniel Sherman, *The Construction of Memory in Interwar France* (Chicago: University of Chicago Press, 1999), 122-25.

23. CAOM, GGI 33413

24. "Le Souvenir Indochinois," BHC.

25. CAOM, GGI 33413

26. CAOM, GGI 33413, Sarraut to Paris #1278, June 21, 1918.

27. CAOM, GGI 33416.

28. Erica Peters, "Negotiating power through everyday practices in French Vietnam, 1880-1924" (Ph.D. thesis, University of Chicago, 2000), 313.

29. On Vietnamese giving to colonial causes in general, see Peters, "Negotiating power," chapter 6.

30. CAOM, GGI 33415.

31. CAOM, GGI 33415.

32. On Freemasonry in Indochina, see Jacques Dalloz, "Les Vietnamiens dans la franc-maçonnerie coloniale," *Revue française d'histoire d'outre-mer* 85 (1998): 103-18.

33. CAOM, GGI 33415.

34. "Le culte des morts de la Grande Guerre" *L'Echo annamite* (January 10, 1920).

35. CAOM, GGI 33415, Hanoi May 22, 1920.

36. Peter Zinoman, *The Colonial Bastille: a History of Imprisonment in Vietnam, 1862-1940* (Berkeley: University of California Press, 2001), 158-99.

37. Hồ Chí Minh, *Œuvres choisies* (Paris: Maspero, 1967), 52-53.

38. "Un projet de monument aux morts pour l'Indochine; Pièce en un tableau par Do-Biet," *L'Echo annamite* (March 23, 1923).

39. Peters, "Negotiating power," 312.

40. CAOM, GGI 33414, Gourdon to Governor of Indochina, January 11, 1919.

41. "L'Œuvre du Souvenir Indochinois" (Paris: Imprimerie nationale, 1942), 2.

42. "La prochaine inauguration du Temple du Souvenir à Nogent-sur-Marne," *L'Echo annamite* (August 13, 1920), 1.

43. On these issues of territoriality and national construction, see Benedict Anderson, *Imagined Communities* (London: Verso, 1991), 131-32; Christopher Goscha, *Vietnam or Indochina? Contesting Concepts of Space in Vietnamese nationalism, 1887-1954* (Copenhagen: NIAS, 1995).

44. CAOM GGI 33414.

45. "Hommage aux soldats coloniaux," *L'Echo annamite* July 20, 1920.

46 "In Memoriam: la consécration du temple aux mânes des Indo-Chinois morts pour la France," *Le Petit parisien* (June 10, 1920).

47. "A la mémoire des héros indochinois," *L'Echo de Paris* (June 10, 1920).

48. "A la mémoire des héros indochinois."

49. "A la mémoire de nos petits frères d'Asie," *Le Figaro* (June 10, 1920).

50. "Les Indochinois ont répondu présent," *Le Monde colonial illustré* (December 1939).

51. BHC, *Souvenir Indochinois: Procès-Verbaux des réunions du Conseil d'Administration depuis le 23 mai 1941*, 4.

52. BHC, *Souvenir Indochinois: Procès-Verbaux des réunions du Conseil d'Administration*, 29, 32.

53. BHC, *Souvenir Indochinois: Procès-Verbaux des Assemblées générales ordinaires depuis le 12 octobre 1965*, 12.

54. BHC, *Souvenir Indochinois: Procès-Verbaux des Assemblées générales ordinaires*, 12.

55. BHC, file labeled "cérémonie de 1980."

56. See the *Bulletin de l'ANAI.*

57. BHC, file labeled "cérémonie de 1981."

58. BHC, file labeled "A.N.A.I., 1981" letter from General Simon, Paris October 10, 1981.
59. "Discours du Général Simon," *Bulletin de l'ANAI* (April-June 1992), 3.
60. See John Gillis, "Memory and Identity" in *Commemorations: the Politics of National Identity* (Princeton: Princeton University Press, 1994), 9.

3

Lines of Communication:
Thematics of Direction and Strategies of Narration in Colonial Indochina

Christopher Robinson

The coordinates for the readings that follow are provided by two quotations:

> Roland Dorgelès: "La route, le télégraphe, l'auto ont bouleversé les
> mœurs. La colonie a plus évolué en quinze ans que l'Europe en un
> siècle" ("The road, the telegraph, the car have revolutionized behav-
> ior, The colony has developed more in fifteen years than Europe has
> in a century").[1]

> Jean-Luc Coatalem: "je réalise que la route qui slalome entre les ri-
> zières et les hameaux est une pelote de fil qui se dévide, que c'est ma
> vie à moi qui s'écoule, s'évanouit au tempo des kilomètres et des se-
> condes" ("I realize that the road which is zigzagging among the rice
> fields and hamlets is a ball of thread which is unwinding, that it is
> my own life which is flowing away, vanishing to the rhythm of the
> kilometers and the seconds.")[2]

What these quotations indicate is that culturally in the West rivers, roads and
railways, telephone and telegraph wires, once they appear in literary texts, serve
a complex mixture of literal (thematic) and metaphoric (symbolic) functions.
Dorgelès underlines the literal point of reference, the perceived importance of
the new systems in Indochina;[3] Coatalem repeats the age-old image of life as

travel in such a form as to tie it specifically to Indochina and to show that roads are in both their literal and metaphorical functions conceptualized as both space and time. At the same time we must remember that, in Southeast Asia, particularly in Buddhist regions such as Cambodia and Laos, Western concepts of roads and travel do not necessarily carry the same metaphoric (or indeed literal) weight: as the mother says to the future Buddhist luminary Angulimala in the recent Thai film of that name (2003), the only significant journey is into the self. And there remains the further problem of how the inherently mobile thematics of lines of communication can be translated into a fundamentally static representation within the pages of books.[4]

If the importance of road and railway construction in colonial Indochina itself justifies the presence of the motif in texts aiming at a realistic presentation of modern life there, the context of literary reception was guaranteed to complicate the ways in which such themes could be written and read. Certainly, roads and railways had become an important thematic element in nineteenth-century fiction. On the other hand, by the outbreak of the first World War the old life-as-a-journey motif, which had already bifurcated in the nineteenth century into the opposing models of Realist progress and Romantic escape, had become a more doubtful and unstable metaphor precisely because of the ways in which speed and mechanization denaturalize the process of journeying and help to fragment experience. At the same time the traditional model of linear narrative, whose forward impetus had already caused problems to a social analyst like Balzac, had been consciously subverted by the Decadents: Joris-Karl Huysmans's *En rade* (1887) by its very title (which connotes both "at anchor" and "stranded") indicates the tension between a desire for movement and an enforced immobility which is reflected in its narrative stagnation. This then is the thematic and aesthetic context into which we have to "feed" the colonial novel and its readers. To this we should add the fact that the construction of roads and railways, at least as far as Laos and Cambodia were concerned, represented a continuation of the "misreading" of the terrain which had marked the French presence in the area since the days of the earliest geographical explorations.[5] It is consequently relatively easy to represent Indochina in terms of tracklessness, the static and the absence of progress, as happens in Jean Ajalbert's *Raffin su-su* (1911) or Roland Meyer's *Saramani, danseuse cambodgienne* (1919), and therefore to dispense (more or less) with linear narrative movement, since in so doing the text at least produces a coherent account of the space of the *indigènes*. A text which focuses on roads or railways is automatically, like its subject matter, going somewhere else, and risks having little to say about the terrain through which it passes. The writers therefore have to juggle with a version of Zeno's paradox. Their thematics ensure that the texts must travel from A to B but their need to evoke indigenous space ensures that at any given point of that trajectory they will be static.

To see how authors dealt with these problems, I want to focus on three texts, Guillemet's *Sur les sentiers laotiens*, Groslier's *La Route du plus fort* and Daguerches's *Le Kilomètre 83*.[6] The first of these I am using as a default text, in that it is an inherently linear travelogue about a journey on pre-colonial tracks. The function of the journey around which *Sur les sentiers* is built is a military expedition (in 1915) to punish a band of Chinese pirates who have attacked the French post at Samnua, killing the Administrator and his troops and making off with money and ammunitions. The linear development is supported paratextually by a map of military activity in upper Laos and intratextually by the intermittent reporting of routes, places and time-spans. This is, if you like, the colonial heart of the text, and we can attach to it a whole rhetoric of superiority which is established from the outset of the text by the application to Laos of a model of what the country should be, in terms of physical geography: both the Mekong and the mountain system are reproached for not allowing the kinds of economic development which the French require of them, either in terms of internal economic development or as part of a route from Yunnan and southwestern China to Saigon. At its worst this rhetoric of superiority generates not just paternalistic imagery—people in the little villages along the Nam Pak who come out to greet the passing troops are described as "une assemblée de fleurs des champs" ("a gathering of flowers of the fields") and are said to be "heureux de la protection que notre présence leur assure" ("happy at the protection that our presence affords them"), but a whole pattern of references to laziness, silence and immobility which stands in explicit contrast with the active life symbolized by Roman legionaries, who embody the military as ideal colonist, an active life defined as "la bonne saine et forte vie qu'ont vécue tous les grands coloniaux au début de leur carrière" ("the good and healthy life that all great colonists have experienced at the outset of their careers"). The message would seem to be that action, particularly as embodied in the forward drive of military adventure, constitutes the positive in life, and that the physical and human geography of northern Laos are inherently inadaptable to such action.

When we look closely at the text, however, we find that the linear narrative structure and the colonial philosophy and attendant rhetoric are actually subordinate to a quite separate set of elements. Even the initial application to Laos of a certain model of *mise en valeur* (valorization—the standard euphemism in colonial discourse for commercial exploitation) is modified by awareness of an alternative perspective: if the Mekong is not the high road to China that the French want it to be, it can still be seen as a source of Laotian prosperity, e.g., "C'est sur ses rives, engraissées par le limon qu'il y dépose, que poussent le coton, le tabac, l'indigo et les légumes d'usage courant. Il est dans une certaine mesure au Laos ce que le Nil est à l'Egypte."[7] (5-6: "It is on its banks, enriched by the mud that it deposits there, that cotton, tobacco, indigo and the commonly used vegetables grow. To a certain point it is to Laos what the Nile is to Egypt"). In other parts of the text this awareness of alternative ways of interpreting the landscape manifests itself as a full-blown espousal of contradiction. This is most noticeable, and most important, in relation to the themes of inaction, immobility and stasis which I invoked earlier. When the focus of the text is on the military narrative, stasis brought about by outside agencies (such as reprovisioning problems or waiting for news from other posts), and the loss of a sense of orderly progression of time which accompanies stasis, Guillemet experiences nothing but a sense of irritation. He goes so far as to define inaction as a "mal qui fait plus de ravages peut-être que le climat" (57: "a disease that is more destructive than the climate"). But against this we can set a contrasting pleasure in certain moments of immobile contemplation and a consequent irritation with those "sujets d'occupation et de préoccupation" (192: "tasks and worries") which, like the mundane experiences in the second half of Baudelaire's prose poem "La Chambre double,"[8] bring the writer back into linear time. The opening of chapter V, "Vers la frontière des Sip Song Pana" with its long description of changing patterns of mist and cloud over an early morning landscape exemplifies this perfectly, culminating in the observation: "Être venus ici et voir cela par de si radieuses matinées infiniment rares en cette saison voilà de quoi nous faire oublier les misères de la route, les grimpades à pic sur des sentiers abominables, la boue, la pluie et la vermine. Heures délicieuses et charmantes dont on voudrait ralentir l'écoulement pour mieux les respirer" (129: "To have come here and seen this on such bright mornings, which are infinitely rare at this season, is enough to make us forget the ghastliness of getting here, the vertical clambering on appalling paths, the mud, the rain and the vermin. Delicious and charming hours, the rhythm of whose passing one would like to slow down so that one might inhale them all the better").

This reevaluation of stasis is accompanied in other parts of the text by a reevaluation of the act of journeying itself. Not only does stasis have an appeal: so does undirected *flânerie*. As the narrative nears its end, Guillemet reflects on the happiness which he is experiencing, despite the fact that nothing out of the ordinary is actually happening. He locates the happiness in the enormous pleasure to be found in a sense of independence, and in the contemplation of the power (his term is *puissance*) of the Laotian landscape. And these two elements he links to the notion of wandering, the nomadic life, the nonlinear, nonteleologically determined journey: "Pour tout dire en un mot, je savoure doucement cette quiétude singulière, cet allègement de tout notre être que donne la vie nomade, qui fut la vie libre et sereine des premiers hommes aux premiers âges"[9] (248: "In a nutshell, I take a quiet pleasure in this singular serenity, this lightening of our entire being that the nomadic life, which was the free and peaceful life of earliest man at the beginning of time, accords"). It would be easy to write this kind of thing down to exoticist rhetoric, especially if we pick out passages which focus on the inviolate state of the landscape or the harking after "coins inconnus où palpite encore l'âme du passé" ("unknown corners where the heart of the past still beats"). But here any insistence on the past is not part of a critique of failure to develop: it is a rejection of the modern in the West. At the end of *Sur les sentiers* in a retrospective view inspired by visiting Laos after the War, Guillemet makes Laotian stasis a paradisiacal feature. The definition is explicitly provocative: "Par un privilège inouï—d'aucuns pourraient la regretter, alors que je m'en réjouis—la roue de fer de la civilisation, qui trouve plaisir à bouleverser tous les éléments d'activité sociale pour le plat triomphe utilitaire de l'uniformité, n'a pas encore passé par là. Par une fortune inespérée cet immense territoire, paradoxalement à la fois très riche et très pauvre, n'a pas bougé" (271: "By an unheard-of privilege—some might regret it, but I rejoice at it—the iron wheel of civilization, which takes pleasure in revolutionizing all aspects of social life for the banal purpose of winning total uniformity, has not yet touched this place. By a stroke of unexpected good fortune this immense territory, which is paradoxically both very rich and very poor at the same time, has remained static"). The explanation for this apparent shift is clear. As the text of *Sur les sentiers* reveals, Guillemet's initial experience in Laos has been followed by service on the trenches. He therefore knows the horrors of externally-imposed negative stasis only too well. What he appreciates in Laos is the possibility of *choosing* stasis.

Alongside this reevaluation of stasis Guillemet continues to acknowledge the inevitability of movement. But he contrasts the modern Westerner, attached to the age of high-speed trains, cars and planes (271) with the close-to-nature Laotian peasant riding his oxcart (a juxtaposition more explicitly explored by Groslier in *La Route du plus fort*). This preference for the meandering progress of the cart, the drifting of a raft (235), the unguided *flânerie* of the nomad, takes us back to the narration itself. When (31) Guillemet initially invites the reader to follow him "dans de longues et lointaines pérégrinations" ("in long and distant peregrinations") the reference appears merely to refer to the six months of the military expedition. In fact it is as much an invitation to wander through a text whose order is as deceptive as its maps are indecipherable, whose narrative is constantly deferred in favor of description and commentary, a text which is couched in a misleadingly uniform present tense which disguises the elongations and ellipses of time, a text in which Zeno's paradox is exemplified to exaggeration point by the constant descriptive and analytical pauses through which the linear narrative is paradoxically conducted. Taking an example more or less at random, if we analyze the relationship between narrative and description in the opening two sections of chapter V ("Vers la frontière des Sip Song Pana"), then despite the disarmingly forward-propelling "towards" of the title the chapter has a complex rhythm:

paras 1 and 2: voluntary stasis—two paragraphs on the beauty of nature;

paras 3-6: involuntary stasis—four paragraphs on provisioning problems, enforced waiting and news of a setback from fellow troops at Long-Nai;

paras 5-13: nine paragraphs of forward narrative;

paras 14-22: nine paragraphs eulogizing the banana palm, the bamboo and the multiplicity of their uses.

In other words, even in a section where the importance of linear narrative is signaled in the title, a framework of reference to the beauty and uses of the natural context and a contrast of voluntary and involuntary stasis put the element of linear narrative into a different perspective.

In practice, then, the shape and rhythm of Guillemet's journey are to a significant degree determined by the landscape through which he moves and his response to it and its human inhabitants as opposed to the military narrative that runs through it. This allows him to modify the classic exoticist view of an indolent, sensuous (though virgin) Laotian paradise by giving more weight to the complexities of its physical and human geography, and by specifically contrasting it with the Europe of World War One. Its narrative strategies in part exemplify the reassessment of the concept of stasis and the preference for nomadic wandering over linear progression which the text in part thematically expounds. Admittedly, in one respect what he produces is redolent of the *mission civilisatrice*: he often seeks to make Laos knowable in terms of European cultural reference, be it by use of cliché (e.g., the jungle as ocean) or by quotation (frequently from Lamartine). But at the same time the text faces up to some of the problems of fitting colonial discourse to experience whose potential meanings risk being obscured by the currently fashionable aesthetics of such discourse. Guillemet, presumably by instinct, offsets the colonial mentality by subverting his own temporal and spatial linear narrative, in an attempt to encompass, define and recreate the autonomous space (physical and human) of Laos in nonlinear ways which make sense of his own awareness of changed values.

Guillemet merely matches his narrative to the demands of a precolonial system of paths and waterways. In contrast Daguerches's *Le Kilomètre 83* and Groslier's *La Route du plus fort* focus on road and railway building in such a way that the thematics of travel also function as a metatext, drawing attention to the broader philosophical and aesthetic issues which their narratives raise. In *La Route du plus fort*, there is a whole thematics of linear versus nonlinear, movement versus stasis embodied in the Ternier/Hélène relationship, and the interpretation of that thematics is made more doubtful precisely by the fact that while Ternier undoubtedly embodies the colonial aspiration toward *mise en valeur* albeit in a relatively philanthropic form, Hélène can be read as both the feminine in general and as the nonlinear values represented by Cambodia. Even granted that colonial discourse, as Nicola Cooper points out,[10] regularly feminizes Indochina, this identification of a French woman, herself inherently also identified with the motif of the motorcar, with the native space of the Cambodian landscape results in a problematic spatial discourse. The fact that the feminine is not necessarily identifiable as the weak (the "plus fort" of the title being subjectable to ironic reading) will complicate interpretation further.

The thematics of lines of communication are peculiarly obtrusive in Groslier's novel. Traveling, touring, road-building, road inspection, cars, carts, elephants: each of these is both a recurrent motif and a particular focal subject at one or more points in the novel. Insofar as Ternier has a character at all it is the linearity of a man with a mission—the opening up of Cambodia by the construction of his road—and the construction of the road itself is a fundamental part of the scientific modernization that includes, for example, the installation of the telephone and telegraph systems. Later the text allows the road to embody these ideas in a more literal way.[11] But just as the other lines of communication, notably telegrams, turn out to be defective and misleading, so the text offers a second discourse on roads which is quite different in tone. The opening chapter in which Ternier, driving a Roland-Gassin while on leave in France, meets Roland Gassin himself and his wife Hélène in a broken-down version of the same

car, can retrospectively be read as deeply ironic. If we bear in mind the road imagery used of Gassin: "Il avait de la vie cette notion souvent hautaine de ceux
qui suivent une voie bien tracée, y triomphent et concluent."[12] (12: "He possessed the frequently haughty view of life of those who follow a clearly-laid
down path triumphantly and reach their conclusion"), we can see that, just as
she steps from one Roland-Gassin into "une seconde voiture, Roland-Gassin
aussi et de même type" ("a second car, also a Roland-Gassin, of the same
model"), Hélène, in exchanging her husband for Ternier, exchanges one linear-
minded man for another. More importantly, Hélène herself rapidly becomes associated with *non*-linearity and a form of positive stasis which recalls Guillemet's defense of Laotian immobility. In chapter 3 where she goes touring in the
environs of Sangké on her own, her linear intentions—she wants to fix and
process what she sees as she travels past it—are disrupted by the multiplicity of
detail: "Trop de choses déroutaient ses regards" (28: "Too many things way-
laid[13] her gaze"). It is only when she stops that she can take in the world: "Elle
fit arrêter la voiture et, tapie dans son coin de cuir, elle ouvrait son intelligence à
cette fécondité" (29: "She had the driver stop the car and, snuggled in her
leather corner, she opened her mind to the fecundity around her"), a process
which directly mirrors the way in which the writer is obliged to stop the narrative in order to create a pictorial sense of the space in which it is taking place.
Hélène is in fact learning to share the stasis of the young Cambodian men
dreaming on a bench and the children who stand motionless around the car.
Groslier goes out of his way to emphasize the wider symbolism of Hélène's little trip: "Tout le Cambodge s'assoupissait là, contenu, symbolisé en un coin de
son territoire . . . C'est partout cette même volupté immobile et simple, la même
poésie qu'enveloppe l'immédiat horizon" (32-33: "All Cambodia was drowsing
there, contained, symbolized in a corner of its territory . . . Everywhere is this
same motionless, simple pleasure, the same poetry that the imminent horizon
envelops"). Hélène's voluntary acceptance of stasis is what allows her to see
Cambodia properly and by implication to understand it. We are offered stasis as
a source of poetic intuition rather than as a marker of stagnation, which is how
it will be portrayed in the following chapter when Ternier takes Hélène to visit
the French quarter and delivers his six page *plaidoirie* on the invigorating benefits of the French presence.

From his first meeting with her Ternier assumes that he can put Hélène on
the right track about Cambodia, and she herself attempts to read it and him in
the same way: "Si les révélations et touches sobres du Résident la déroutaient
encore, elles l'invitaient à s'avancer désormais dans tout cet inconnu en dé-
marches logiques, sur des routes bien établies, éclairée d'un tranquille bon sens"
("If the revelations and sober touches of the Resident still threw her off course,
they also bade her go forward from this point on into the unknown in logical
steps, by well established roads, illuminated by a tranquil good sense"). By the
end she is able to offer her own reading: when Ternier, Hélène and the road itself are brought to a stop by impenetrable forest, Hélène's "Ainsi la route
s'arrête ici" ("So the road stops here") defines not just the physical road but her

relationship with Ternier, her life story, even the narrative itself, all of which have been slowing down or fading out for some time. Ternier responds in terms of the challenge of the unknown; Hélène on the contrary sees it as the victory of the unknown. Ternier's frantic journey back to Sangké to get drugs and medical instruments to deal with Hélène's appendicitis, while Hélène is ironically condemned to "l'immobilité la plus absolue" (219: "the most absolute immobility") stages the fatuity of the man of action. Ternier pursues his goal to no end. If this were simply part of the story of Ternier and Hélène it might matter little, but Groslier himself underlines the symbolism, first in addressing Ternier ironically as conqueror—"Cours conquérant sur ta route" (226: "Hurry on your way, conqueror"), then in defining Hélène's symbolic rôle as an effort defeated by another effort, and finally by suggesting that Hélène can be read as "la fleur secrète de cette région ouverte par ton soc" ("the secret flower of this region, exposed by your ploughshare"). The act of opening up Cambodia is merely destroying what it is supposed to "mettre en valeur" ("valorize"), because Ternier is guilty of running counter to the natural rhythms inherent in the environment.[14]

The reader might expect the literary structures and devices of the novel to offer some resolution to the problem of these contradictory discourses. Solange Thierry in her postface to the Kaïlash edition, writes of two *fils conducteurs* ("narrative threads") but in fact the novel barely possesses a linear narrative any more than it possesses developing (or knowable) characters. The *données* of the story are slight and the explanation of what happens is all dependant on two letters to which Ternier and the reader only have access in the last chapter. Characters mouth a discourse of forward movement (road-building, social progress) but speech is itself a static element. Description, on the other hand, which, as Hélène discovers, requires standing and looking, is the element on which the reader's progress in understanding is predicated. Moreover, in the third of the book devoted to the final journey along the road and the undeveloped tract which is its continuation, not only is description the only significant "event," but the division between organic, inorganic and human dissolves, as the road takes on a mind of its own and the human and the organic fuse: "l'homme et la forêt s'assemblent pour se mouvoir ensemble" (172: "man and forest come together to move together"). Lyrical evocations of the countryside and people (notably a distinctly homoerotic hymn to the naked male Cambodian body), by invoking such concepts as positive silence (202), weight the text in the direction of the discourse represented by Hélène. The text is thus divided between the natural linearity of its apparent plot and dominant road imagery and the competing desire to stroll, to stop, to fragment, such that the conclusion provided by the letters seems an arbitrary and almost unnecessary imposition of conventional literary shaping.

Whether there is, in the strict sense, a metatext about forms of narration in *La Route du plus fort* is open to discussion. Whether there is one in Daguerches's *Le Kilomètre 83* on the other hand is not. The reason for this is obvious. Daguerches's text is dominated by a need to justify and make sense of the model represented by the railway both thematically and aesthetically. *Le Kilomètre 83* opens with a key passage for the interpretation of the aesthetics of the novel and their relationship to its thematics. Daguerches introduces a Chinese artist, An-hoan, whose task is to decorate the kilometer stones that mark the railway's progress. The central function of these decorations is to establish a link between the Asian cultural context and the Western artifact that passes through it: the stones bear either a motif relating to the area they represent or some "unreadable" Chinese symbols. But An-hoan (whose cross-cultural link-function is emphasized by the doubling of his name with its Western approximation Antoine) has died on the day he finished kilometer-stone 82. The expressed function of the narrative that is to follow is to constitute the Western analogue of an An-hoan decorated stone: "La borne du kilomètre 83, dont An-hoan a laissé vierge la tablette de grès, je veux la dresser dans ma mémoire"[15] ("An-hoan has left the sandstone facing of kilometer stone 83 unmarked; I want to create it in my memory"). It is culturally a Western analogue precisely in that the narrator refuses the possibility of pure decoration and insists on the realism, the paradoxically both momentary (static) and yet linear (mobile) nature, of what he will produce. It is a realism which emphasizes movement and progression in both space and time: "Mon désir est qu'elle réverbère avec clarté, miroir successif et fidèle, les images mobiles enregistrées au fil de l'heure et de ses mille mètres de rails" ("My desire is that it should clearly reflect, in its faithful sequential mirror, the moving images recorded on it by the passage of time and of its thousand meters of rail"). Significantly, moreover, the project announces its own inevitable failure in terms which are echoed at the end of the novel. The passage is worth quoting in full because its details are important:

> Désir naïf, demain déçu! Mais n'est-ce pas assez qu'il en subsiste, maintenant que le vieil Asiatique n'est plus là pour dégager le signe essentiel, tout au moins une assez belle confusion d'hiéroglyphes, quelque sœurs de ces stèles que l'on trouve, chues dans l'herbe, au cœur touffu de la forêt d'Angkor, et que les touristes qu'elles font rêver appellent des "Mains de Bouddha"! (245)

> (Naïve aspiration, which the morrow will overthrow. But, now that the old Asian is no longer with us to bring out the essential sign from the stone, is it not enough that a trace of it should remain, in the form of a quite pretty hotchpotch of hieroglyphs, sisters to those inscribed columns that are found lying in the grass in the dense heart of the Angkor forest and which the tourists who are set dreaming by them, call "Buddha's hands"!).

Although there is an acknowledgment that only an Asian mind (and by implication an Asian aesthetic) could get to the heart of understanding and representing what the novel will seek to portray, the aspiration to such a suggestive power (the Flaubertian *faire rêver*: the power to set readers dreaming) is significantly linked not to the modern environment explored but to the art of Angkor which is so often used to suggest "real" Cambodian meaning. We are being invited, in other words, to read a failed attempt to impose a Western model on the representation of a Cambodian environment, but one which the narrator hopes will compensate at the level of intuition and suggestion for what it fails to produce at the level of explanation and narration.

There is one further section of the novel that serves as a commentary on the aesthetic dilemma outlined in the opening section and on the apparently rather curious solution adopted. The second engineer to die in the course of building kilometer 83, Georgie, is in his private persona a sculptor, but his sculptures precisely embody the disastrous effects of attempting to apply the Western mind directly to Cambodian material through a Cambodian medium. When Georgie dies, his studio, to which noone has previously been admitted, proves to be full of horrendous representations of marsh fauna modeled in the local clay. The artist's imagination applied directly to his environment can only create something close to madness in its rejection of order and balance: "la fantaisie tératologique de l'artiste avait renchéri sur celle de la nature. Une ingéniosité abominable, amalgamant le démesuré et le disproportionné, greffant le biscornu sur l'amorphe, avait trouvé le moyen d'épanouir, jusqu'à la splendeur, la monstruosité" (208: "the artist's teratological imagination had added to that of nature herself. An abominable ingeniousness, amalgamating excessiveness and disproportion, grafting the bizarre onto the shapeless, had contrived to make monstrosity blossom into splendor"). The narrator promptly destroys the dead man's chamber of glyptic horrors in the same way that the narrative struggles against any tendency to disorder and disproportion. And just as the saving grace for the progress of the railway itself is the rediscovery of the ancient Cambodian causeway by which the marsh can be crossed and the power of the legend of the malevolent gong dispersed, so the model for averting the inevitable defeat of a linear realistic narrative *à la française* must be found in an aesthetic evocative of the suggestive power of fragments of ancient Cambodian sculpture, and not in any attempt to work with the material of the contemporary world.

The text clearly problematizes its own representation, but it does so in the voice of a narrator whose own idealistic view of railway building is as destined to failure as he claims the aesthetic intentions behind the narrative to be. The nature of the aesthetic failure is perhaps not immediately obvious, given that the mobility and temporal/spatial progress expressed in the concept of "images mobiles enregistrées au fil de l'heure et de ses mille mètres de rails" ("the moving images recorded on it by the passage of time and of its thousand meters of rail") is evidently present at one level of the text. Insofar as the novel recounts the race to complete the line in the face of the curse of the legendary gong it constitutes a fine example of the "beating-the-odds" sub-genre of the adventure story. However, this model only applies to Part II (more or less exactly the second half of the novel in page terms): part I, as far as the railway is concerned, is a narrative of stasis. Its events do involve developments in time and space and these linearities are repeatedly underpinned by journeys, but they do not advance the construction of kilometer 83. They create sub-narratives, which, though helping to define space and character, all peter out or are held in suspension, the real focus being on description.

If we do focus on the railway-building narrative proper (i.e., the second half of the novel), we find that it has no less than three separate climaxes. Daguerches is, in effect, offering us three "endings," each corresponding to a different concept of the thematic value of the railway. The first, the building of kilometer 83, is represented as a triumph of French endeavor, though Vigel's celebratory rendering of the Schumann *Carnaval de Venise* variations, with its masked Marseillaise motif, comments ironically on the limitations of its Frenchness, and more broadly as a monument to human achievement (or at least the narrator's concept of that progress). The second, the completion of the building of the line from Battambong to the border, which is itself only a stage within the structure Phnom-Penh to Bangkok, of which the Siamese stretch is under separate construction, serves to present the railway not as disinterested human achievement or even as *mise en valeur* of the territory, but as part of a movement-beyond which is tied to the concrete aims of international capitalism. Even if the railway is embedded on an ancient Cambodian causeway (a motif recalled by the fact that the second celebratory scene is staged among Angkorian ruins), it is a project which overarches the environment, i.e., it provides a way of ignoring Cambodia rather than of exploring, expressing or even constraining it. It is however the third ending which is perhaps the most interesting. This scene is pure melodrama: the deranged Fagui throws the points and almost derails the train, precipitating Vigel's quick action to save both the boss's daughter and the situation, which will be rewarded by an Homais-like sanctification by career success. The two short action-and-detail-packed paragraphs speed the narrative up grotesquely and then as abruptly cut it off. Insofar as the narrator's vision has been of the railway as an end in itself and not as a process, the "real" railway has its narrative end in a completely unreal event and in the ironic future triumph of the one engineer who, having been constantly orientalized in the details of his representation, cannot fulfill a representative colonial function.

This succession of "endings" to the linear narrative obliges the reader to accept that the role played by the linear narrative, like that played by the railway itself in the context of the environment, is ambiguous. As a tool for creating meaning in the novel, it is less than satisfactory. The real dual focus of the text for most of its duration is the antagonism between Western characters and Cambodian environment, and the image which explains the organization of these mutually antagonistic dimensions of the novel is not the railway but the river, particularly as explored in Part 1,12 (137-39), where it represents both singular forward movement, "l'énorme continuité glissante et rectiligne" ("the vast mass slipping onward in a continuous straight line"), and multiplicity of swirling disorder, "tournoiement, remous, dislocation dans l'innommable cohue tourbeuse" ("swirling, eddying and dislocation in indescribable confusion"). The accumulation of characters and their consequent dissolution, concomitant though it is on the building of the railway, does not follow the linear processes of its construction (which are hardly touched upon, but constitutes a series of eddies in the narrative current, closely bound into elaborately hostile evocations of the power of the environment.[16] The "belle confusion de hiéroglyphes" ("pretty hotchpotch of hieroglyphs") announced in the opening definition of the function of the pseudo-kilometer stone we are reading, is located in the hieratic figures of the Forest, the Sun, the River and the Marsh, and the legend of the Gong is only "explained away" in the sense in which rational explanations are inadequately imposed on inexplicable forces in the *contes fantastiques* of Mérimée.[17] Thus, far from directing the narrative, the railway underlines the superficiality of its function, just as the structure of the novel emphasizes the alien status of the railway.

Given the Dorgelès quotation with which I started this chapter, one might have supposed that the use of roads or railways as the basis of a novel or travelogue would be guaranteed to promote the progressive image of the colonial presence, and at the same time to offer a means of ensuring the forward thrust of a realistic narrative while permitting enough space and time for the assimilation of the terrain covered. Interestingly neither of these assumptions holds good for any of the texts I have examined. In all of them, in very different ways, an awareness of the ambiguities involved in imposing linear models on environments which are in significant respects geographically and culturally resistant to linearity is matched by some sense that linear narrative can only misrepresent the complexities of the colonial experience as reflected in the lives of individuals. The disruptive effect that this in turn imposes on the reading experience highlights the discontinuities and uncertainties within the value systems of the texts. The fact is that roads and railways in the colonial novel serve a very different set of functions from their equivalent in metropolitan texts, where at most they indicate cultural difference in terms of modernity. In our texts roads and railways are definitely alien spaces which impinge on but are not fully part of the world which they ostensibly delineate. The very methods that facilitate possession of the region indicate the lack of communication between the clearly separated communities—the Siamese prince's outrage that Cambodians should be allowed to take their bullock-carts onto the new road in *La Route du plus fort* is a backhanded reference to the issue.[18] Daguerches and Groslier are very conscious of this problem of alien space: all three use diachronic time and the concept of the road (or in Daguerches's case the line which the railway follows) as a four-dimensional space in order to open up a line of communication between the French and the *indigène*. Guillemet, Groslier and Dorgelès also establish an evident relationship between the problems of narration, the tension between the forward movement of storytelling and the stasis of description and analysis, on the one hand and the thematics of constructing roads and railways on the other (or in Guillemet's case the thematics of their absence). Thus despite the problems of being both on the road and moroccobound, the road novel and its equivalents have a constructive if ambiguous part to play in helping writers and readers assimilate the integration of colonial space, the space of individual lives and the space of narrative.

Notes

1. *Sur la route mandarine* (1925), quoted here from the Kailash edition (Paris/Pondicherry, 1995): 39. All translations in this paper are the author's own.

2. *Suite indochinoise* (1993), quoted here from the Le Dilettante edition (Paris, 1999): 81.

3. For further evidence of this, see for example Marin Stuart-Fox, *A History of Laos* (Cambridge: Cambridge University Press, 1997), 46-50, and Robert Aldrich, *Greater France: A History of French Overseas Expansion* (London: Macmillan, 1996), 190-91.

4. The title song of the 1942 Hope, Crosby and Lamour film *The Road to Morocco* makes the point memorably, precisely because it encapsulated it in a joke: "We're off on the road to Morocco/ Like Webster's Dictionary, we're [M]morocco-bound."

5. For the comic attempt to make sense of a river by adding a railway, see Milton Osborne's account of the Khone Falls railway in *The Mekong: Turbulent past, uncertain future* (Sydney: Allen and Unwin, 2000), 136-53. It is notable that in neighboring Siam roads were perceived as a way in which outsiders could penetrate the kingdom, probably for hostile purposes. Their development was consequently very late—Reginald Le May in *An Asian Arcady* (1926) says that in 1913, in order to reach the northern capital of Chiang Mai from Bangkok, he had to walk the last 120 miles from Den Chai, where the new railway (itself only begun in 1898) stopped: the walk was on jungle paths.

6. Médecin Lieutenant-Colonel (Eugène) Guillemet, *Sur les sentiers laotiens* (Hanoï-Haïphong: Imprimerie d'Extrême-Orient, 1921); Georges Groslier, *La Route du plus fort* (Paris: Emile Paul, 1925); Henri Daguerches, *Le Kilomètre 83* (Paris: Calmann-Lévy, 1913).

7. The end of the quotation still betrays the application of an external model—the Nile *is* navigable in the way desired.

8. In this poem from his collection of prose poems *Spleen de Paris*, Charles Baudelaire (1821-1867) juxtaposes real time, with its relentless linear dripping away, and a suspended form of dreamtime.

9. One can connect with this nostalgia the harking after the potential alternative narratives offered by the journeys of others which he cannot follow up, as in the lines of Méos and Mans encountered (37-38).

10. Nicola Cooper, *France in Indochina: Colonial Encounters* (Oxford/New York: Berg, 2001), 133ff.

11. For example, "droite comme une belle idée" (156: "straight like a beautiful idea") and "Cependant la piste hardie et souple sait où elle va et sa tête intelligente s'est avancée dans ce désert, car son but s'étend au-delà" (184-85: "However, the bold supple track knows where it is heading and its intelligent head has pressed forward into this desert, for its goal lies beyond"), an image then expanded into a whole paragraph.

12. All quotations from the novel are given from the Kailash edition (Paris/Pondicherry 1997; original edition Paris: Emile Paul, 1925).

13. In this and the following quotations from this novel there is a constant play on the word/stem "route" which cannot be consistently rendered in English translation.

14. "Tout est logique qui se soumet au rythme de la terre et de la lumière et tu n'aspires qu'à contrarier ce rythme" (201: "Everything that submits itself to the rhythm of the land and of the light is logical and you only aim to break that rhythm").

15. Alain Quella-Villéger, *Indochine Un rêve d'Asie* (Paris: Omnibus 1995), 108. All the quotations from *Le Kilomètre 83* are given according to the version in this edition because the Kaïlash edition (1996) is defective at a key point, omitting most of the account of Georgie's sculptures. The original edition is Paris: Calmann-Lévy, 1913.

16. The only character to be allowed a proper linear dimension associated with the railway is Vigel—but the linearity is illusory, since the character most close to the environment is thus propelled by an arbitrary event into the most colonial of futures.

17. Prosper Mérimée (1803-1870) produced the classic examples of nineteenth-century short stories on fantastic themes, where logical explanation cannot quite account for every element of the supernatural which the story evokes.

18. *Indochine Un rêve d'Asie*, 163—the choice of a Siamese voice for this highly colonial idea is of course merely a piece of political sniping, which the text underscores by suggesting that to the Siamese the Cambodians were still no better than slaves. There is no reason to suppose that the majority of French colonists would have thought any different.

4

Automobiles and Anomie in French Colonial Indochina

David Del Testa

At first glance, the author of "Automobilistes, ayez pitié!" ("Drivers, have pity!"), a front page article in the Thursday July 1, 1937 issue of the biweekly Hanoi newspaper *L'Annam Nouveau*, might seem only to be making a simple plea for public safety.[1] He begs his readers to reduce their driving speed for the poor who often walk along the edges of "the colony's" roads. However, as with much of the discussion of transportation in French colonial Indochina, a close reading of the article reveals a strong social critique. The author noted that he had driven hundreds of thousands of kilometers all around the world but had never seen driving as poor as that in French Indochina. He also noted that the relatively lower costs of the colony permitted Europeans who might otherwise ride trains at home to own cars and drive them poorly at the expense of "our brothers of Europe and Asia." Likewise, those Europeans who could only afford small cars in Europe had large, chauffeur-driven cars in the colony. Their owners forced chauffeurs to drive them at "un train d'enfer" (like a bat out of hell). To the author of this article, it seems, bourgeois prudence did not accompany colonial *embourgeoisement*.

Transportation modernization and its cultural, social, political, and economic importance have received a great deal of attention from scholars in the humanities and social sciences.[2] In particular, these scholars have analyzed how modern transportation altered the sense of time and space in which its primary elements (new lines of communication, the machines themselves) and secondary influences (the rapid movement of people and information, enforced timeliness) have become influential.[3] Much of the scholarship around this topic has revolved around several broad themes, including railroads as an environment for change; the railroad station and its positioning as a symbol of changing social and political relationships; and automobiles as a mechanical symptom of cultural change. Regionally, the effects of transportation modernization in Europe, the United States, and Japan have received the most attention.[4] In addition, many works on European, Japanese, and American colonialism have touched upon the economic consequences of transportation modernization in the colonial world. Among these, however, only a few have directly analyzed the cultural and social impact of transportation modernization in the colonial world.[5] This chapter attempts to augment the latter scholarship.

I argue that many French and Vietnamese artists and authors of the colonial era used modern roadways and railroads as stages on which they might freely discuss the tensions, transformations, and conflicts of colonialism. Relatively little work beyond narrative description has yet appeared on colonial-era roads and railroads in French Indochina and their reconstruction and refiguring during the postcolonial period. This seems strange since many of the essential events of recent regional history occurred on or along imperial roads and railroads: the Mandarin Road, the Ho Chi Minh Trail, the Street without Joy, the *Transindochinois*, the Reunification Express.[6] Transportation was one of several essential backdrops—along with villages, courtrooms, schools, brothels, opium dens, and most importantly, domestic settings—on which colonial-era authors frequently relied as backgrounds for such discussions about colonialism. The use of transportation in this way started because both the French and the Vietnamese valorized modern transportation as universally beneficial, leaving it open as a category through which writers and artists might safely discuss colonialism with less fear of censorship or approbation. Here, I examine how Vietnamese authors use modern transportation as a way to criticize colonialism and the situations it had created in colonial Vietnam. Although it targets roadways and railroads, this chapter also encourages scholars to explore the supposedly "safe spaces" of the colonial world—hospitals, orphanages, schools—and help nuance scholarly understanding of the Franco-Vietnamese relationship during the colonial period.

Although water was the preferred method of long-distance transportation wherever possible, precolonial Vietnamese certainly used roads, including those connecting Hanoi with Saigon and Vinh with Thakhek in Laos. These precolonial roads did not have the same grand sweep or permanence that the French accorded their own designs, for their engineers purposefully designed them to intrude as little as possible on valuable agricultural land. Despite changing transportation needs, the French did not initially improve transportation but instead relied on existing footpaths and navigable rivers. Two governors-general, Paul Doumer (governor 1896-1902) and Albert Sarraut (governor 1911-1914, 1916-1919), gave transportation development in French Indochina an impetus.[7] Between 1917 and 1954, the French built or improved over 9,000 kilometers of roads and 3,800 kilometers of railroads throughout Indochina and became known throughout Southeast Asia for their "folie des chemins" (road craziness). The railroads alone cost nearly six billion 1939 francs, and road construction perhaps three billion more.[8] These arteries had multiple explicit purposes for the French: economic armature for the export of raw materials, strategic network for the transport of troops against foreign aggression and domestic unrest, and framework of the *mission civilisatrice*. They also had many other intended and unintended social and economic consequences.

Transportation modernization was one element in the wholesale transformation of Vietnamese society during the colonial period. Elsewhere, I proposed the concept of the "Imperial Corridor" for French Indochina's colonial-era transportation infrastructure.[9] "Imperial Corridors" are linear zones or environments of cross-cultural contact and political struggle that emanated from the railroad lines and roadways in a colonial context. They create a subset of the larger public sphere and cross-cultural discourse that emerged as the French and Vietnamese struggled to deal with the impact of colonialism and modernity. In conceptualizing "imperial corridors," I drew heavily from the work of John Stilgoe and Mary-Louise Pratt.[10] In addition to Stilgoe and Pratt, Michel de Certeau's discussions of how railroads allow their users to objectify and alienate themselves from the landscape and people they pass have inspired me in my thinking of the consequences of modern transportation development in French Indochina.[11] In this framework, Certeau's conceptualization of the railroad carriage as space-outside-time and the world exterior to that carriage as a violent struggle seem particularly applicable to understanding personal relations in the colonial context. In this way, the vehicles themselves are simultaneously symbolic of tension while being environments for it and generators of it. I see Vietnamese artists and writers turning very early in the colonial period to transportation as a way to explore the challenges of individuality, commodification, and cross-cultural exchange it created.

Trường Chinh, an early revolutionary and compatriot of Hồ Chí Minh, anticipated Certeau and one potential impact of the "imperial corridors" created by roadways. While in hiding in 1937-1938, he wrote his book *Peasant Question*, where he described, among other concerns, how,

> [Vietnamese] aristocratic and bourgeois writers set out in their cars and speed through the countryside; they see the green and fragrant fields, the thick smoke rising from the thatched roofs in the evening and immediately invent a picture full of "poetic flavor," but they don't know . . . that at times the peasant can only eat one meal every two days . . . the children have bloated bellies . . . the houses are ramshackle.[12]

The membrane of the windowpane and the privileged private space of modern transportation allowed observers to objectify and thus romanticize the world they envisioned and cathect with it their desires for bucolic simplicity and an organic social order with themselves primary. Because the automobile did not discriminate against its owners and Vietnamese using automobiles often adopted the same cultural values associated with colonial car ownership, the automobile facilitated an objectification of Vietnam by the Vietnamese that perhaps would not have otherwise occurred in the automobile's absence. Certeau suggests that the windowpanes of the railway carriage, a commodified space, silence the world passing before the passenger's eyes, allowing him or her to capture and control it and objectify it. Tension originates because the rails on which the trains roll compel movement and make that visual control simultaneously evanescent and ephemeral. To Certeau, the increasing size, speed, and capacity of a particular conveyance led to its increased capacity to separate, objectify, and alienate. In the automobile, however, observers could more easily objectify and romanticize the spaces through which they passed.

Although scholarly discourse and popular unrest had challenged the French for decades, military pacification and local collaboration had silenced most forms of public criticism by the late 1890s. Written criticism of any sort might bring at the very least stiff approbation and at worst a long prison sentence.[13] In the context of increasingly harsh control of the free circulation of opinion and knowledge after 1900, cartoons and satirical images apparently survived as a public medium for criticism of colonial occupation.[14] I argue that Vietnamese artists at this time used modern transportation as a site for their criticism because, much like the topics artists criticized, it embodied the mixed feelings many Vietnamese had about colonialism, the benefits it brought, and the perils it created. This is because it was modern transportation—railroads, bicycles, and rickshaws at first and automobiles and motorcycles later—that served as the setting in which many Vietnamese encountered the French for the first time and where the sharpest day-to-day encounters between the French and Vietnamese occurred. In addition, the Vietnamese very quickly adopted and adapted to modern means to meet their transportation needs.[15] They soon dominated the public spaces provided by modern transportation, especially those provided by the railroads. As early as 1916, author Maurice Rondet-Saint already noted how with trains the Vietnamese were "très nombreux, très voyageurs aussi, comme presque partout dans les contrées exotiques." ("very numerous, very keen on traveling, as is the case in almost all exotic countries").[16] This adaptation to new transport systems reinforced to the French that transportation modernization was a good investment, while it revealed to anticolonial patriots that modernization coupled with the idea of independence might arouse Vietnamese patriotism.[17] At the crossroads of independence, collaboration, and cultural change, transportation certainly served as an important tool of social critique. It maintained this role throughout the colonial period, although the media through which critics used transportation as a vehicle for their criticism and the kinds of transportation emphasized changed.

Before discussing individual Vietnamese examples, it is important to draw attention to the trains in particular as their own source of symbolic power and fascination. Railroads represented collective effort and served as a moving tableau of the intentions and potential of colonialism as much as its failures and weakness. Rondet-Saint confirms what I would argue about the symbolic importance of the railroads in Indochina: that is, that the French built them to serve as a symbol of power as much as a tool of development. In his 1916 *Choses de l'Indochine contemporaine*, Rondet-Saint observes that "[l]es locomotives sont énormes" ("the locomotives are enormous").[18] A 1928 Art Deco-style cover illustration for an advertising brochure of the government-run *Compagnie Chemins de fer de l'Indochine* ("Rail Company of Indochina") confirms Rondet-Saint's earlier observation. It shows a huge ten-wheel Continental (2-4-0) locomotive practically leaping off the page as it steams westward along the picturesque quay of the central Vietnamese town of Qui Nhơn.[19] Indeed, throughout the colonial period, the French continued to deploy big Continental and Pacific-class (2-4-2) locomotives on a narrow-gauge rail network that never allowed those engines to go over 60 kilometers an hour in a shallow curve. The railroads embodied a sentiment of a caged tiger but also Certeau's *primum mobile*, the god from which all action proceeds.[20] These locomotives specifically, and the whole railroad system in general, served as a visible reminder of the power of the French state to shape the physical and social environment of Vietnam for the good of its people as well as a reminder of the mechanical violence the state could unleash if it chose to do so.

By contrast, automobiles spoke much less of collective power and much more of individual strength and the private world. Automobiles attracted Europeans and those Vietnamese who could more easily afford them and who frequently chose to separate themselves from local society by using an automobile. Automobiles more than railroads served as both a locus of public leisure for colonial society and a point of contact between the French and a few Vietnamese. Many clubs existed for automobile owners and enthusiasts, including the *Union automobile et touristique du Tonkin*, the *Automobile Club Annam-Tonkin*, and the *Club automobile et motorcycliste du Tonkin-Annam-Laos*. Enthusiasts also had available to them a whole variety of guidebooks in French, such as Claudius Madrolle's *Les Routes Automobiles d'Indochine* ("Automobile Roads of Indochina") and Georges Norès' *Itinéraires automobiles en Indochine* ("Automobile routes in Indochina").[21] The registered membership of these clubs and the authors of the guidebooks are overwhelmingly male and French, and they follow a tradition of fraternity social clubs in France of the time.

A privately-owned automobile has a whole suite of values associated with it the consideration of which is germane to this discussion. Private possession of an automobile reveals that the owner has the resources to purchase and maintain the vehicle, and tacitly agrees with the system of consumption and usage that private automobiles imply. Because they normally have a limited seating capacity, automobiles reinforce an egocentric positioning of individuals in the world. Because society views them as an extension of the individual, automobile owners often take great pride in maintaining their appearance, keeping them in a manner that reflects their own worldview and advertises it to the world. They provide a shield from the world around them and thus serve as a kind of armor against the outside world, and can limit contact between individuals and an unknown, potentially threatening public. Automobiles provided not only individual mobility but gained their owners private space more or less under their own control. Thus automobiles advertise not only control of distance but offer control of space, which sells at a premium throughout the world.

With French Vietnam, the general characteristics of the automobile transferred from metropole to colony and took on unique characteristics that had layers of meaning building on one another like the layers of an onion. First of all, automobile ownership indicated for both Europeans and Vietnamese relative wealth, but also relatively greater complicity and success in the colonial system. It took serious money to buy and maintain an automobile in the colony, and the colonial economy was practically the only avenue to the acquisition of that kind of money.[22] Among its therefore relatively wealthy owners, automobiles also served as an advertisement of the real or pretended economic success of an individual within that colonial economy. Marguerite Duras presented this perfectly in *Un Barrage contre le Pacifique* (*The Seawall*) by contrasting how desperately the *déclassé* family of the character Suzanne clung to their aged and exhausted Citroen B11.[23] Jean-Jacques Maitam, whose memoir *House Divided* offers interesting insight into the world of wealthy *métis* in colonial Vietnam, recalls how important owning the colony's only Lincoln was to the status of his wealthy father.[24]

Likewise, just as a private automobile revealed one's place in the colonial economy, it also served as a marker of one's place within the colonial social hierarchy, a system linked to but not necessarily dependent on monetary wealth. In this context, the perception of one's racial background influenced the symbolic service an automobile provided to its owner, but the interior of an automobile provided a rare unracialized space to which only money limited access. Like whiteness, an automobile might serve a French person as a constant value within a fluctuating moral economy whose elements—money and its availability, military rank or family background, and one's favor within the court of the colonial social network—underwrote the colonial social hierarchy. Thus, many French were desperate to acquire an automobile as soon as they could, to fit into the social hierarchy in which automobile ownership provided valuable access to colonial social circles but also the means to escape the hothouse environment white colonial society created. Thus, as indicated in her memoir *Notre Indochine* ("Our Indochina"), Madeleine Jay was very happy when her husband Antoine acquired a used automobile so they could escape the endless social calls she found so distressing.[25] Jay does not acknowledge, however, how such an automobile also provided public acknowledgement of their social station. For *métis* and Vietnamese, an automobile might serve as the brevet necessary to occasionally join the ranks of white colonial society or, if they remained independent of that society, an essential element of respectability and upward social mobility. For instance, the scene of Mr. Jo inviting Suzanne into his enormous Léon-Bollé in Duras' text the *L'Amant de la Chine du Nord* (*The North China Lover*) provides an excellent fictional representation of the blurred boundaries modern transportation created in the colonial world.[26] For *métis* and Vietnamese, an automobile might serve as the brevet necessary to occasionally join the ranks of white colonial society or, if they remained independent of that society, an essential element of respectability and upward social mobility.

Throughout the colonial period, Vietnamese and French artists and writers both used themes and images of transportation as a way to critique colonialism, but before 1920, as far as I can tell, only woodblock prints and cartoons were used as a medium of critique. After 1920, modern transportation appeared increasingly as a literary backdrop, although the woodblock prints and cartoons of the earlier period continued to appear occasionally. Most notable about this second phase is the growing usage of the automobile as a trope, although railroads figure regularly through the mid-1930s. This gradual switch from visual to written criticism and the growing predominance of the automobile corresponds both with the sudden efflorescence of literary production after 1930 and the rise in ownership of automobiles by the Vietnamese themselves.[27] As images of transportation became a more common way to discuss conflict in colonial Indochina, the images became increasingly self-referential.[28]

In an environment in which few French or Vietnamese spoke each others' language and the Romanized Vietnamese (*quốc ngữ*) had not yet come into wide use, cartoons and other satirical imagery had an advantage in that they communicated to the widest possible public—both lettered and illiterate—feelings about particular colonial encounters. Although my survey of topics is certainly not exhaustive, of the prints that have a modern theme, images using transportation have an important presence. Woodblock prints had long served as a medium to express popular concerns of the day in Vietnam. In addition to representing classical themes useful for illustrating folktales or providing examples of *hán nôm* (Vietnamese expressed in a hybrid Chinese script) to students, woodblock prints had long served as a medium to express subtle social, political, and cultural criticism. Here, I will use examples of twentieth-century woodblock prints emanating from the Đông Hồ paper village near Bắc Ninh, twenty kilometers northeast of Hanoi, as the source of my examples.[29]

Đông Hồ artisans produced a well-known series of four prints entitled "The Progress of Civilization" sometime just before or after World War I.[30] It is not clear what stimulated the production of these prints, but the tradition of using woodblock prints to subtly criticize Vietnamese society in combination with the increasing cultural penetration of European cultural mores at this time would seem sufficient to stimulate their production. In this series, the first two prints are entitled "The Automobile, the Bicycle, and the Hunt (or, if read differently, 'Courtship')." The left-hand print presents a dapper Frenchman lighting a cigar or cigarette in front of his two-door roadster. On the other side of his car, a young woman who appears Vietnamese shades herself with a parasol and proffers a small bouquet of flowers. Its caption, in colloquial Chinese-derived *hán nôm* script, reads "I couldn't give a damn." Although neither of the people portrayed is assigned the caption, my reading is that it indicates the Frenchman rejecting the flowers and preparing to speed away. This was a common and much commented-upon problem of the time, in which French men who had taken Vietnamese lovers often abandoned them and the offspring of their union. The right hand panel presents a similar scene, this time with a mustachioed Frenchman in hunting garb holding a rifle at rest by the muzzle with his left hand while holding up a bicycle by the handlebars with his right. Another, more elaborately gowned Vietnamese woman has rested her hand on the hand the Frenchman uses to support the bicycle. Its caption reads, "You watch it!" To whom the command is meant is unclear, but since the woman's hand rests on top of that of the Frenchman, it may either indicate the man rejecting the advances of the woman or a generalized warning for Vietnamese women and French men to avoid this kind of contact. By using modern transportation prominently, the woodblock artist can more delicately approach problems of the colonial period such as sexual concubinage, abandonment, the denaturing of Vietnamese women through western influence, and, by suggestion, *métissage.* Among many other woodblock prints of the time that criticize this "progress of civilization," transportation figures prominently.[31] French artists before World War I used modern transportation in a similar way.[32]

After this early burst of social criticism centered on transportation modernization, artistic uses of transportation as a site of criticism become less common among the Vietnamese. Although still a site of visual criticism, the increase in literacy in *quốc ngữ* and French as well as the explosion of the printing industry and proliferation of written materials of all sorts made the printed word the site of criticism of colonialism.[33] If anything, however, the printed word received from colonial censors a great deal more attention than allegorical images, and so criticism of the colonial state, Franco-Vietnamese relations, or modernity had to remain somewhat circumspect. In this case, modern transportation maintained its role as providing the perfect site for such criticism. Although perhaps not the most important trope of criticism—concubinage or abusive labor practices or excessive Westernization for Vietnamese served more frequently as site of discussion—modern transportation continued to serve as a site on which writers inscribed in fictional works their ideas about the tensions and anxieties of colonialism.

In my by no means exhaustive survey of Vietnamese fiction of the colonial-era, automobiles, railroads, and rickshaws served as the most important venues for authors to set their stories, although boats and airplanes also occasionally served as well. Of a hundred or so colonial-era novels, short stories, plays, and poems by Vietnamese authors I have examined so far, about 25 use modern transportation as a setting for the majority of or an important part of the action in their stories.[34] With Vietnamese authors, there is a subtle difference between portrayals of the trains and automobiles. Reflecting their more public presence, trains serve as a microcosm of all of the tensions and ambiguities of that colonialism created in Vietnamese society, whereas automobiles appear to serve as sites particularly of symbolic, physical, and sexual violence.

As mentioned earlier, the railroad system in French Indochina enjoyed enormous popularity, and increasingly became a "Vietnamese" space during the 1920s and 1930s. In this context of "Vietnamization," authors often addressed the ambiguous mixture of progress and perils that railroads created for Viet-namese. Many Vietnamese writers used railroads as a background for their sto-ries of love, life, and conflict during the colonial era.[35] For some, the railroads provided a stage on which they might describe the illusion or impact of "pro-gress" under colonialism. Trọng Lang, in his "Trên Xe Hoả" (On the Train), describes how hucksters peddle patent medicines to the poor riding in Fourth Class.[36] He notes how perfectly good Vietnamese traditional medicines exist whose effects endure rather than evaporating quickly. Mạnh Phú Tư, in *Life as a Concubine*, documented the fictional life of a young Vietnamese man of mod-est means who rose from a servant fanning a French railroad company supervi-sor to a middle-aged deputy station supervisor who shaved income from ticket sales.[37] For Tư, the railroad bureaucracy provided a classroom for teaching young Vietnamese the kinds of corruption and nepotism necessary for success in the colonial world. However, resignation is just as powerful as collaboration in implicating the Vietnamese in tolerance for colonial occupation. In his "Đi Tây" (Going West), the author Nhất Linh wrote that "[i]n our country, the first time we sit on a hard [train] seat and our buttocks hurt, we console ourselves: it hurts a little, but it won't kill us. After that we don't feel any more discomfort, and by the third time it even feels quite smooth. So our buttocks make progress in becoming used to pain, but we make no progress at all."[38] According to Nhất Linh, the colonial train system, like the rest of colonialism, numbed Vietnamese into inaction and tolerance of an intolerable situation.

In his novel *Giông Tố* (*The Tempest*), the writer Vũ Trọng Phụng begins by describing the random rape of a peasant woman on the backseat of a wealthy man's car while his driver and aide look on and snigger.[39] In this way, automo-biles represent the terrible price of wealth and individuality that colonialism has brought and the sharp social divisions it has created (or at least exposed). Like-wise, Phụng, in the novel *Làm Đĩ* (To Work as a Prostitute), presents the grad-ual descent of a woman, Huyền, into life as a prostitute when she enters into marriage with a man, Kim, she does not love.[40] The only place she can find a few furtive moments with her lover, Tân, is in Mr. Tân's automobile. Once again, Phụng celebrates the freedom automobiles provide, but also the potential immorality they may provoke.

Of all the Vietnamese commentaries on the railroads, Nhượng Tống, an anticolonial activist and writer, provided perhaps the richest example of how the railroads in Indochina hosted the evils of colonialism. In his autobiographical story Đời Trong Ngục: Hoả Lò, Côn Đảo, Hòn Cốm (*Life in the Clink Hoả Lò, Côn Đảo, Hòn Cốm*), Tống, recounted a train ride from Hue to Hanoi he took as a prisoner in 1933.[41] Tống portrays the train ride, which forms about a third of the whole story, as a cipher for understanding the complex tensions of colonial Indochina during the 1920s and 1930s.

After being hauled in for questioning in the imperial capital of Hue by Lucien Sogny, the head of internal security for the Annam Protectorate, Tống is arrested and sent to the central prison in Hanoi for arraignment on charges of sedition by rail. During the first day of travel, Tống meets many pleasant and sympathetic people. After lunch and a pleasant conversation, Tống's guards say that they, "do not get the chance to eat with someone of [his] class very often," a statement which evokes emotion and shame in Tống. Here the railroad brings Vietnamese who might not otherwise meet into contact with one another. The scene also evokes the continuing disunity of the Vietnamese people and their division along educational and class lines. Further along in the journey, a group of students boarding Tống's train show him a great deal of respect after finding out that he was made a prisoner because of his political beliefs. These youths profess proudly that they are members of Hồ Chí Minh's "Thanh Niên" movement. Just as the train pulled into Vinh station, a sympathetic young woman, having overheard Tống's conversation with the students, gives Tông some money to help him during his imprisonment.[42]

Tống and his guards stop for the night in Vinh, where his time is not as pleasant as it has been on the train. A new guard sent to take Tống to the city jail for the evening is menacing. The guard addresses Tống with the pejorative pronoun "mày" (you-there) and roughhouses him.[43] A thief who shares Tống's cell for the night lies about being a member of the Thanh Niên in order to elicit some sympathy from him. The thief is the first of many false friends Tống meets on his way to Hanoi. In fact, the closer Tống gets to Hanoi, the worse the journey becomes for him.

The next morning, back on the train to Hanoi, Tống again encounters more of his fellow citizens, all of whom are unsympathetic. At one point during the trip, Tống comments audibly to his guards that a couple sitting across from him look Japanese because of their western clothing and appearance. The husband of the couple responds that they are in fact Vietnamese, "Vietnamese who are French," and that they learned Vietnamese after learning French and living in France.[44] This couple represents to Tống the worst possible consequence of colonialism, mất nước (the loss of country), a topic that many other colonial-era authors addressed in great detail. When the westernized Vietnamese ask why Tống was a prisoner and he responds that he is a political activist, the couple instantly turns cold and silent. The westernized couple disembarks at Phủ Lý, a town near Hanoi, and speed off in their waiting automobile. When Tông reaches Hanoi, he is hurried into chains and off to prison.

The train ride Nhượng Tống took from Hue to Hanoi via Vinh provides insight into the social environment that the railroads had become by the early 1930s. The train itself is a microcosm of the particular tensions of colonialism in Indochina of the time, including racial and political tension between the French and the Vietnamese, the emotional tension between Vietnamese over collaboration, and the economic tension engendered by the Depression. The political climate created by colonialism and the division of society, replicated on the train itself, created strong emotions among the Vietnamese. According to Tống, for example, the couple that berated him for his political meddling has surrendered their national identity, and thus their self-esteem, in return for material wealth.[45] The type of surrender to colonial repression manifest in the wealthy couple shows up again in the form of the gentle but duty-bound guards who accompany Tống from Hue to Hanoi. However nice they are, they are still guards working for the French. The Vietnamese have to confront one another and the reality of their choices on the train.

It might seem strange that the only French person encountered by Tống is Lucien Sogny, the notorious head of the *Sûreté* for Annam Protectorate. By making the French so rare in their own colony and by populating the train and his entire journey almost exclusively with Vietnamese, Tống signaled how the Vietnamese were oppressing themselves within the colonial system. Although Tống meets many "good" Vietnamese along the way, most Vietnamese serve as people who aid and abet the French—as guards, as thieves, and as sycophants of a foreign culture. The train had developed into a container for all the complexities of colonialism for Vietnamese during the 1920s and 1930s. No longer an icon of a utopian "association", the railroads systematized and deepened the colonial presence. The railroads became for Vietnamese authors a symbol of disappointment with the promises the French had implicitly made with their colonial mission and with other Vietnamese for allowing the kind of oppression and division encountered on the trains to continue.

Modern transportation, especially railroads and automobiles, provided French and Vietnamese artists and authors with an important stage on which they might reveal the tensions and struggles of colonialism. They typically used railroads as a background on which to describe collective syndromes or tensions while they used automobiles as a site to discuss more individual struggles or problems. Rather than addressing alienation from nation or tradition as with railroads, Vietnamese authors often used automobiles as symbolic of the yawning economic and cultural divisions and individual violence they believed colonialism encouraged. These authors could engage in this kind of criticism using modern transportation as a background because of its universally positive valorization. Images of trains and cars in colonial-era Vietnamese cartoons and literature reveal a society profoundly at war with itself over the values its members wanted to promote—technological advancement, political unity, social equality—and the challenges its members faced in deciding what vehicle—individual competition, collective action, traditional values—to use to achieve those goals.

Notes

This chapter originated as a paper given at the *France, India and "Indochina": Cultural Representations* conference at the University of Newcastle-upon-Tyne, September 2003. California Lutheran University supported the cost of travel to and attending this conference. My sincere thanks to the editors of this volume Dr. Kathryn Robson and Dr. Jennifer Yee of Newcastle for their patience, support, comments, and effort. My thanks as well to Dr. Peter Zinoman for providing additional comments for a draft of this paper.

1. F.A.C., "Automobilistes, Ayez Pitié," *L'Annam Nouveau*, July 1, 1937.

2. See Michael Adas, *Machines as the Measure of Men: Science, Technology, and the Ideologies of Western Dominance* (Ithaca: Cornell University Press, 1989); Daniel R. Headrick, *The Tools of Empire: Technology and European Imperialism in the Nineteenth Century* (New York: Oxford University Press, 1981) and Leo Marx, *The Machine in the Garden: Technology and the Pastoral Ideal in America* (New York: Oxford University Press, 1964).

3. See in particular Stephen Kern, *The Culture of Time and Space, 1880-1918.* (Cambridge, Massachusetts: Harvard University Press, 1983).

4. For France, see Marc Baroli, *Le Train dans la littérature française* (Paris: Editions N.M., 1964); André Escolan, "Le train dans la littérature française," *Revue générale des chemins de fer* 1994, no. 4 (November-December): 89-98; Margot B. Stein, *The Social Origins of a Labor Elite: French Engine-Drivers, 1837-1917, Garland Series of Outstanding Dissertations* (New York/London: Garland Publishing, Inc., 1987); Christophe Studeny, *L'Invention de la vitesse: France, XVIIIe - XXe siècle* (Paris: Gallimard, 1995); Eugen Weber, *Peasants into Frenchmen: The Modernization of Rural France, 1870-1914* (Stanford, California: Stanford University Press, 1976).

5. See Laura Charlotte Bear, "Traveling modernity: Capitalism, community and nation in the colonial governance of the Indian railways" (Ph.D. thesis, University of Michigan, 1998).

6. The Mandarin Road was the precolonial route for imperial officials and scholars between Hanoi and Saigon. The "Street without Joy" refers to a particular part of this road during the First Indochina War north of Hue where heavy fighting occurred between the French and Việt Minh. The Ho Chi Minh Trail refers to a collectivity of hidden trails and roadway in the highlands of Vietnam, northeastern Cambodia, and Laos that allowed the infiltration of soldiers and supplies into South Vietnam from North Vietnam between 1959-1975. The *Transindochinois* was the rail line connecting the eastern border of China with Saigon via Hue that the French built between 1898 and 1936. The Vietnamese government reopened this line on December 31, 1976 as the "Reunification Express."

7. Doumer favored railroads over roads. He had close links with France's steel industry, automobiles had not yet become a common mode of transportation, and his father had been a railroad worker. See Michel Bruguière, "Le Chemin de fer du Yunnan: Paul Doumer et la Politique d'Intervention française en Chine, 1889-1902," *Revue d'Histoire Diplomatique* 77 (1963): 23-61, 129-61, 252-78.

8. See the statistical tables in the appendices of David W. Del Testa, "'Paint the Trains Red': Labor, Nationalism, and the Railroads in French colonial Indochina, 1898-1945" (Ph.D., University of California, 2001).

9. See David W. Del Testa, "'Imperial Corridor': Association, Transportation, and Power in French Colonial Indochina," *Science, Technology, and Society* 4, no. 2 (1999): 319-54.

10. See Mary Louise Pratt, *Imperial Eyes: Travel Writing and Transculturation* (New York: Routledge, 1992), John R. Stilgoe, *Metropolitan Corridor: Railroads and the American Scene* (New Haven/London: Yale University Press, 1983).

11. In particular, Chapter Eight, "Railway Navigation and Incarceration," in Michel De Certeau, *The Practice of Everyday Life*, trans. Steven Rendell (Berkeley: University of California Press, 1984), 111-15.

12. Trường Chinh, *The Peasant Question, 1937-1938*, trans. Christine Pelzer White, vol. 94, *Data Paper—Southeast Asia Program, Cornell University* (Ithaca, New York: Cornell University Press, 1974), 9.

13. See David G. Marr, "A Passion for Modernity: Intellectuals and the Media," in *Postwar Vietnam: Dynamics of a Transforming So*ciety, ed. Hy Văn Lương (Singapore: Rowman & Littlefield Publishers, 2003), 257-95, 260- 61.

14. Woodblock prints and other satirical images may be seen as one of the earliest forms of popular criticism, and certainly entered public awareness before the popularity that Marr or Nguyễn Văn Ký ascribes to them beginning in the 1920s. See Marr, "A Passion for Modernity" and Nguyễn Văn Ký, "La Société vietnamienne face à la Modernité: Le Tonkin de la fin du XIXe siècle à la seconde guerre mondiale," *Recherches asiatiques*, ed. Alain Forest (Paris: Harmattan, 1995), 193-228.

15. For traffic rates on Indochina's railroad, see David W. Del Testa, "Some preliminary findings on the relationship of railroads to the economies of Tonkin and Annam Protectorates, French Indochina, 1919-1937," in *Research on Vietnam's Quantitative History*, ed. Jean-Pascal Bassino, Asian Historical Statistics Project Working Papers (Tokyo: Hitotsubashi University, 2000), 63-96.

16. Maurice Rondet-Saint, *Choses de l'Indochine contemporaine* (Paris: Librarie Plon, 1916), 131. Translations from this text are my own.

17. Many Vietnamese anticolonial figures celebrated the idea of modern transportation as a way to strengthen Vietnam and ensure its independence. See Phan Bội Châu's *Tan Viet Nam* (1907) and Phan Chu Trinh "Letter to Governor-general Paul Beau" (1907) as cited in Trương Bửu Lâm, *Colonialism Experienced: Vietnamese Writings on Colonialism, 1900-1931* (Ann Arbor: University of Michigan, 2000), 105 and 125-26, respectively. French colonial authorities proposed transportation modernization as a way of improving Franco-Vietnamese collaboration. See Paul Doumer, *Indochine française (souvenirs)* (Paris: Editions Vuibert et Nony, 1905), 308.

18. Rondet-Saint, *Choses de l'Indochine contemporaine*, 113. Translations from this text are my own.

19. Tô Ngọc Văn, *Chemins de fer de l'Indochine* (Hanoi: G. Taupin et Cie., 1928).

20. De Certeau, *The Practice of Everyday Life*, 113.

21. Similar guides may have existed in Vietnamese, but I have not found any.

22. In the 1930s, the least expensive second-hand automobile cost about 600 piastres, equivalent to three months wages of a French civil servant and twenty-four months wages of an average Vietnamese

23. Marguerite Duras, *Un barrage contre le Pacifique* (Paris: Editions Gallimard, 1950); *The Sea Wall*, trans. Herma Briffault (New York: Harper and Row, 1986), first publ. 1952.

24. Jean-Jacques Maitam, *A House Divided (Viet Nam)* (Greensboro: Tudor Books, 2002).

25. Antoine Jay and Madeleine Jay, *Notre Indochine 1936-1947* (Paris: Les Presses de Valmy, 1994).

26. Marguerite Duras, *The North China Lover*, trans. Leigh Hafrey (New York: The New Press, 1992).

27. Marr illustrates this in "A Passion for Modernity," 260-65.

28. In particular, the automobile and discussion of it served to intensify the objectification of the Asian landscape into its most Oriental configuration. For the French, this perhaps appears obvious. Automobiles allow French drivers and passengers to tour in comfort and take in the Oriental scenes. In particular, Roland Dorgelès' 1925 critical travelogue *Sur la route mandarine* ("On the Mandarin Road") (Paris: Albin Michel, 1925) stimulated many French in the colony to attempt to recreate his trip. The memoirs of André Angladette, *Du Nord au Sud de l'Indochine par la route mandarine . . . il y a près de soixante ans*, cite Dorgelès as a source of inspiration for touring Vietnam by car,

as does Claudie Beaucarnot's vacation diary. See André Angladette, "Du Nord au Sud de l'Indochine par la route mandarine . . . il y a près de soixante ans," *Mondes et cultures* XLIX, no. 3 (1989).

29. The craftspeople of Đông Hồ village specialize in the production and sale of paper and woodblock prints.

30. The car uses a style of suspension that appeared around 1912, so the print could be no earlier than that. Color reproductions of the first two images can be found in Nguyễn Văn Huy and Laurel Kendall, eds., *Vietnam: Journeys of Body, Mind, and Spirit* (Berkeley: University of California Press, 2003), 28. Black and white representations of these and all other images here can be found in Maurice Durand, *Imagerie populaire vietnamienne*, vol. 47, *Publications de l'Ecole française d'Extrême-Orient* (Paris: Ecole française d'Extrême Orient, 1960).

31. Woodblocks criticize "modern customs" by illustrating French men conversing—one smoking and one with a very large brindled mastiff—in front of a sedan; a woman on a bicycle in western clothes and an umbrella; a rural scene that injects a phaeton into a village and juxtaposes a young boy in western clothes with a traditionally-dressed scholar. Durand, *Imagerie populaire vietnamienne*.

32. So far, I have only a few sources on which to base my claims. In particular, an artist by the name of Pierre Rey, who went by the penname André Joyeux, drew a number of devastating satirical sketches of the conflicts colonialism produced using, among other settings, modern transportation. In one image entitled "Tarif militaire" ("the military fare"), Joyeux shows a French soldier wearing a dress uniform over his bare chest kicking a rickshaw-puller in the back. In another illustration, a pair of elephants violently defecates cannonballs and rips up railroad tracks to the caption of, "Same thing the railroad workers." See André Joyeux, *La Vie Large des Colonies* (Paris: Maurice Bauche, 1912).

33. See for example a cartoon in a 1932 edition of the magazine *Phong Hoá*. Commenting on the cruelty of rickshaw transportation, the caption of the cartoon reads "a one manpower five-seat animal cart." Likewise, in a style that imitates the exploits of a famous Vietnamese cartoon character Lý-Toét, a 1939 issue of a national high school newspaper, *Học-Sinh*, shows a man dressed in the garb of a traditional mandarin missing a train because he doesn't understand why it doesn't stop for him on the side of the tracks. See "Mr. Tu Huy goes for a Rest (by Train)," *Học-Sinh*, June 1, 1939.

34 Unfortunately there is no space within this chapter to include the titles of these works.

35. The authors Vũ Trọng Phụng, Hoàng Đạo, and Trọng Lang often set their stories in the context of modern transportation. See, for example, Trọng Lang, "Trên Xe Hoả," in *Tổng Tập Văn Học Việt Nam*, ed. Nguyễn Đăng Mạnh (Hanoi: Nhà Xuất Bản Khoa Học Xã Hội, 1997), Thế Lữ, "Câu chuyện trên tàu thuỷ," in *Tổng Tập Văn Học Việt Nam*, ed. Hà Minh Đức (Hanoi: Nhà Khoa Văn Xã Hội, 1994), Vũ Trọng Phụng, "Lấy vợ xấu," in Vũ Trọng Phụng, *Truyện Ngắn - Kịch - Tạp văn* (Hanoi: Nhà Hội Nhà Văn, 1996, first published 1937).

36. Trọng, "Trên Xe Hoả."

37. Mạnh Phú Tư "Life as a Concubine," in *Vietnamese Women in Society and Revolution*, ed. Long Vĩnh Ngô (Cambridge, MA: The Vietnam Resource Center, 1974), 110.

38. Greg Lockhart, "Broken Journey: Nhất Linh's Going to France," *East Asian History*, 8 (1994): 73-134, 127.

39. Vũ Trọng Phụng, "Giông Tố" (1936), in *Tổng Tập Văn Học Việt Nam*, ed. Nguyễn Đăng Mạnh (Hanoi: NXB Khoa học xã hội, 1997).

40. Vũ Trọng Phụng, *Làm Đĩ* (Hanoi: Mai Linh, 1939).

41. The VNDQQ (Viêt Nam Quốc Dân Đảng) was an anticolonial nationalist group founded by Nguyễn Thái Học and others in 1927. Mostly dissipated by the French in 1930, the party continued its activities in Indochina and then South Vietnam until the 1950s. See Danny J. Whitfield, *Historical and Cultural Dictionary of Vietnam*, ed. Basil C. Hedrick, (Metuchen, N.J.: The Scarecrow Press, 1976), 323.

42. Nhượng Tống (Hoàng Phạm Trần), *Đời Trong Ngục* (Hanoi: Nhà Xuất Bản Văn Hoá Mới, 1935), 14 and 15.

43. Tống, *Đời Trong Ngục*, 15.

44. Tống, *Đời Trong Ngục*, 18.

45. Tống, *Đời Trong Ngục*, 18.

5

Disturbing the Colonial Order:
Dystopia and Disillusionment in Indochina

Nicola Cooper

Although official France attempted to produce its own truths about Indochina, and to articulate indisputable forms of knowledge about Indochina, it was ultimately unable to marshal all discourses on Indochina to a homogeneous and monolithic colonial image of French imperial identity. While official French discourse achieved a relatively high degree of internal consistency, divergent discourses emerged in a variety of sources, thus destroying the monolithic and essentializing desire of what Said has termed "orientalism."

These divergent discourses manifested themselves in multifarious ways, and embodied, for the most part, concerns and fears which arose from the often anxious response to colonization on the part of settlers and colonial agents. Although they may not necessarily have challenged the premises of colonialism, the narratives which deviated from the received ideal of Indochina and of French identity nonetheless disturbed and undermined many of colonialism's orthodoxies. They violated the norms of the official discourse of French rule in Indochina. Indochina thus remained uncontainable and unknowable, in spite of efforts to understand and define it, and to fix and codify its colonial identity.

Of course, no matter how absolute a system of domination aspires to be, there will always be areas it cannot control. Thus the colonial production and domination of Indochina was often challenged unconsciously from within French colonialism's own ranks. The counter-narratives under discussion here reveal a complex and unstable web of responses to empire in Southeast Asia, many of which called into question the fundamental principles of colonial rule: the superiority of the colonizing nation and its agents; the difference between colonizer and colonized; and the binary oppositions between Western civilization and Eastern barbarity. Some of the themes expressed through these counter-narratives might be read as early, and tentative, avatars of the ideas and issues which were to amplify to form the basis of anticolonial thought in France.

From the turn of the century onward, a variety of colonial and governmental sources in France had combined to produce an image of France as an imperial nation in Southeast Asia, and of Indochina as the nation's showcase colony. France had evolved a colonial doctrine which revolved around a trinity of values or attributes: duty, responsibility and generosity. French colonial rule in Indochina was viewed as harmonizing, liberatory and fraternal. The *mise en valeur* (development) of Indochina, and the application of metropolitan values of progress, development and technological aid which were brought to bear, were perceived as acts of altruistic generosity and fraternal sharing. The notion of *la Plus Grande France* (greater France) functioned both to protect and develop Indochina. Many images, perceptions and representations of Indochina in popular cultural media or elsewhere reinforced and/or mirrored this state-sanctioned "official" version of the territories' identity which colonial France had constructed.

Nonetheless, however rigorously the nation's policymakers, its colonial lobby and its colonial administrators may have thought they had defined and fixed the identity of the colony and set the terms of the relationship between France and Indochina, Indochina always eluded those definitions, and undermined the conceptual foundation which had been constructed for it. This occurred either through the refusal to comply on the part of the colonized peoples; or through slippages—linguistic, cultural, and ideological. These took the form of counter-narratives which disturbed the colonial order and threatened to undermine that officially conceived identity. What emerges is a plethora of competing images of Indochina: some reiterative of official discourses and largely stereotypical, others paradoxical and antithetical. Thus in spite of the widely disseminated pro-colonial propaganda, and a strong underlying commitment to the French colonial doctrine, counter-narratives and discourses which undermined or disturbed both the prevailing colonial orthodoxy and received ideas about Indochina were manifest.

The following chapter analyzes the discomfort, unease or dissent which occurred in seemingly procolonial texts; the voices which provide a counterpoint, however hesitatingly, to the prevailing ideological hegemony. These voices reveal the instability of the colonial project; they are voices which point to an altogether less universal acceptance of France's colonial ideals, and which provide alternative discourses to the established myth of French colonial identity and the nation's role in Indochina.

Colonial propaganda had succeeded not only in drawing up and disseminating the image of the colony as a field for French civilizing and constructive ac-

tion, it had also constructed an ideal image of the settler: hardy, virile, and en-
terprising—an intrepid bushman (*broussard*) or a talented engineer or busi-
nessman. Many were seduced by the colonial dream and the exotic charm of a
life overseas. For those imbued with the state's colonial ideology, the appeal,
not to say challenge, of colonial emigration often stemmed from the goal of
fulfilling France's mission overseas, and living up to that idealized image of the
French settler abroad.

In Marguerite Duras's *Un barrage contre le Pacifique* (*The Sea-Wall*), a
retrospective portrayal of settler life in Indochina, the appeal and influence of
the colonial "dream" is evident. For a young, idealistic couple, Indochina presented an outlet for ambitions and energies which could not be fulfilled in the
mainland:

> Certains dimanches, à la mairie, elle rêvait devant les affiches de
> propagande coloniale. "Engagez-vous dans l'armée coloniale," "Jeu-
> nes, allez aux colonies, la fortune vous y attend." . . . Elle se maria
> avec un instituteur qui, comme elle, se mourait d'impatience dans un
> village du Nord, victime comme elle des ténébreuses lectures de
> Pierre Loti. Peu après leur mariage, ils firent ensemble leur demande
> d'admission dans les cadres de l'enseignement colonial et ils furent
> nommés dans cette grande colonie que l'on appelait alors
> l'Indochine française.

> (Occasionally on Sunday, she stopped to gaze at the Colonial propa-
> ganda posters in front of the town hall. "Enlist in the Colonial
> Army!" said some. And others: "Young People, a Fortune awaits
> you in the Colonies!" . . . She married a schoolmaster who was as
> sick as she was of life in the northern village and as victimized as
> she was by the maunderings of Pierre Loti and his romantic descrip-
> tions of exotic lands. The consequence was that, shortly after their
> marriage, they made out a joint application to be sent, as teachers, to
> that great Colony then known as French Indo-China.)[1]

The charm and allure of Indochina, and of the trappings of settler life, both fed
by the exoticism of writers such as Loti, and by colonial propaganda, create a
compelling portrait of the colonial ideal. This initial appeal, in both Duras's
work, and also, as we shall see, in earlier narratives, is however rapidly displaced by feelings of disappointment, failure and impotence. The propagandist
value of the colonial dream was often rapidly dissipated on contact with the
colony. For belief in France's colonial ideal, and Indochina's status as France's
colonial *perle* ("pearl"), the most precious and successful of the overseas possessions, were dealt perhaps the severest blow by tales of settler life in the colony.

Apart from some small colonial enclaves in the Pacific Ocean, Indochina
was the farthest flung of France's overseas possessions, and this sense of distance is itself an important aspect of the metropolitan image of Indochina. Much
popular literature was concerned with themes of exile and nostalgia for the

homeland. Metropolitan settlers felt cut off from the homeland: boat journeys to
Indochina took four weeks, and regular air transport to Indochina was not established until 1938.[2] Unlike many of the French overseas territories, particularly
Algeria, Indochina was never a settlement colony. The metropolitan population
was perhaps more isolated or insular in Indochina, as figures for French settlers
never exceeded 42,000.[3] Whereas Algeria had a far larger metropolitan population, was geographically closer to the mainland, and enjoyed a political status
which ensured that the territory was closely linked to France in the metropolitan
imagination, Indochina remained distant both spatially and conceptually.

In much popular fiction concerning Indochina, distance from the mainland
is repeatedly shown to have a disorienting and debilitating effect on the French
settlers. This sometimes manifests itself as a form of counter-exoticism: it functions not as an escape from ennui experienced in the mainland, but as the fear of
departure. In Georges Groslier's *Le Retour à l'argile*, Raymonde Rollin's anxiety about her future colonial life commences before her departure for Indochina:

> Elle imagina un affreux exil, se vit campée dans la brousse mena-
> çante, loin de tout confort, épiée par des indigènes sournois, par la
> fièvre et les bêtes.

> (She imagined a frightful exile, saw herself camped out in the men-
> acing bush, far from all comforts, spied upon by shifty natives, prey
> to fevers and wild animals.)[4]

Where colonial propaganda had emphasized the authority and superiority of the
colonial settler, Raymonde imagines menace; where colonial propaganda had
emphasized the fortune awaiting settlers, Raymonde imagines only loss and
deprivation. Raymonde's is a partially self-fulfilling prophecy, for once in Indochina she "vit mal, en proie à un ennui qu'entretiennent ses regrets de la
France" ("lives unhappily, prey to an ennui which her nostalgia for France kept
alive"), and remains convinced that she lives "en pays ennemi" ("in an enemy
country").[5] Whilst difference and alterity have often been viewed as constituting
part of the appeal of colonial migration, here the different and the inhabitual are
sources of anxiety. The move toward the Other embodied in exoticism is here
displaced by an inward-turning and anxious response to difference. Western
imperialism's traditional desire to know is replaced by a fear of knowing. In
spite of the widespread appeal of settler life conveyed through colonial propaganda, official discourses of colonialism could not entirely dissipate the anxieties provoked by emigration and colonial otherness.

Elsewhere, even if colonial propaganda has succeeded in its objective to
popularize metropolitan emigration to the colonies, writers are quick to highlight the disjunction between the colonial ideal and the reality of settler life in
Indochina. Once that unknown becomes known, and experienced at firsthand,
the illusion or dream of Indochina recedes rapidly, resulting in nostalgia and
spleen. In Jean Jacnal's "Dans la boue" ("Amidst the Mud"), the isolation suffered by the white settler in Indochina exacerbates the sense of disorientation:

Il est dans ce pays des étranges silences,
Où l'on sent mieux son cœur qui pleure dans l'exil,

(It is in this country of strange silences
That one feels most strongly one's heart weep in exile.)[6]

This isolation is often reflected in the novel titles themselves, such as Jean Dorsenne's *Loin des blancs* ("Far from White Men").[7] Similarly, in Pierre Loti's *Un Pèlerin d'Angkor*, his travel diary of his journey to Angkor Wat, the author emphasizes the inward-turning and sorrowfully reflective response to the migratory experience: "comment dire la tristesse, le recueillement songeur, pendant les nuits, de ces coins de la France, de ces semblants de patrie égarés au milieu de la grande brousse asiatique, isolés de tout" ("how can I tell of the sadness, the pensive contemplation, during the nights, of these lost corners of France, these shadows of homeland scattered in the middle of the great Asian bush, isolated from everything").[8] These portrayals of settler life in Indochina run counter to the traditional view of the imperial nation's desire to dominate the colony, and to impose itself both physically and metaphorically upon the colonized territory. Loti's portrayal of those "coins de la France" scattered throughout the vast space of Indochina provides a counterpoint to the nation's self-affirming belief in its transformative enterprise in Indochina. Settlers are fearful of the challenge of colonialism, and fearful about the colonizer's ability to fulfill his functions: they display a less than unshakeable belief in the possibility of carrying out France's colonial mission.

Portrayals of nostalgia for the homeland amongst settlers in Indochina also bring to light the notion of time wasted in Indochina. Of the French members of the expeditionary corps, Loti produces a sentimental view of nostalgia for the homeland and the comforts of France: "pauvres garçons . . . qui vont consumer ici une ou deux des plus belles années de leur vie!" ("poor boys . . . who will here squander one or two of the best years of their lives!").[9] This is mirrored in Jeanne Leuba's attempt to convey the settler's apprehension concerning time spent in Indochina to the metropolitan reader:

> Je voudrais qu'il aperçut confusément un peu de cette existence qui est la nôtre, un peu de ce pays où nous vivons—où nous souffrons— l'exil volontaire où nous passons nos jeunes, nos fortes années à lutter contre le spleen, la chaleur, les maux physiques, les énervements, les incompréhensions, les hostilités de la nature et des hommes.

> (I want him to grasp vaguely a little of this existence of ours, a little of this country where we live out—where we suffer—that voluntary exile in which we spend our youth, our years of strength, battling against melancholy, the heat, physical ills, irritations, misunderstandings, the hostilities of men and nature.)[10]

The notion of time misspent, with its emphasis on wasted youth, clearly runs counter to popular colonial propaganda in which the young and virile European found in the colony a worthy outlet for his energies. This very sense of waste implicitly calls into question the purpose and value of France's civilizing mission.

Indeed, not all representations of Indochina conformed to the positive view of the colony as a space for male action and adventure, a privileged site for development. Traditional rhetorical oppositions had construed France as an energetic European nation reinvigorating and improving a backward, impoverished and slothful Asia. While the principle of *mise en valeur* was thought to embody this ideal version of French intervention in Indochina, many fictional or autobiographical representations of life in Indochina showed that behavioral patterns amongst settlers ran counter to this model. Many fictional accounts of settler life in Indochina highlighted the way in which the alienation of the settler community militated against their potential to carry out their idealized functions. A sense of creeping passivity and lassitude often overwhelmed the European French in Indochina. Coupled with their sense of disorientation and gradual dislocation from Western life, and the attendant anxieties of living a life of exile in a foreign country, the colonizer's authority, and his ability to function as an agent of the nation's principle of *mise en valeur*, were sapped.

Contact with the colony is shown to distort time, and seems to effect a physical and psychological disjunction in the French settler in Indochina. Indeed, in the novel *Raffin-Su-Su*, Jean Ajalbert's eponymous protagonist loses any sense of time once he arrives in Laos:

> Le temps ne compte plus au Laos comme ailleurs. On ne le détaille pas. On ne le découpe pas en parcelles précieuses, minutées, sous globe, comme chez nous.

> (Time is not important in Laos as it is elsewhere. It is no longer broken down into minutes and hours. It isn't separated out into neat parcels and kept in a glass case as it is at home.)[11]

Time and exile combine to produce a sense of alienation and lassitude. Raffin's initial energy is frittered away by the intangible yet inexorable effect of the climate and atmosphere of Indochina. Whilst Raffin still felt a tangible contact with the mainland—here through his attempt to woo a Frenchwoman ("Madame Français")—who surely signifies for Raffin an idealized version of an imperial *mère-patrie*—he could motivate himself to fulfill his function as model settler:

> Sous l'empire idéal de "Madame Français," Raffin se gardait actif et volontaire, avec mille projets de routes, de chemins de fer, de cultures, d'élevages, d'exploitations minières, forestières, d'assistance médicale, de relèvement physique, intellectuel et moral de l'indigène . . . La paresse ambiante souriait de tant de zèle, qui se calmerait.

> (Under the model influence of Madame Français, Raffin kept him-
> self active and deliberate, with hundreds of projects for roads, rail-
> ways, crops, breeding, forestry and mining concerns, medical aid,
> the physical, intellectual and moral improvement of the natives . . . .
> The pervading laziness smiled at such zeal, which would eventually
> die down.)[12]

The narrator's ironic intervention at the end of the quotation undermines our faith in the transformative power of the male colonizer and of colonialism and calls into question the maintenance of the initial impetus of *mise en valeur*. Life in Indochina for Raffin is like a long siesta, where a carefree laziness takes over from the missionary vigor of building, exploring, and improving.[13]

The type of slothful, passive idleness to which Raffin succumbs is viewed as a harmful yet often inevitable feature of colonial life in Indochina. Far from underwriting the utopian vision of Indochina as an outlet for male creative energy, many portrayals present the reverse: the colony becomes a dystopic reality of exile and disillusionment.

The dissipation of the initial energy and commitment to the French colonial project of the white European newly-embarked in Indochina partially constitutes what Marguerite Duras was later to call "le vampirisme colonial" ("vampirism of colonialism"). Duras charts the initial hope and expectation of idealistic parents, imbued with official France's missionary zeal, on their way to bring French civilization to Indochina; and their gradual disappointment, loss of hope and despair as their projects fail.

In *L'Eden Cinéma*, the stage version of *Un Barrage*, the ideal of *mise en valeur* in its various manifestations is constantly invoked. The tenacity of this ideal, and its appeal to the good faith (*bonne foi*) of the idealistic settler is reflected in the Mother's consistent refusal to lose faith in her project to build her barriers and cultivate her land. The Mother's idealism seems unshakeable; the colonial ideal of progress, development and *mise en valeur* is pursued without heed: "Elle était sortie de la nuit de l'Eden ignorante de tout. Du grand vampirisme colonial. De l'injustice fondamentale qui règne sur les pauvres du monde" ("She emerged from the darkness of the cinema not knowing anything. Not knowing anything about the great vampire of colonialism. About the fundamental injustice that reigns over the world's poor").[14] In *Un Barrage contre le Pacifique*, the death of the family's horse symbolizes at once the good intentions and ideals of the European migrant to Indochina, and their failure: "Il essaya honnêtement de faire le travail qu'on lui demandait et qui était bien au-dessus de ses forces depuis longtemps, puis il creva" ("Faithfully, for a week, he had tried to do all the work required of him, but it was much beyond his strength—such strength as he had had for many years. And then he died").[15] Like her horse, the Mother becomes a victim of the nation's colonial design: she struggles to realize a hopeless project, succumbs to a seemingly inevitable outcome: madness and death. The overarching despair of the settler, and the inevitability of the failure of both the Mother and colonialism, are mirrored in Duras's prematurely closed narrative: "C'est là que nous avons été jeunes. Que la mère a vécu son espoir le plus grand. C'est là qu'elle est morte" ("It's there that we were young. There that the mother lived her greatest hope. There she died").[16]

The colonial dream, however, is in part betrayed by the very sense of superiority and its attendant arrogance which the successful inculcation of France's colonial doctrine appears to have produced. The Mother consults no one about her project and persuades the local populations that "les enfants morts de faim, les récoltes brûlées par le sel, non ça pouvait aussi ne pas durer toujours" ("the children dying of hunger, the harvests burned by salt, no, that couldn't go on forever"), and they believe her.[17] The figure of the Mother—always referred to as *the* mother, *la mère*, generic and universal—can be viewed as a debased version of *la mère-patrie*. The Mother also embodies that Western arrogance which refuses to accept the inexorability of Nature, as she battles on even though the ocean repeatedly pours through the barrages, destroying the crops. The refrain in *L'Eden Cinéma*, which recalls the ocean's destruction of the barrages, emphasizes the aggression of nature, and its repetition also expresses the Mother's implacable struggle to fulfill the colonial ideal: "La marée de juillet monta à l'assaut de la plaine et noya la récolte" ("The July tides come up over the plain and drown the harvest").[18]

In Duras's retrospective counter-narrative to the ideal of *mise en valeur*, this portrait of abject colonial failure functions not only as a *mise en scène* of the psychological, individual, sexual and social impact of the failed colonial dream, but also as an indictment of the corruption of colonial administrations in Indochina. Duras's epithet of "vampirisme colonial" thus also contains the notion of the settler's energy worn away by the struggle against the fraud and swindling of a rotten colonialism: "Pour avoir une concession fertile il fallait la payer deux fois. Une fois ouvertement, au gouvernement de la colonie. Une deuxième fois en sous-main, aux fonctionnaires chargés du lotissement" ("To get a fertile concession, then, in French Indochina, you had to pay twice. Once, openly, to the colonial authorities. And then again, under the counter, to the officials of the Land Commission").[19] In *Eden Cinéma*, the Mother's monologue concerning her unsent letter of recrimination to the colonial authorities reveals her indignation at her situation.[20] Although it appears that the reader is intended to sympathize with her, and to condemn the colonial authorities for their "vampirisme," the Mother too, is clearly guilty of a sort of "vampirisme manqué." The irony of her monologue (which might be read as a retrospective indictment of colonialism as a whole) is that she is unable to recognize how she is implicated in the "crime" she accuses the colonial authorities of perpetrating. The Mother is indignant, I would argue, precisely because she has been prevented from gaining her share of the colonial spoils. The Mother envies the richer white settlers, and attempts to emulate them. The family's poverty creates distance between them and other white settlers, and instead creates a form of reconciliation and closeness with the natives: they are united in their poverty. Thus although the monologue stresses the harmful effect upon the natives of corrupt colonial practices, and reveals a well-intentioned colonialism on the part of the Mother, her bitterness is nonetheless rooted in her inability to secure and profit from the capital gains she implies are the due of the colonizer.

In this rather ambiguous portrayal of colonial failure and disillusionment, the only outcomes for impoverished and unfortunate settlers are madness, corruption or death. In Duras's work, the authority and confidence of the colonizing nation is thus shown to be partial and precarious; the economy of capitalism which underpins colonialism militates against the universal success of the colonizer.

In earlier narratives, the latent doubts over the realizability or advisability of the colonial project manifest themselves in anxiety and fear, and in both physical and psychological debilitation. This gradual debilitation suffered by white settlers in Indochina is blamed on a variety of sources, including Indochina's climate and natural features. Many novelists presented the metropolitan settlers' lives abroad as a constant struggle against the maleficent forces of nature. The image of the intractable forest serves as a metaphor for Indochina, and France's relationship with the colony:

> Si familier que je croie être avec la forêt . . . il y en a, en elle, je ne sais quelle réserve de vie primordiale, dont la masse m'impressionne toujours, je ne sais quel air de bête feuillue, crochée au sol . . . de bête intuable . . . au point que je regarde avec admiration, à notre droite et à notre gauche, les deux bourrelets de chair écailleuse et brillante, qui ne demandent qu'à se refermer sur le dérisoire estafilade infligée par les ingénieurs du Siam-Cambodge.

> (However familiar I believe myself to be with the forest and all its myriad forms, there remains within it an unknowable reserve of primordial life, whose mass still impresses me, a certain intangible presence like a leafy beast, crouched on the ground . . . an immortal beast . . . to such a degree that I watch with admiration, to our right and left, the two rolls of scaly, shiny fat, our weather-strips, which ask only to close themselves over the derisory gash inflicted by the engineers of the Siam-Cambodia railway.)[21]

The forest emblematizes the ambiguous hold that the metropole has over Indochina. However familiar the French settler might feel he has become with the country, there is a certain element of it which forever escapes his grasp. In these metaphorical portrayals, colonialism is not presented as a durable force: Indochina is waiting to close in over the French presence. Analogous to France's relationship with its indigenous subjects, this evocation of the forest recalls the series of antitheses which mark French colonial discourses concerning Indochina. It concretizes a view in which Indochina is familiar yet unknowable, held in check but constantly threatening to break loose from metropolitan control.

In the Indochina of Boissière's short stories, "règne, en souverain orgueilleux et absolu, le végétal" ("the plant reigns a proud and absolute monarch"), with its "meurtrière émanation" ("deadly odors").[22] The organic omnipotence of Indochina's vegetation at once threatens and dethrones French control. Similarly, in Malraux's rather anachronistic *La Voie royale*, it is the insuperable organicism of the forest which signals the threat of decomposition of the self. Malraux's protagonists believe that only through the assertion of will can "déchéance" or submission be avoided, yet this is thwarted precisely by the sinister power of the Cambodian forest, which negates the will to overcome and dominate:

> La forêt et la chaleur étaient pourtant plus fortes que l'inquiétude: Claude sombrait comme dans une maladie dans cette fermentation où les formes se gonflaient, s'allongeaient, pourrissaient hors du monde dans lequel l'homme compte, qui le séparait de lui-même avec la force de l'obscurité . . . L'unité de la forêt, maintenant s'imposait; depuis six jours Claude avait renoncé à séparer les êtres des formes, la vie qui bouge de la vie qui suinte.

> (The heat and the never-ending forest harassed them even more than their anxiety. Like a slow poison, the ceaseless fermentation in which forms grew bloated, lengthened out, decayed, as in a world where mankind has no place, wore down Claude's stamina insidiously; under its influence, in the green darkness, he felt himself disintegrating like the world around him . . . Claude was growing aware of the essential oneness of the forest and had given up trying to distinguish living beings from their setting, life that moves from life that oozes.)[23]

The pervasive formlessness of the decomposing vegetation seems to affect Claude Vannec both physically and psychologically. It is beyond his control and threatens both his physical and mental integrity:

> Quel acte humain, ici, avait un sens? Quelle volonté conservait sa force? Tout se ramifiait, s'amollissait, s'efforçait de s'accorder à ce monde ignoble et attirant à la fois comme le regard des idiots, et qui attaquait les nerfs.

> (Here what act of man had any meaning, what human will but spent its staying power? Here everything frayed out, grew soft and flabby, tended to assimilate itself with its surroundings, which, loathsome yet fascinating as a cretin's eyes, worked on the nerves.)[24]

Thus the forest attacks the European's mental faculties through his enfeebled bodily responses. The virility of the adventurer is challenged and his lucidity questioned. The pervasive decomposition of the forest and the excessiveness of the vegetation have an almost infectious capacity: they threaten mental decay and idiocy.

As in much colonial literature, and most particularly in the context of *fin-de-siècle* fears about European degeneration, this battle against nature is also presented as a psychological struggle. It might be argued that the themes of sickness, mental disturbance and death are related to the psychological trauma experienced by those individuals who constituted the early wave of departure to the colonies. Reflecting an almost unconscious unease with Empire and the colonial situation in Indochina, the psychological changes which occur in the characters of Henry Daguerches's novels, for instance, are always imputed to Indochina, and most often to its climate, as "L'âme et l'esprit s'anémient ici" ("The soul and the spirit are weakened here").[25] These fears mirror the concerns expressed in contemporary health and hygiene manuals which also associated climate with mental and physical degeneracy. Indochina is here compared to a debilitating virus which gnaws away at the psychological stability of the European settlers. Enfeeblement, mental anemia, and spinelessness work from the interior to weaken the psyche, and are evoked in physiognomic terms, as exterior signs of deterioration: sagging and spinelessness. Whilst fictional portrayals of Africa reflected fears of cannibalism, and possible death by wild animals, in the case of Indochina, the notion of insidious disease appears to have constituted the most acutely felt anxiety.

The perceived insalubrity of Indochina is frequently evoked in fiction and memoirs. Its exotic appeal was both seductive and debilitating. As is the case with many of France's overseas possessions, the first mass metropolitan experience of Indochina was almost inevitably that of war and conquest, thus adding to the association between Indochina and death. Later, the first fictional metropolitan representations of Indochina date from the period of pacification and take the form of autobiographical *récits*, journals and diaries, giving highly subjective accounts. Loti, for instance, candidly documents his dislike of Indochina, and states clearly the personal origins of this antipathy: his elder brother was killed in 1865 while returning in ill health from Indochina, where he had been a naval officer. Arriving in Saigon, Loti notes: "Une ville . . . dont le nom seul jadis me paraissait lugubre, parce que mon frère . . . était allé, comme tant d'autres de sa génération, y prendre les germes de la mort" ("A city whose very name of old seemed lugubrious to me . . . because my brother had been there, like many others of his generation, and picked up the germs of death").[26] This personal experience of loss is echoed in *Pêcheur d'Islande*, where the hero dies on board the ship headed for France as a result of a tour of duty in Tonkin.[27] The ship for France becomes a "hôpital mouvant" ("moving hospital"), an "étouffoir de malades" ("stifler of the sick"), in which many died.[28]

As noted above, while fear of sickness in any of the French overseas territories may have been a common theme in colonial literature, it is particularly noticeable in the case of Indochina, which is often evoked through allusions to insidious sickness leading to death.[29] The association of Indochina with death certainly originated in metropolitan France with the popularization of literature which reported the exploration and conquest of the territories. This image was perpetuated by the parliamentary colonial debate of the late nineteenth century, which pitched convinced colonialists against those who deplored the sacrifice of "l'or et le sang français" ("French blood and French gold") in foreign territories. As Malleret notes:

> Les souvenirs colportés par les soldats qui firent la rude expédition de Cochinchine et la pénible guerre du Tonkin, ont laissé jusqu'à nos jours une trace profonde dans les esprits. Incapable de s'affranchir de cette notion formée aux premiers jours de la pénétration coloniale, le public a confondu pendant longtemps, tous les pays indochinois dans un ensemble qui conservait, à ses yeux, la même signification sinistre.

> (The memories brought home by the soldiers who made the harsh trip to Cochinchina and took part in the difficult war in Tonkin have left deep imprints to this day. Incapable of moving beyond the notion formed during the first days of colonial penetration, the public has long confused all the Indochinese territories, blurring them into one mass, which retains, to the public's mind, the same sinister signification.)[30]

Clearly these initial portrayals of Indochina as a vast burial ground for young French men are important, yet the question remains as to why this "first impression" was never truly replaced, even once Indochina had been "sanitized," with a less maleficent representation. The durability of the association between Indochina and death, between Indochina and disease and suffering suggests a residual unease with the experience of colonial expatriation.

The hostility and threat of Indochina's environment is often coupled with anxiety regarding the population. Although most sources between the turn of the century and the early 1920s confirmed a view that French rule in Indochina was successful and that the Indochinese populations were peaceable and appreciative subjects, there nonetheless occurred rather less explicit indications of anxieties related to intercultural encounters. On the one hand, commentators seemed to agree that Indochina in the 1920s was a model of Franco-indigenous collaboration and harmony. Paul Claudel, for example, visiting Indochina in 1921 as part of his duties as French Ambassador to Japan, was full of praise for the colony:

> On assiste au mouvement d'un peuple entier dont le désir le plus profond, semble n'être que d'adopter notre culture et notre langue elle-même.

> (We are witnessing the movement of an entire people, for whom the most profound desire seems only to be to adopt our culture and our language itself.)[31]

He demonstrates the accepted view of the indigenous populations of Indochina as peacefully collaborating with their French rulers. Similarly, the visual representation of native Indochinese populations at the colonial exhibition of Vincennes had perpetuated this image of a docile peasant people: malleable *figurants* who actively sought the guidance of the superior imperial nation. Other, more anthropologically-minded texts often offset these positive attributes against a disparaging résumé of the natives' less desirable and potentially menacing qualities. Writing a history of the French overseas possessions, Gaffarel states:

> Les Annamites ont des qualités: ils sont gais, braves, entreprenants, polis, hospitaliers, dévoués à leur famille, avides d'instruction et passionnés pour le progrès: mais ils sont aussi malpropres, gloutons, disputeurs, inconstants, ingrats, cruels, voleurs, menteurs et débauchés. Ces défauts disparaîtront ou diminueront peut-être avec les progrès de l'instruction.

> (The Annamites have certain qualities: they are cheerful, courageous, enterprising, polite, hospitable, devoted to their families, keen on education and passionate about progress. But they are also dirty, greedy, argumentative, fickle, ungrateful, cruel, thieves, liars and debauched. These faults will perhaps disappear or diminish as their education progresses.)[32]

Here, those negative qualities are seen as being held in check by French civilizing action and education. The analysis leaves unspoken the potentially negative consequences for French rule in Indochina should that "instruction" not be successfully accomplished.

Views and representations such as these reinforced the founding colonial premise of imperial superiority and authority over the subjugated colonized. On the other hand however, much colonial fiction and travel writing nonetheless revealed what might be construed as a far less firmly held belief in the innate authority of the colonizer. As we have seen, fictional responses to settler life exposed anxieties related to the experience of living as an ethnic minority in a dominated territory: these responses range from Raymonde Rollin's extreme fear of living in "an enemy country," to less overt instances of tension and apprehension.

Contemporary commentators have noted that one of the ways in which colonial authority manifests itself is through the commanding gaze of the European. To be an observer is to reenact the power hierarchy of the colonial relationship. The act of observing implies a position of authority, through which a sense of mastery over the unknown is conveyed. Natives are "obligated to show themselves to view for the white men, but they themselves lack the privilege of the gaze . . . gazed upon, they are denied the power of the gaze."[33] The colonial gaze becomes a means through which to control, and to enact disciplinary surveillance over subjugated populations. For the European in Indochina however, this economy of the colonial gaze often appears to be reversed: the European becomes the object of study, and is imprisoned by the gaze of the Other; the European is stripped of the authority and privilege traditionally preserved for the Western observer.

Fears concerning the potential hostility of the native Indochinese populations reflect the latent discomfort of the conquering nation vis-à-vis its own role and actions, revealed through individual accounts of physical isolation and excessive visibility. Anxiety is often provoked in crowd situations where the disequilibrium of the minority/majority equation for the European becomes most tangible. Viollis for example, describes one crowd as consisting of "milliers de jaunes visages impassibles où guettent les prunelles aïgues" ("thousands of impassive yellow faces where sharp eyes lie in wait").[34] When visiting Hué, she and her companions feel "la sensation d'être guettés par des centaines d'invisibles prunelles" ("the sensation of being watched by hundreds of invisible eyes").[35] The experience of living or traveling as a minority group amongst the overwhelming numbers of the Other subverts the power of the European gaze. Experiencing the surveillance of a numerically superior population provokes doubt concerning the authority of the representative of the ruling colonial nation. In Duras's *L'Eden Cinéma*, the unbreachable distance between European and native populations confirms the impossibility of authentic complicity within the hierarchical confines of the colonial relationship. The end of the text emphasizes the inevitable distance between the two communities and denies the possibility of harmonious integration:

> Elle était blanche. Même si elle vous [les paysans indigènes] aimait. Même si son espoir était le vôtre et si elle a pleuré les enfants de la plaine, elle est restée une étrangère à votre pays . . . Nous sommes restés des étrangers à votre pays. Elle sera enterrée dans le cimetière colonial de Saïgon.

> (She was not of your race. Even though she loved you, even though her hope was your hope and she mourned the children of the plain, she was not of your race. She was always a stranger in your country. All of us were always strangers in your country. She'll be buried in the French cemetery in Saigon.)[36]

The disillusionment and disappointment unveiled in many accounts of Indochina thus provide a counterpoint to the quasi-utopic portrayals of French Indochina disseminated by official sources. Indeed, these texts often present the very antithesis of the official version of Indochina as the "perle" of the Empire. Indochina becomes, on contact, a veritable dystopia: its defining features are disease, debilitation, threat and isolation. Thus although official portrayals were perhaps the most widely disseminated sources of metropolitan knowledge about Indochina, there nonetheless existed a series of narratives which strongly reflected colonial doubts and unease.

Notes

This chapter is reprinted with some revisions from Nicola Cooper, *France in Indochina: Colonial Encounters* (Oxford and New York: Berg, 2001). Thanks to Berg for permission to reproduce.

1. Marguerite Duras, *Un Barrage contre le Pacifique* (Paris: Gallimard, 1950), 23; *The Sea Wall*, trans. Herma Briffault (New York: Harper and Row, 1986), 17.

2. Philippe Franchini, "La Cité blanche," in *Saigon 1925-1945: de la "Belle Colonie" à l'éclosion révolutionnaire ou la fin des dieux blancs*, ed. Philippe Franchini (Paris: Editions Autrement, 1992), 69.

3. The metropolitan population in Algeria during the same period was estimated to be 946,000.

4. Georges Groslier, *Le Retour à l'argile* (Paris: Kailash, 1994), 15 (first edition Paris: Emile Paul, 1928).

5. Groslier, *Le Retour à l'argile*, 25 and 26.

6. Jean Jacnal, *Rêves d'Annam* (Paris: A. Challamel, 1913), 112.

7. Jean Dorsenne, *Loin des blancs* (Paris: Fayard, 1933).

8. Pierre Loti, *Un Pèlerin d'Angkor* (Paris: Kailash, 1994), 15 (first edition Paris: Calmann-Lévy, 1912).

9. Loti, *Un Pèlerin d'Angkor*, 15-16.

10. Jeanne Leuba, *L'Aile du feu* (Paris: Plon-Nourrit, 1926), 242.

11. Jean Ajalbert, *Raffin Su-su* (Paris: Publications littéraires et politiques, 1911), *Raffin Su-su suivi de Sao Van Di*, (Paris: Kailash, 1995), 7.

12. Ajalbert, *Raffin Su-su*, 17.

13. Ajalbert, *Raffin Su-su*, 25-26.

14. Marguerite Duras, *L'Eden cinéma* (Paris: Mercure de France, 1977), 18 *Eden Cinema*, in *Marguerite Duras: Four Plays*, trans. Barbara Bray (London: Oberon Books, 1992), 50.

15. Duras, *Un Barrage contre le Pacifique*, 13; *The Sea Wall*, 9. This translation is problematic on two levels: firstly because it attributes a timescale (a week) which is not present and particularizes the quotation so that the sentiment expressed can only be attributable to the horse. In the original, however, the quotation may be understood metaphorically: the horse symbolizes the colonizer's attempt to work diligently, but to no avail. Secondly, the clause referring to the horse's ability to work is a mistranslation and should read: "He tried honestly to do the work that was asked of him and which had been beyond his capacities for a long time."

16. *L'Eden cinéma*, 30. *Four Plays*, 53.

17. *L'Eden*, 25. *Four Plays*, 52.

18. *L'Eden*, 19. *Four Plays*, 50.

19. *L'Eden*, 21-22. *Four Plays*, 50-51.

20. *L'Eden*, 127-33. *Four Plays*, 86-88.

21. Henry Daguerches, *Le Kilomètre 83* (Paris, Kailash, 1993), 65-66 (first edition Paris: Calmann-Lévy, 1913).

22. Jules Boissière, "Dans la forêt" in *Fumeurs d'Opium* (Paris: Kailash, 1993), 9 (first edition Paris: Flammarion, 1895). His protagonists are prey to "jungle fever," and the threat of malaria, producing a sense that sickness in Indochina is again organic and omnipresent: "bue dans l'eau des ruisseaux et respirée dans les brouillards du matin" (11: "drunk in the water of the streams and breathed in the morning mists").

23. André Malraux, *La Voie royale* (Paris: Grasset, 1930). *The Royal Way*, trans. Stuart Gilbert (New York: Random House, 1955), 84-85. I am very grateful to Paul Michael Sager of New York University for helping me to obtain these translations of Malraux.

24. Malraux, *Voie Royale*, 67. *Royal Way*, 85-86.

25. Daguerches, *Le Kilomètre 83*, 135.

26. Loti, *Un Pèlerin*, 10.

27. Pierre Loti, *Pêcheur d'Islande* (Paris: Booking International/Classiques français, 1994), 125-71 (first edition Paris: Calmann Levy, 1893).

28. Loti, *Pêcheur*, 127.

29. Boissière, "Dans la forêt," 11.

30. Louis Malleret, *L'Exotisme indochinois dans la littérature française depuis 1860* (Paris: Larose, 1934), 12.

31. Paul Claudel, *Œuvres complètes de Paul Claudel: Tome 4, Extrême-Orient* (Paris: Gallimard, 1952), 333. Claudel was first Ambassador to China (1895-1909), then to Japan (1921-1927). He visited Indochina on a number of occasions, making six short trips, and three longer visits in 1903, 1921 and 1925. It was his 1921 trip which gave rise to written reflections on the colony, which appear as a combination of the *récit de voyage* with a *rapport de mission*. These first appeared in May 1922 in *La Revue du Pacifique*.

32. Paul Gaffarel, *L'Algérie et les colonies françaises: lectures géographiques et historiques* (Paris: Garnier, 1888), 582-83.

33. David Spurr, *The Rhetoric of Empire: Colonial Discourse in Journalism, Travel Writing and Imperial Administration* (Durham: Duke University Press, 1994), 13.

34. Andrée Viollis, *SOS Indochine* (Paris: Gallimard, 1935), 30.

35. Viollis, *SOS*, 50.

36. *Eden*, 154. *Four Plays*, 95.

6

Of *Le Cafard* and Other Tropical Threats:
Disease and White Colonial Culture in Indochina

Michael G. Vann

In both contemporary historical accounts and the memories of popular culture, the colonial experience was replete with numerous clichés and stereotypes. For many former colonials, as well as many other Westerners desirous of the colonial lifestyle of apparent ease and luxury, the images of the colonies that come to mind are of spacious villas staffed by numerous servants; being pulled around in a rickshaw while dressed in pristine white clothes attesting to the lack of labor of a life of idleness; or enjoying relaxing cocktails—a gin and tonic for the British and an aperitif of Pernod or Ricard in the French empire—as the tropical sunset indulged in its spectacular nightly lightshow. In short, the images are ones of various manifestations of power: military and political power, economic and material power, and cultural and racial power. In the height of the age of empire, colonial whites ruled the tropical world. In this world that they dominated, they required daily reminders of their power. Frantz Fanon described the colonial settler as "an exhibitionist" whose "preoccupation with security makes him remind the native out loud that he alone is master."[1] However, there was always a certain vulnerability—what Milton Osborne termed a "background anxiety"—in the minds of the colonials.[2] Thus, despite the clichés and stereotypes of white power and comfort, feelings of unease, apprehension, and fear were common. The perceived vulnerability of colonial whites took

various forms. From the threat of native violence in the form of crime or political rebellion to the general uncertainty about being a stranger in a strange land,
the white communities in the colonies were frequently on edge. This vulnerability can be most clearly seen in the white colonial obsession with perceived
threats to their health. Using the French community in Hanoi as a case study,
this essay considers this constant tension between power and vulnerability and
argues that said tension was central to the culture of colonial whiteness.

A combination of historical, biological, and ideological factors, with health,
illness, and death playing a central role, formed the culture of French Hanoi.
For the colonial whites, the state of their health and the omnipresent threat of
tropical disease produced a constant anxiety. With the perpetually busy hospital
and rapidly expanding graveyard as reminders of white mortality, pessimism,
fatalism, and depression darkened the white experience in the city.[3] At better
moments, the colonials responded to their sad state of affairs with gallows humor. Either way, the collective obsession with their own mortality stood in stark
contrast to the comfortable lifestyle and relatively high standard of living they
enjoyed as the colonial ruling class. The perceived health crisis exposed white
vulnerability in the tropics, a vulnerability which political, military, and economic force could not erase.[4]

Arrival in the colonies placed the European at risk. The white man suddenly found himself in a land of pathogenic danger. In addition to keeping one's
distance from the supposedly unhealthy natives, conventional wisdom and expert opinion advised the colonial to take a variety of special precautions to protect themselves. Climate was a primary concern. For decades, Europeans considered the intensity of the sun's rays to have potentially life-threatening
consequences for whites. Ignorant of the very real risk of skin cancer and the
origin of many diseases, medical authorities believed tropical heat and humidity
to be the source of a variety of ailments. The term *l'anémie coloniale* served as
a catch-all phrase for a general malaise which affected whites in the tropics.[5] In
order to protect their fragile bodies, colonial whites made the pith helmet the de
facto uniform of European colonization. Indeed, it is difficult for many to imagine a scene in the era of High Imperialism without at least one character wearing the pith helmet.[6] Other authorities advised whites to wear a spinal pad made
of cloth to protect one's nervous system from the damaging solar rays.[7] Evidently experts believed that the thick pad running down the spine would provide
the needed barrier to keep these dangerous rays at bay (one can only imagine
the discomfort such an accessory would create in the hot and sweaty tropics). In
addition to the heat and humidity, the level of electricity in the air also worried
Europeans.[8] It seems that the spectacular thunderstorms of the tropical world,
natural phenomenon that have amazed generations of Southeast Asian inhabitants and travelers unused to their power and ferocity, appeared as some sort of
threatening omen to the sophisticated men of science newly arrived from
Europe. For these Europeans it seemed as though the air, land, and sky were
conspiring against the European body. In such an environment, where the very

forces of nature threatened one's health if not one's very life, fear, anxiety, and vulnerability infected the mind of the white colonial.

In response to these various threats, medical experts tried to devise standards and practices to help the vulnerable white body. Unfortunately, as late nineteenth and early twentieth century medicine often failed to understand the true nature of most tropical diseases, colonial physicians, officers, and administrators could only suggest comforting measures that eased the suffering or treated the symptoms rather than removing the threat of disease. As long as the vectors in the propagation of disease and the nature of the pathogen remained a mystery, white colonial bodies would remain vulnerable. Thus, to maintain their health, Europeans were advised to take plenty of time to rest during the day and to get away to misty mountain retreats or to beaches cooled by seabreezes. Accordingly the colonial state made the development of hillstations and coastal retreats a priority for the success of the imperial mission.[9] To ensure the survival of the colonial overlords, sufficiently comfortable accommodation had to be constructed in the hostile tropical environment. This accommodation included spacious and well-ventilated villas, state-of-the-art urban infrastructure such as running water and sewers, and access to relaxing resorts. As such things had not existed in the colonies prior to the European conquest, few if any of these measures were deemed necessary for the indigenous populations. Put simply, whites required better treatment in the colonies; better than they needed at home and better than the indigenous people. In the experience of daily life, these medical guidelines worked as a justification for the luxury and leisure of the colonial lifestyle. The disproportionately high standard of living amongst white colonials became an acknowledged medical necessity. In order to preserve themselves, whites had to be pampered.

Faced with an onslaught of pathological threats, disease came to play an inescapable, if not central, role in the formation of white colonial identity. While dramatic epidemics, which caused serious conflicts and threatened to spread chaos through the streets of Hanoi, captured the attention of most observers, endemic illnesses made an equally great impact on the colonial body and mind. With an imperfect supply of drinking water playing host to a variety of amoebas and the humid air buzzing with mosquitoes, the adult European without the benefit of childhood immunities was subject to countless maladies. While some of these were relatively minor ailments to be sure, these nonlife-threatening sicknesses caused undeniable discomfort. At the top of this list we could place dysentery, the great plague for Europeans in the tropical world. Leading to painful stomach cramps, general physical weakness, and acute diarrhea, dysentery's real threat lay in dangerously severe dehydration. Dysentery might be followed by dengue fever, a more serious ailment. Only occasionally fatal, this mosquito-borne disease cripples the patient with intense fever, migraine headaches, and pains in the limbs and joints; hence its appellation "bone-break fever." To make matters worse, dengue fever, like its mosquito-borne cousin malaria, has a tendency to come back and reinflict its woes upon the patient. Such recurrent diseases must have drained not just the physical strength of the white colonials, but also their mental and emotional strength. The daily fatigue caused by battling a variety of ailments taxed the morale of the white community. Near-constant diarrhea, intestinal pains, and low-grade fevers contributed to the general sense of ennui known as *le cafard*, the colonial blues.

The susceptibility of colonial whites to the quotidian illnesses of the tropics reveals the essential paradox of the colonial order: despite the triumphs of Western technology, science, and medicine; despite the French command of overwhelming military force; despite the colonial state's monopoly of political power; and despite the radically unequal standards of living between whites and non-whites, the European colonial was vulnerable to multiple debilitating and potentially deadly biological threats to his very body. Learning to live with this inherent contradiction, an inconsistent balance between power and weakness, was a central aspect of becoming colonial. Such a paradox required the Europeans to recognize the limits of their power. However, the colonials did not have to merely accept these threats. It was hoped that specific measures could be enacted to protect the white community. Colonial medicine thus became a central front in the battle to build the colonial empire.

Death was ever present. In Hanoi, local historical memory created a pantheon of colonial heroes felled by disease. At the top of this hagiographic list was Paul Bert. Despite his active lifestyle and the mark he left on the city, the republican Gouverneur Général d'Indochine (GGI) survived only a few months in Hanoi. Considered a martyr for the cause of French colonization, he was killed not by enemy fire but by dysentery in the 1880s. Another colonial administrator but also a literary figure, the celebrated Jules Boissière managed to pen several novels of colonial life, including *Fumeurs d'opium*, before intestinal problems struck him down at the young age of thirty-four. Many white colonials wanted public commemorations of their fallen comrades. In 1913, a certain Dauffes, president of *L'Association amicale de la Garde Indigène de l'Indochine*, wrote to the GGI. He petitioned for the erection of a monument to the French officers killed in action. To bolster his case, he noted that at least twenty-five percent of the two hundred dead Frenchmen died due to enemy fire.[10] The overwhelming majority of the men to be memorialized died from illness. Taking some responsibility for the danger it placed its civil servants in, the *Administration* assumed the cost of burials of *fonctionnaires* and their family members who died in the colony.[11]

Memoirs of life in French Hanoi are filled with anecdotes about the fragile health of the colonials. When Marius Borel, who survived more than five decades in Indochina, recorded his life in the colony, he noted the sickness or death of most of his close friends. The rate at which fevers, diarrhea, dysentery, and malaria took their toll on his countrymen attests to the constant danger to their health. When Borel secured a small plantation in the Tonkinese highlands, he still found himself making regular treks to Hanoi to be treated for everything from stomach trouble to a dog bite. He recorded these trips to the capital in search of medical assistance with a glum resignation. In the city, he frequently visited friends in the hospital or in rented hotel rooms during their illnesses. He noted these visits and the frequent failure of his friends to recover with a somber grief. For Borel and other whites living in provincial Tonkin, Hanoi was associated with sickness and death, making the city a place of suffering and sadness, at least for the duration of these visits.[12] The portrait that emerges from his firsthand account of over half a century of life in the colony is one of the constant presence of disease and death.

Suffering through these constant illnesses, the white colonials were enraged when they encountered metropolitans, or worse Parisians, criticizing the supposed decadent luxuries of the colonial lifestyle. Back in France, it seemed that those not familiar with the tropical reality thought that the colonial life was simply a series of parties with easy jobs that required little of the colonial civil servant. Such colony-metropole disputes could take the form of public debates in which the colonials tried to defend themselves and their lifestyle against the condescending ignorance of those who did not understand life in the colonies. In an angry 1912 polemic entitled "Le Risque colonial," Jean Ajalbert bitterly complained about the lack of sympathy and understanding in Paris. He fumed against the work of Maurice Viollette, a fellow polemicist who wrote that: "in the cities, where they crowd together, where sinecures are created at will, they have theaters, promenades, a worldly and luxurious existence; they do not suffer from . . . a precarious situation, a murderous climate, the absence of medical help, the scarcity of provisions." To protect themselves, the Parisian flippantly suggested that the colonials wear *casques*, pith-helmets. In defense of the colonials, Ajalbert cited several GGIs who died from illnesses, as well as countless *colons*, soldiers, and *fonctionnaires*. Acknowledging that there were grand cities in the colony, he argued that dysentery still created widows and orphans, as did malaria, liver abscesses, hepatitis, and the ubiquitous anemia. According to Ajalbert, the condemnation of "la vie large des colonies" by metropolitans who did not understand the "risque colonial" only added to the demoralization of colonial exile.[13] The same themes persisted a generation later when Christiane Fournier, a more sensible and moderate voice, politely condemned the exoticist image of the colony as a fantasyland of sacred ruins, sensual dancing girls, and glorious temples. "All that exists. And also wood fever, malaria, dysentery, and the heavy torpor of hot lands."[14] Adding to the paradox of colonial health, defensive colonials almost seemed to cherish their suffering, considering it a sign of their sacrifice to the colonial cause and using it as a guilty denial of their privileged status. Such tensions between colonials who felt that they had to defend themselves against metropolitans ignorant of their supposed suffering resonated with the culture divide between frontline soldiers, *les poilus*, and the home front in the First World War.[15]

Humor was a common means of expressing the colonials' relationship with disease and death. In *La Vie large des colonies*, an anthology of cartoons about life in Indochina, the artist André Joyeux won the praise of critics such as Jean Ajalbert. Ajalbert applauded the irony of the title as well as the fact that the author juxtaposed many of the colony's difficulties and dangers with the supposed colonial good life.[16] Much of Joyeux's work points to the bitter ironies and hypocrisies of life in the colonies. With a dark humor, his sketches show the common colonial obsession with the state of one's health. In a section entitled "La Joie de vivre," Joyeux's tragi-comic pen lampooned the constant ailments that weakened the European (see figure 6.1).[17]

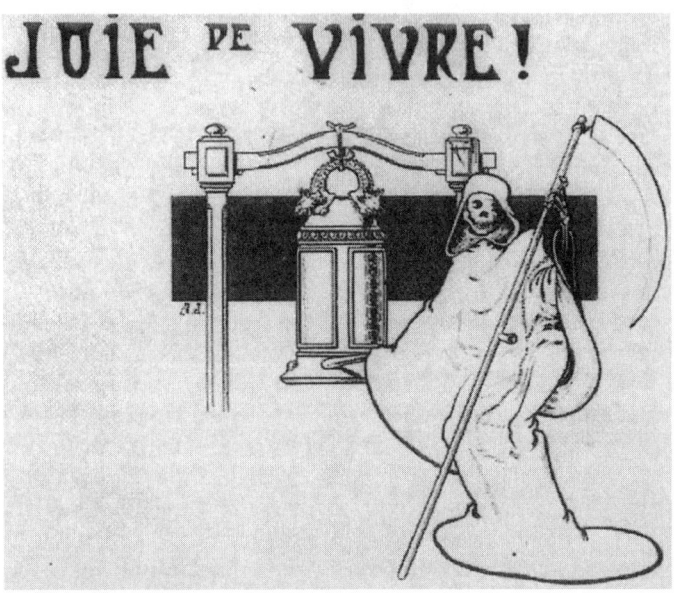

Figure 6.1: "The Joy of Living!" (André Joyeux, *La Vie large des colonies*)

"The Small Miseries" (see figure 6.2) shows a sophisticated group of colonials at an elegant formal dinner. As a well-dressed woman removes her gloves, a gentleman seated next to her asks, "So, my dear Madame, how is your *cochinchinette*?" The joke lies in the fact that *cochinchinette* was the local slang for a severe intestinal problem often associated with dengue fever. The ailment normally caused severe abdominal pains, sudden bouts of diarrhea, and frequent fevers. Unfortunately, the state of colonial medicine in the early twentieth century offered little relief for such ailments. Having a *cochinchinette* meant that one would be in a constant state of discomfort, making even the most basic daily chores a burden, let alone dressing for a formal dinner affair. The punch line lies in the fact that such a vulgar and disgusting topic could be part of polite dinner conversation, suggesting the mundane and commonplace nature of these severe health problems. The ailment was so common that one need hardly blink an eye nor blush when the subject is brought up at dinner.

"The Table of Advancement" (figure 6.3) is a more scatological cartoon. The title refers to the chart of raises and promotions in the colonial civil service. Viewed as obsessed with their promotions, many colonials laughed at the civil servants who, with little else to do, spent much of their time keeping track of their slow rise up through the colonial bureaucracy, as well as the career trajectories of their friends and their rivals. However, in this case the term refers to something much more sinister.

Figure 6.2: "Les Petites misères" ("The Small Miseries").
"And so, Madame, how is your *cochinchinette*?" (André Joyeux, *La Vie large des colonies*)

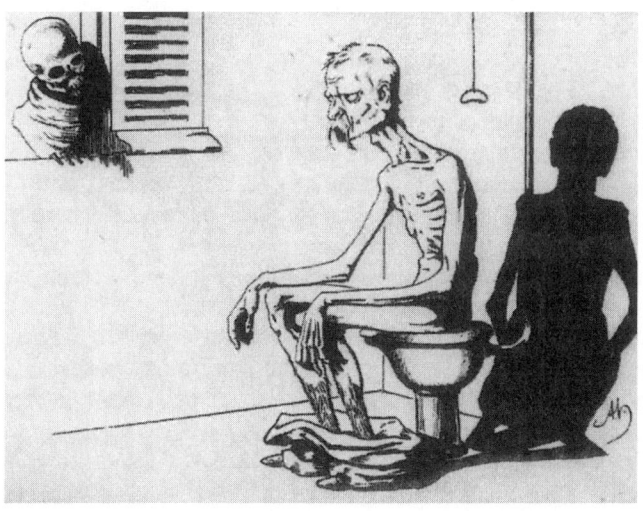

Figure 6.3: "Le Tableau d'avancement" ("The Table of Advancement").
(André Joyeux, *La Vie large des colonies*)

In the cartoon we see a man seated on a toilet. He is emaciated and has a look of angry resentment upon his face. Indeed he seems to be little more than a skeleton with an exaggerated Gallic moustache. At the window Death looks in, as if checking on the advancement of the disease that is causing the man to wither away. We can almost feel the man's life force flow out of him and down the pipes. The image is one of sad resignation and fatalism, tinged with a dose of toilet humor.

Another cartoon comments upon the heavy drinking which frequently contributed to the ill-health of the colonials. Indeed, many commented upon the heavy drinking of soldiers, civil servants, and settlers who seemed to have devoted an unusual and unhealthy amount of time to drinking in cafés and bars in the larger colonial cities. Figure 6.4, "Hepatite suppurée," shows a patient being carried off after surgery. His friend asks the doctor if he found anything on the patient's liver? "Yes," the doctor replies as he wipes the blood from his hands, "a liter of Pernod." Again, the humor here lies in the fatalism of life in the colonies. The cartoon tells us that if colonial diseases don't get you, the conditions will drive you to drink and thus destroy your health.

— Vous lui avez trouvé quelque chose au foie?
— Oui, un litre de Pernod.

Figure 6.4: "Hépatite suppurée" ("Suppurated Hepatitis"). "Did you find anything in his liver?" "Yes, a liter of Pernod." (André Joyeux, *La Vie large des colonies*)

Joyeux also commented upon the continual presence of death in the colony. "En Mer: au retour" (figure 6.5) contains a French pun: "Un voyageur descend à contre-voie"; literally, "a traveler goes down on the return trip." The image of a coffin plunging into the sea as it slides off a steamer accompanies this statement; a comment on the many ailing colonials who left Hanoi for France but never made it home. To remind the reader that these are serious and tragic issues, Joyeux closes with "The Risks" (figure 6.6). It shows two men leaving a villa where a woman cries as a baby plays innocently on the floor. The caption reads simply: "M. Fisc, twenty-eight years old, customs commissioner, died of dysentery this morning at the military hospital." Both these last images, coming at the end of the generally humorous section on health, come as a sharp slap in the face. Here we are reminded that many colonials not only suffered from the various ailments of the tropical world but that they also succumbed to the deadly power of these poorly understood exotic diseases.

Un voyageur descend à contre-voie.

Figure 6.5: "En mer: au retour" ("At Sea: The Return"): "A traveler goes down on the return trip." (André Joyeux, *La Vie large des colonies*)

White colonials held that the combined effects of the constant battle against illness, the constantly lurking grim reaper, the sense of exile, and the alienation of being surrounded by racial Others, whom you could neither trust nor communicate with, let alone understand, created a common depression known as *le cafard*. In a melancholy essay, Fournier proposed a satirical scientific classification of the *le cafard*. She divided the emotional state into melancholy *cafard*, chronic *cafard*, and violent *cafard*. Fournier advised the reader to understand these conditions as they were an essential and inescapable part of the colonial experience.[18] As late as 1938, *le Médecin-Colonel* Abbatucci deployed a medical discourse to explain *le cafard*. Linking it to colonial anemia, he pointed to the excessive heat and humidity, the intensity of the light, sudden barometric fluctuations, and changes in the electric field as causes of the condition. Supposedly, these forces could impact the central nervous system producing *le cafard*, "a sort of misanthropy, aggressive surliness, which can sometimes drive you to impulsive and violent actions." He warned that few colonials could escape this behavior but noted that with proper rest and relaxation, it could be overcome.[19]

M. Fisc, 28 ans, commis des Douanes, est mort ce matin de dysenterie à l'Hôpital militaire...

Figure 6.6: "Les Risques" ("The Risks"). "M. Fisc, twenty-eight years old, customs commissioner, died of dysentery this morning at the military hospital." (André Joyeux, *La vie large des colonies*)

One Joyeux cartoon suggests that many colonials had other means, such as heavy drinking, to take care of *le cafard*. "Braf lechions" depicts a worn out colonial soldier drinking heavily with the caption "Pour tuer le cafard . . ." The comment here is that self-medication (here with alcohol but in other cartons with opium) is necessary to survive the psychological discomfort of life in the colonies. This logic views alcoholism—or opium addiction—as not a moral failing but rather a necessary evil in the colonial world. One had to drink or to smoke in order to survive in such difficult conditions. The belief that one was at odds with the environment in the colonial tropics served to rationalize various forms of addictions. Such an attitude shows the special culture of colonialism.

By medicalizing this psychological state, the discourse of *le cafard* exculpated the colonial from rude, reckless, and violent behavior. Violence, so common in the streets of Hanoi, was not really the fault of the white colonial, but due to a health condition from which he suffered. The feverish white man, at once a symbol of European civilization and yet driven to irrational decadence and barbarism by the onslaught of the tropical environment, could be saved. But salvation could only come through the creation of an infrastructure of comfort. Conveniently, treatment and a possible cure were at hand. By prescribing rest and relaxation in comfortable surroundings, at home in the villa, or on vacation at the hill station, this medical discourse rationalized the dramatically higher standard of living enjoyed by the white population. Indeed, more than rationalize it, expert opinion made it a requirement for the survival of whites in the colonies.

In the case of the colonial community's relationship with disease we see the complex logic of colonial whiteness. The main issue is that of the paradox of power. French colonials felt themselves to be at once powerful and vulnerable. While whites saw themselves as economically, militarily, and morally superior to the natives, they still feared the biological threats of the tropical world. This vulnerability was essential to white colonial experience and directly influenced the structure of the colonial order of things. Responding to this perceived vulnerability, white colonials sought to reinforce and underline their existing power. To ward off disease, French colonials constructed what they saw as an infrastructure of health that both protected their fragile European bodies and displayed their power as the conquering elite. In order to preserve themselves, whites had to protect their health with a certain degree of luxury and leisure. Thus, the palatial villas and numerous material comforts were not simply aspects of colonial vanity, but an essential survival tool in the dangerous colonial world. By definition, colonials required a certain degree of material superiority. Race, a cultural construction, thus worked to create the material manifestations of colonial whiteness. Yet, despite the material benefits of colonial rule, fear of tropical disease was always gnawing at the back of the colonial community's mind. Thus, even in the great sites of colonial power, there was always the concern—if not obsession—with health. As this anxious concern manifested itself in a variety of forms, not the least of which was the gallows humor of the colonial press, we see the colonial paradox in action.

Notes

1. Frantz Fanon, *The Wretched of the Earth* (New York: Grove Press, 1963), 53-54.
2. Milton Osborne, *From Conviction to Anxiety: Reassessing the French Self-Image in Viet-Nam* (Flinders University Asian Studies lecture 7, 1976) and Milton Osborne, *Fear and Fascination in the Tropics: A Reader's Guide to French Fiction on Indochina* (Madison: University of Wisconsin, 1986).

3. Actually more than one graveyard, as the numerous fatalities rapidly filled each new establishment to capacity, Centre Archives d'Outre-Mer (hereafter CAOM), Gouverneur Général d'Indochine (hereafter GGI), dossier 7768: "Frais d'inhumations des membres des familles de fonctionnaires" (1904).

4. As an introduction to the growing literature of colonial medical history, one should consult David Arnold's two anthologies: *Imperial Medicine and Indigenous Societies* (Manchester: Manchester University Press, 1988) and *Warm Climates and Western Medicine: The Emergence of Tropical Medicine, 1500-1900* (Amsterdam: Rodopi, 1996).

5. Frédéric Baille, *Souvenirs d'Annam* (1886-1890) (Paris: Plon, 1890), 145.

6. By the 1930s Christiane Fournier wrote that the pith helmet had become too much of a cliché and no fashionable colonial would be seen wearing one, *Perspectives occidentales sur l'Indochine* (Saigon: La Nouvelle Revue Indochinoise, 1935), 96-98.

7. Dane Kennedy, *Islands of White: Settler Society and Culture in Kenya and Southern Rhodesia, 1890-1939* (Durham: Duke University Press, 1987), 110.

8. Challan de Belval, *Au Tonkin, 1884-1885: Notes, Souvenirs et Impressions* (Paris: Plon, 1904), 165 and 179.

9. Baille, *Souvenirs d'Annam*, 144. See also Dane Kennedy, *The Magic Mountains: Hill Stations and the British Raj* (Berkeley: University of California Press, 1996).

10. CAOM, GGI, dossier 16930: "A.s. de l'érection d'un monument à la mémoire des morts de la Garde indigène" (1913).

11. CAOM, GGI, dossier 7768: "Frais d'inhumations des membres des familles de fonctionnaires" (1904).

12. Marius Borel, *Souvenirs d'un vieux colonialiste* (Rodez: Imprimerie Subervie Rodez, 1963): 41, 54, 86, 93, 103-5, 111, 169-99, 203, 209-10, 221 and 233-34.

13. Jean Ajalbert, *Les Nuages sur l'Indochine* (Paris: Louis-Michaud, 1912), 5-8.

14. Christiane Fournier, *Perspectives occidentales sur l'Indochine*, 9.

15. Stéphane Audoin-Rouzeau, *Men at War, 1914-1918: National Sentiment and Trench Journalism in France during the First World War* (Oxford: Berg, 1992) and Patrick Fridenson, *The French Home Front, 1914-1918* (Oxford: Berg, 1992).

16. Ajalbert, *Les Nuages sur l'Indochine*, 203-34.

17 André Joyeux, *La Vie large des colonies* (Paris: Maurice Bauche, 1912).

18. Fournier, *Perspectives occidentales*, 133-34.

19. S. Abbatucci, "Le Climat tropical—l'Acclimatement" in Fédération Française de l'Enseignement Ménager, *La Vie aux colonies: Préparation de la femme á la vie coloniale* (Paris: Larose, 1938), 46-57.

7

French Women and the Empire

Marie-Paule Ha

In his 1897 inaugural speech for the Societé française d'émigration des femmes (hereafter SFEF),[1] Joseph Chailley-Bert, one of the foremost colonial propagandists of the time and secretary-general of the Union coloniale française,[2] explains that after two decades of military expansion, France should now engage in the economic *mise en valeur* of her overseas possessions. To this end, besides sending forth settlers, France should also, Chailley-Bert argues, dispatch to the colonies French women whose presence was essential to the success of this new phase of the colonial venture. Hence the need to create the SFEF, whose main mission was to facilitate the emigration of French women to the outposts of the empire. Even though the Society had a rather ephemeral existence,[3] its creation by the all powerful Union coloniale française bespeaks the importance that was attributed to women in their role as "helpmates" to the key actors of colonial development, i.e., the *colons* (the settlers).

The objective of this chapter is twofold: I will first investigate the reasons for what seems to be a total about-face from, in the words of Ann Stoler, the "strident misogyny of imperial thinkers and colonial agents,"[4] the group notoriously known to blame women for the "ruin" of the empire as epitomized in the "myth of the destructive females."[5] Why did the Union whose membership was made up precisely of these very same staunch colonialists promote and support colonial female emigration? What roles would they want women to play in the empire? What types of women were considered to be "appropriate" candidates for emigration? What were the problems confronting the SFEF? In the second half of this chapter, I will examine the experiences of different groups of French women residing in Indochina during the late nineteenth century and the early decades of the twentieth century. Using Indochina as a case study, I will argue that there existed significant discrepancies between the goals of the SFEF and the reality of the colonial world, which might in turn account for some of the Society's difficulties in implementing its program.

In order to appreciate fully the role of the SFEF, it would be useful to examine briefly the political platform of its parent organization, the Union coloniale française. Founded in 1893, the Union was, according to Charles-Robert Ageron, the most prominent colonial lobbying group of the time, counting among its select members leading merchants, important financial houses and major chambers of commerce in France and the empire.[6] It wielded so much influence in colonial affairs that it was seen by its contemporaries as "le véritable ministère des colonies" ("the real ministry of the colonies"), being even better funded than the actual ministry of the colonies.[7] Under the able and strong leadership of Chailley-Bert, the organization became within a few years of its creation the most effective colonial propaganda machine in France. Besides sponsoring numerous banquets, lectures and congresses to promote the colonial idea, the Union also put out several publications such as the *Guides de l'Emigrant*, manuals on colonial hygiene, *Le Régime commercial des colonies* and the highly influential bimonthly periodical, *La Quinzaine coloniale*. The chief goal of the Union was to push for the colonial *mise en valeur* through lobbying for measures on land policy, railroads and tariff reforms favorable to settlers and colonial corporations.[8]

The founding of the SFEF in 1897 was intended to service the Union's economic development plan. In his SFEF inaugural speech, Chailley-Bert prefaced his discussion of the Society's role and functions with a brief presentation of the Union's agenda. He started by informing his audience of the recent changes in the "politique coloniale" which now came to mean "organisation politique et administrative et l'exploitation économique de nos colonies" ("political and administrative organization and economic exploitation of our colonies").[9] To bring about the successful implementation of this new program, it would not be sufficient, in the Union's view, to send to the colonies merely hardworking individuals with no particular professional training, as used to be the case. For the new overseas possessions were quite different from the old ones in at least two respects: unlike the colonies of settlement such as Canada which were both sparsely populated and situated in the temperate zone, the territories acquired in the nineteenth century already had a highly dense indigenous population and were located mainly in the tropics, where the climate made it hard for Europeans to engage in physical work. Consequently, the new settler could not be the modest worker of yore, but must be well equipped with skills and financial resources so that instead of doing the work himself, he could hire the natives to do the heavy chores for him.[10]

While the recruitment of settlers with capital was undoubtedly the sine qua non of the successful economic development of France's overseas possessions, it alone would not be sufficient to effect true colonization. To bring about the latter, Chailley-Bert claims, "il y fallait encore envoyer ce qui constitue la famille, ce qui en est la base: des femmes" ("it was necessary to send there the elements that would constitute the foundation of the family, namely women"); for without the family there would be no long-term commitment to the colony. Hence, the need to dispatch to the outposts of the empire "femmes d'un âge tel qu'elles puissent être pour les colons des auxiliaires de travail et des compagnes de vie" ("women of an age to become both workmates and wives to the settlers").[11]

But at the turn of the century, as stated in the pamphlet of the SFEF, the availability of eligible French women willing to emigrate was highly limited given the uncertainties and difficulties of such a venture.[12] The problem of female emigration was further complicated by the Union's view that given their higher economic status, the new settlers would need as companions women from a more "reputable" background than those the *Ancien Régime* used to send to its North American colonies. For the latter, Chailley-Bert reminds his audience, were persons "dont le moins qu'on puisse dire, c'est qu'on redoutait d'en savoir trop long sur elles" ("about whose past one would want to know as little as possible").[13] One of the major tasks entrusted to the SFEF was then to ensure that no modern-day Manon Lescaut would be shipped off to the colonies.

Indeed, Chailley-Bert made it amply clear in his speech that the chief objective of the creation of the Society was to remake a new virginity for the female colonial migratory movement. To this end, even though the Society was de facto "une sorte d'agence matrimoniale," ("a sort of matrimonial agency") it could not present itself as such, but had to "revêtir certains déguisements qui feront des jeunes personnes qui recourront à elle des complices inconscients de notre but" ("be disguised in such a way that the young women who will use its service will become unwitting accomplices of our undertaking").[14] The disguise of the Society was that of a placement agency that would help women to look for employments in the colonies. By operating under such a cover, the SFEF was said to achieve a one-stone-two-bird result: "Donc, en principe, la position première procurée par nous; éventuellement et par surcroît, le mari gagné par elles" ("Hence, in principle, the post initially supplied by us, with the potential addition of a husband won by them").[15]

In order to confer a semblance of respectability to its endeavor, the SFEF put in place a series of highly stringent measures designed to ascertain the reputable character of its applicants. Upon receiving the applications, the Society would send to the candidates a questionnaire enquiring about their character, morality, health, family background, education, occupations and motives for emigration. The information thus gathered would be verified by the committees set up by the SFEF throughout France. It was on the basis of these findings that the Society would vet the applications. The successful applicant would then move on to the second phase of the background check, for which she would be asked to provide several references testifying to her "good" health and morality. At the last stage of the vetting the applicant would be required to send a picture of herself to the Society. The justification for such a request is that, the general-secretary of the Union contends, marriage in the *métropole* took the form of a business transaction in which the value of the dowry rather than the woman's looks was the primordial concern whereas in the colonies where no wealthy *héritières* would be available, an attractive physique would make up for the lack of fortune.

In providing this placement *qua* matrimonial service to French women and the settlers, the SFEF claimed to be guided by the two objectives of patriotism and philanthropy. It fulfilled its patriotic duty by contributing "au développe-ment et à la prospérité des colonies, l'honneur de la France y étant engagé—son intérêt aussi" ("to the development and prosperity of the colonies, at stake are also the honor and the interest of France").[16] Women could do their patriotic share by reconstituting French life and reproducing the French race in the out-posts of the empire. The end result might be the emergence of "Frances nou-velles" ("New Frances") around the world, which in turn would bring about the global spread of the French language and the French race. Indeed, the maintain-ing of racial purity was one of the chief concerns of colonial officials such as General Gallieni. In a meeting with the SFEF, Gallieni, then serving as the gov-ernor-general of Madagascar, conveyed to Mme Pégard, the secretary-general of SFEF, his vehement objection to interracial miscegenation that would breed a mixed-blood population: "Je veux empêcher, par tous les moyens en mon pou-voir, les soldats dont je fais des colons, à l'expiration de leur congé, de se mettre en ménage irrégulier ou même régulier avec des femmes malgaches, je ne veux pas que l'île soit peuplée par une race de métis, mais bien par une pure race française" ("I want to prevent by all possible means our soldiers, who will be-come settlers at the end of their leave, from living legitimately or illegitimately with Malagasy women, I want the island to be populated by a pure French race and not mixed-bloods").[17] One way to forestall these undesirable results would be to make more French women available in the colonies, who would then cre-ate nice homes filled with, in the words of the Jesuit, J. B. Piolet, "de jolies têtes blondes et souriantes" ("happy pretty blond heads").[18]

The Society's philanthropic initiative, on the other hand, was said to bring relief to what it presented as the "problem" of "excess" unmarried females be-tween the age of 25 and 50 in mainland France, whose number, according to the SFEF pamphlet, exceeded a million and a quarter at the turn of the century. The assumed plight of these single women had also been reviewed by Chailley-Bert, who identified two causes to the problem. One was the inability of many par-ents in the *métropole* to provide an attractive dowry, without which they could not marry off their daughters. The second reason was the increasingly large number of well-educated young women who could not find employment in spite of their academic achievements. This situation gave rise to, in the words of Chailley-Bert, a "stock" of young women without employment and future. The concern was, as the Comte d'Haussonville put it in his brief address preceding Chailley-Bert's speech, that these single women who were *non-classées* would run the great risk of becoming *déclassées*. The only remedy to this predicament was marriage. What better place to unload the *métropole*'s "overstock" of single females than the colonies, which suffered a severe shortage of French women with a gender ratio as low as one female to ten males in some regions. At the time of its founding, the SFEF had received strong endorsement from powerful politicians in both the *métropole* and the colonies. In her piece in the January 1898 issue of *La Quinzaine coloniale*,[19] Mme Pégard informed her readers that the Society counted among its members Félix Faure, then president of the French Republic, his wife and daughter, the minister of the colonies, and numerous chambers of commerce across the nation. In the colonies, the Society was likewise patronized by the spouses of high-level officials such as Mme Doumer, wife of Paul Doumer, governor-general of Indochina.

With what seemed to be such a promising beginning, why didn't the SFEF fare better than it did? As acknowledged by its secretary-general in both her article in *La Quinzaine* and her speech to the Congrès international des oeuvres et institutions féminines, the Society faced serious obstacles from the very start. Foremost among the problems was the scarcity of jobs suitable for French women in the colonies. As the Society presented itself as a placement agency, successful employment procurement would be essential to its survival. But its efforts at securing jobs met with little success. On the administrative front, even though Lebon in his capacity as minister of the colonies did write to the colonial administrations to request them to set aside a number of posts for the SFEF, most of the responses were lukewarm at best, if not outright negative.

In the private sector, Mme Pégard identified two elements that were not conducive to French women's employment. With the exception of Algeria and Tunisia, both of which had a relatively large European population, most of the other new colonies did not have a critical mass of French families requiring the service of French women. This explanation seemed to imply that the latter could only be employed by French residents themselves. A second problem had to do with the fierce competition from the native population. According to the secretary-general of the Society, Malagasy and Annamite women were very quick at picking up different skills and were willing to work for a pittance whereas their French counterparts would demand a salary many times higher. As a result, for the cost of hiring one French woman worker, one could have as many as four or five native employees. In fact, the issue of salary was a concern not only of the private sector, but also of the colonial administration, which likewise would prefer to engage natives in order to bring down cost.

The other equally thorny problem confronting the Society was the lack of adequate funding. According to Mme Pégard, the women who sought the SFEF's services were very often in a state of extreme destitution and many of them had neither resources nor skills. As a result, the Society had to provide them with financial assistance and pay for their training. In her article in *La Quinzaine*, Mme Pégard described briefly the backgrounds of the women the Society had been helping. A number of them came from the lower end of the social spectrum such as Mlle. L., a former lace-maker, who because of her poor eyesight, could no longer earn her living and found herself in the direst of situations. The Society found her a place as a governess in a colony, but had to help her pay the rent she owed her landlord. Another similarly indigent woman to whom the SFEF lent a helping hand was a certain Marie C. P., who had been married off to a scoundrel at the age of fifteen and lived in a state of utter misery. Interestingly enough, besides women of the lower class, some of the Society's "clients" were destitute members of the middle or even upper middle class. Such was the case of Mme B., the widow of a once wealthy industrialist and mother of a ten-year-old boy, who likewise found herself in dire need and had to make a living as a dressmaker. She was due to emigrate, but needed the Society to raise funds for her journey. Equally unfortunate was Mlle S., who was from an ancient aristocratic family that had been ruined in the stock market crash of 1893. She was promised a position as dressmaker and was placed in a Parisian couture house to learn the trade before heading for the colony.

From Mme Pégard's report, it is clear that the Society seldom attracted the type of women that the Union would consider as "suitable" to the settlers. In "La Colonisation du Tonkin," Chailley-Bert claimed that the prospect of marrying settlers would be most attractive to "les jeunes filles de la petite bourgeoisie" ("the young women of the petite bourgeoisie"), who were in his words "tout indiquées pour nos colons" ("all earmarked for our settlers").[20] Yet, the reality turned out to be quite different, as many of the "good" families refused to let their daughters emigrate. Even women from the lower social strata, such as the farm girls whom the SFEF tried to recruit, were on the whole unreceptive to the colonial venture. As a result, the Society had to look for candidates among female orphans who, it was thought, could be more easily persuaded to emigrate given the fact that they had no prospects for their future. In her report summarizing the achievements of the Society during the first three years of its existence, Mme Pégard concluded with the following observation: "aujourd'hui toutes les femmes que des épreuves, des malheurs immérités, l'absence de toute fortune, la misère et l'abandon ont cruellement éprouvées, tournent leurs regards vers les Colonies comme vers une nouvelle Terre promise" ("today all the women who have known a life of trials, undeserving hardships, poverty, destitution and abandonment turn to the colonies as a new Promised Land").[21] In other words, most of the women who were susceptible to the idea of colonial emigration came from socially unaccounted-for groups and therefore fell well below the class level the Union had set for the prospective mates of the settlers.

We have noted earlier that the effort to enlist "respectable" females to the outposts of the empire was informed by class concern, as it was believed that the new settlers who came from the petite bourgeoisie would want to marry persons of similar social standing. In other words, one of the main tasks women were asked to perform in the outposts of the empire was to recreate a middle-class habitus with bourgeois morality and norms. Besides the imperative of upholding bourgeois propriety, the SFEF was also concerned with the need to maintain white prestige in the colonies. Indeed, nothing was more threatening to the colonizers' sense of superiority than the presence of poor whites in their midst.[22] The January 1905 issue of *La Quinzaine coloniale* featured a report of a court case in Hanoi involving a number of impoverished white males who were reduced to living off both public and private charity. The chief concern of the author of the report was with the disastrous impact these poor whites would have on French prestige, as a number of them "se sentant déplacés parmi leurs compatriotes, se mêlent à la population annamite ou chinoise" ("feeling estranged from their fellow compatriots, would mix with the Annamite or the Chinese"). The spectacle of their material and moral degradation would certainly do little to "fortifier notre bon renom et pour rehausser notre prestige" ("strengthen our good reputation and enhance our prestige").[23] This anxious determination to maintain white prestige required that white women should stay within the bounds of the European community and be paid high enough wages to allow a standard of living that would set them apart from the colonized. Such restraints indeed made the work of the SFEF doubly hard as they reduced considerably the employment opportunities of French women in the colonies. These and other difficulties eventually brought about the undoing of the Society.

§

While at this stage of my research I have not yet been able to establish the actual causes of the demise of the SFEF, I propose to evaluate the Society's efforts using Indochina as a case study of French women's colonial experience. My choice of Indochina was not simply a random selection from among two dozen possibilities. Besides the fact that it happens to be the principal area of my research, this Asian colony also presented a great deal of interest to the SFEF. In his inaugural speech, Chailley-Bert listed Tonkin as one of the four outposts of the empire (the other three being Algeria, Tunisia and New Caledonia) suitable for European settlement.[24] In fact, according to the statistics Mme Pégard provided in her 1900 report, out of the sixty female emigrants the Society dispatched to the colonies during the first three years of its existence, one third (the largest number) were sent to Indochina.

What was the French female population in Indochina between the late nineteenth century and the first decades of the twentieth century? There is no straightforward answer to the question for, as both Gilles de Gantès and Aurélie Gfeller point out in their respective studies of the French population in Indochina, the census was carried out in a variety of ways that changed according to periods and regions, and very often individuals were classified by race and status at the same time.[25] In other words, some counting would limit itself only to ethnic French, whereas others would include naturalized French and Eurasians. According to Gfeller, the European community underwent an important expansion during the 1920s, as shown in the 77.6 percent increase between 1921 and 1930. Translated into actual numbers, there were 15,116 French civilians in Indochina in 1913 and 33,501 in 1933. Gfeller attributes this upsurge to the accelerated economic growth of the colony during the 1920s. The gender ratio had likewise improved: in 1886, Tonkin had a ratio of 13 women to 100 men, which then doubled in 1907 while in 1922 the ratio across Indochina was 40.8 percent. The actual numbers for 1922 are provided by de Gantès in "Coloniaux, gouverneurs et ministres": 1,018 men and 429 women in Annam, 3,862 men and 2,155 women in Cochin-China, and 2,563 men and 1,981 women in Tonkin. Two factors brought about the increase in the female population according to Gfeller: better living conditions and the introduction of measures forbidding interracial union between civil servants and natives by the government of Paul Doumer in 1901. Two other features characterized the distribution of the French civilian population in Indochina: first, they were very unevenly spread out in the five parts of the Union, with the heaviest concentration in Cochin-China followed by Tonkin, Annam, Cambodia and Laos; secondly, within each region the French tended to congregate much more in urban centers.

Even though statistically the French made up a minute portion of the Indochinese population they formed a highly complex community whose story has yet to be fully studied. To date most of the works that deal with this community pay scant attention, if at all, to its female elements. When they do, they seem to treat them as a homogenous group comprised mainly of spouses of colonial administrators, settlers, and professionals. Such a social and class mapping of the female colonial population in Indochina characterizes not only the narratives of the colonial writers of the past, but also recent works.[26] There are different explanations for the phenomenon of class homogenization in earlier studies of female colonial experiences. One reason has to do with documentation, as many of the sources about or by colonial women tend to focus on the middle or upper-middle class groups.[27]

A case in point is the extensive interview conducted by Sylvie Locret-Le Bayon on one hundred former *coloniales*. The majority of her informants presented themselves as middle-class. More than a fifth of the interviewees lived in Indochina during the first half of the twentieth century. In their accounts, they all concurred that they had a very privileged life in the colony and many admitted that they were relieved of most of the household chores by their numerous native domestics. As a result, they were left with a great deal of free time that was spent in social activities. A few even contended that it would have been detrimental to French prestige if French women were seen going to the market. Many talked about the frequent balls, receptions and dinners they either attended or organized. Apparently, this lavish lifestyle was made possible by the high incomes of the fathers or husbands, many of whom occupied middle or upper-middle level positions in the army or the administration.[28] Only two of the interviewees mentioned their employment as teachers. Other personal narratives by French women I have access to present the same picture of "la vie large coloniale" ("the colonial good life"). For instance, in *Notre Indochine 1936-1947*,[29] Madeleine Jay's narrative of her life in Saigon was also filled with stories of soirées, visits and parties. Like the women interviewed by Locret-Le Bayon, Madeleine had several servants to look after the house and her three children. Her husband, Antoine, an engineer with a diploma from the Ecole des

Ponts et Chaussées, became the director of the Saigon railways system at the end of his second year of service in Indochina. Given Antoine's high position, the Jays' circle of friends not surprisingly was mostly comprised of members of the upper echelon of the civil service and big companies such as Shell and the Banque de l'Indochine. Apparently, the "colonial good life" lasted until the Japanese occupation, which effectively put an end to the privileged existence of these *coloniales*.

One feature common to the accounts of middle and upper-middle class colonial wives of their lives in Indochina was the importance of socializing. I have argued elsewhere that these social activities, far from being mere amusements to fill up the women's free time, actually served the highly strategic purpose of establishing "civilized" bourgeois norms in the outposts of the empire.[30] Some *coloniales* in fact made a point of observing bourgeois social rituals in exact accordance with the metropolitan standard. Such is the case of the mother of one of the women interviewed by Locret-Le Bayon. A teacher in Hanoi, she religiously held "her day" fortnightly for her friends and acquaintances. The daughter remembered the occasion as being very formal and that the visitors were comprised mainly of "dames" ("ladies"). The mother also considered it her duty to call on the "days" of the wives of her own superior and that of her husband, as well as those of her colleagues. Apparently, bourgeois norms seemed to be so well anchored in the colony that a certain Mani, who published several articles on Indochina in *Le Monde colonial illustré*, reassured his readers that the rumors about colonial orgies were totally unfounded for "Le vrai milieu saigonnais est un milieu bourgeois aux habitudes établies, aux distractions saines, aux occupations réglées scrupuleusement. Monsieur a son bureau; Madame, sa machine à coudre, son piano, ses courses, ses visites, et surtout ses enfants" ("the real Saigonnese milieu is a bourgeois milieu with established customs, healthy distractions, and well-defined occupations. The husband has his work and the wife her sewing machine, her piano, her shopping, her visits and most importantly her children").[31]

If one were to rely on the sources that have been discussed thus far one might be led to conclude that the majority of French colonial women were middle-class. Yet some documentation points to the existence of another group of French women, who did not know the "colonial good life," but had to work to make a living for themselves and their children. Many were wives and daughters of the "petits blancs" in the colony.

At this stage of my research, I do not have enough data to allow me to come up with even a rough estimate of the social and numerical makeup of these women. The group that I will discuss in the last section of this chapter concerns the widows and daughters of deceased civil servants, who for different reasons decided to stay in Indochina rather than returning to France. My study is based on the archival materials of the Indochinese colonial government located in the Centre des Archives d'Outre-Mer (hereafter CAOM) in Aix.

As early as 1903, the governor-general of Indochina wanted to introduce a policy whereby the government services and departments would set aside a number of posts for the surviving wives and daughters of deceased civil servants and settlers, who were left without resources. In 1904, a circular to this end was issued to the section heads across Indochina.[32] But the majority of the responses were less than encouraging as some departments claimed that they had either no vacancies or no situations "suitable" for women. Other officials such as the *résident supérieur* of Annam replied that they could not afford to employ French women who would cost them four times more than their Annamese counterparts.

From the documents I had access to it seems that the first government service that recruited a fair number of French women was the Douanes et Régies (customs and state industries, hereafter D&R). According to their personnel files, they started employing women as early as the 1890s. The majority of their female employees were widows with children. In their dossiers they all indicated their strong desire to stay in the colony. A few among them were divorcees and single women. Some were hired as *journalières* (day workers) and some as permanent staff. Most of them were employed in the opium factory,[33] the matchstick factory, the weighting and welding workshops and the dispatching service. A number of them served as supervisors (*surveillantes*), others were bookkeepers. Their earnings ranged between 2,400 to 3,000 francs. Besides their work records, their dossiers sometimes also included evaluations of both their work performance and their personal conduct. For example, one woman, a divorcee, had her performance rated as "very good," but her private conduct as "laisse à désirer, douteuse" ("leaving much to be desired, suspect"). Another was described as "employée sans autorité auprès des indigènes qui ne la considèrent pas comme supérieure à leur race" ("having no authority over the natives who do not consider her as their racial superior"). A third, who worked at the welding workshop, was criticized for "moralité douteuse, conduite mauvaise, caractère mauvais, tenue inconvéniente [*sic*]" ("suspect morality, bad conduct, bad character, unseemly clothing"). A *surveillante* at the matchstick factory was faulted for her "tenue et habitudes sociales: laissent à désirer, inintelligente, paresseuse" ("clothing and social habits which leave a great deal to be desired, unintelligent, lazy").[34] One could read these comments about the inappropriateness of the women's behavior not only as evidence that the administration was using bourgeois social and moral yardsticks to evaluate their female employees, but also as an indication of their apprehension about the impact that such "improper" women might have on white superiority. In other words, the anxiety was induced by a conflation of racial and class markers.

Starting in the late 1910s onwards, two other departments employed an increasing number of French women. They were the postal, telephone and telegraph services (hereafter PTT) and the educational service (*Instruction publique,* hereafter IP). While many of the PTT posts went to indigent widows and daughters of deceased civil servants, the IP had to be much more selective in their hiring, as the teachers had to have the appropriate training, a requirement that disqualified those with a low educational level. The personnel files of the PTT provide interesting data on the group of women who sought the help of the administration to get a job or renew a contract. For example, in a petition written by an employee of the D&R pleading for a position for his niece, the uncle informed the director of PTT that since the death of his brother, who was also an employee of D&R, he had to take care of his two orphaned nieces while having a child of his own. But recently, as he had been redeployed to Haiphong where the cost of living was much higher than that of the province where he used to work, he could no longer support the two girls.[35] There were also several cases concerning widows in needy conditions. Such was for example the situation of a widow of a former D&R employee with two dependent children, who had no resources. Her file contained a letter by the governor of Cochin-China explaining that the widow in question had been employed as laundress (*lingère*) and housekeeper (*femme de charge*) at the Ecole primaire supérieure des filles de Saigon (Girls' junior high school) until 1929 when she requested leave for health reasons. After her departure, the positions she occupied were given to mothers of other necessitous families, but the administration indicated its willingness to put her on the waiting list for a PTT position as "dame téléphoniste."[36] Equally hard pressed was the situation of another young widow, a *métisse*, with four small children between the ages of seven years and six months, whose husband, a former employee in a forestry plantation in Bien Hoa, died without leaving any money. The head of the Service de sûreté wrote on her behalf to the governor to apply for a position of telephonist.[37] Some older widows also found themselves in similarly precarious plights. Such were the cases of two women aged 58 and 59, whose deceased husbands had served respectively as postal worker and chief conductor at the public works. Both requested the renewal of their contracts with the PTT on the ground that their livelihoods depended entirely on their pay.[38]

Since many of the PTT positions were created to provide financial relief to widows and female orphans in need, both categories were required to give up their employments once they found a husband. A few of the former widows who got remarried applied to keep their jobs on the ground that they could not make ends meet with their spouses' incomes alone. Such was the rationale behind the request of Mme D., a widow who married a clerk in a commercial firm. In her petition to the governor-general, she contended that her new husband's monthly salary of 150 piastres was insufficient to meet the expenses of the couple and their six-year-old child.[39] Consequently, she would need to retain her job, which would bring them the needed supplementary income. A similar request was put forward by another widow whose second husband, also a commercial clerk, earned a salary of 250 piastres, an amount judged likewise as inadequate for a family of four.[40] A third young woman, Mme F., formerly employed as temporary telephonist, made the same appeal to keep her position after she married an employee of the Société des Verreries d'Extrême-Orient. While the husband had an income of 300 piastres, he had to take care of a ten-year-old boy. Mme F. explained that since she also had to help out her widowed mother and her brother, a student at the Lycée Albert Sarraut, the couple would not be able to cover all their expenses with her husband's salary alone.

Given the limited scope of this chapter, it has not been possible to provide an exhaustive account of the conditions of the "needy *coloniales*" in Indochina, but the cases discussed above do give us a sense of the heterogeneous character of the French female population. While it is necessary to exercise some caution in interpreting the letters that were written to convince the administration that their authors did deserve its sympathetic intervention, it is clear that the petitioners did rely on their employment to earn a living for themselves and their families. These archival materials do allow us to infer the existence of a sizeable group of French women whose colonial experiences were quite a distance away from those of Madeleine Jay and Locret-Le Bayon's informants.

From this study of the conditions of French women in Indochina, we may appreciate some of the obstacles the SFEF encountered in implementing its objectives. On the job placement front, it is obvious that the Society could not count on the colonial government to hire their applicants, given the fact that Indochina, which was considered as one of the *métropole*'s "wealthiest" colonies, had its own share of women "in need" who heavily depended on the administration's support. As for the SFEF's goal of providing marriageable women to single French males, the situation was no less complicated. From Mme Pégard's own account, most of the women that the Society managed to recruit did not have the requisite social and cultural profile to be the spouses of middle and upper-level officials and administrators, as they were expected to embody a specifically bourgeois notion of Frenchness and femininity. On the other hand, the personnel files of the PTT indicated that there existed in the colony a number of young widows and single women (daughters of deceased civil servants) who contracted marriage with the local French males of more modest background. This group of women who had either grown up or lived for a number of years in Indochina would no doubt be perceived as much more acculturated to the native environment and would make more "suitable" companions to local Frenchmen than the candidates of the SFEF. While we cannot yet ascertain the actual reasons for the demise of the Society, it is clear that the placement and matrimonial services it offered found few takers in Indochina.

Notes

My research for this chapter was made possible by a grant from the University of Hong Kong.

1. *L'Emigration des femmes aux colonies. Allocution de M. le Comte d'Haussonville et discours de M. J. Chailley-Bert à la conférence donnée le 12 janvier 1897 par l'Union coloniale française* (Paris: Armand Colin, 1897). The only work I know of that provides more than occasional references to the Society is Yvonne Knibiehler and Régine Goutalier's *La Femme aux temps des colonies* (Paris: Stock, 1985), 88-91.

2. For detailed discussions of Chailley-Bert's contributions to the colonial lobby and the Union coloniale française, see Raymond F. Betts, *Assimilation and Association in French Colonial Theory 1890-1914* (New York: Columbia University Press, 1961) and

Stuart M. Persell, "Joseph Chailley-Bert and the Importance of the Union coloniale française," *The Historical Journal* 17, no. 1 (1974): 176-84.

3. At this point of my research, I have not yet been able to ascertain the exact duration of the Society's existence. But periodicals such as *La Quinzaine coloniale* and *Le Conseil des femmes*, which covered the Society's activities, stopped reporting about them after 1905. In *La Femme aux temps des colonies*, Knibiehler and Goutalier also stated that there was no more news of the Society a few years after its creation.

4. Ann Laura Stoler, *Carnal Knowledege and Imperial Power: Race and the Intimate in Colonial Rule* (Berkeley: University of California Press, 2002), 42.

5. The phrase "the myth of the destructive females" was coined by Margaret Strobel in her *European Women and the Second British Empire* (Bloomington: University of Indiana Press, 1991). For discussions of the negative image of white women in colonial discourse, besides Strobel, see Claudia Knapman, *White Women in Fiji 1835-1930: The Ruin of Empire?* (Sydney: Allen & Unwin, 1986); and Stoler, *Carnal Knowledge.*

6. For details on the history and membership of the Union, see Stuart M. Persell, *The French Colonial Lobby, 1899-1914* (Dissertation, Stanford University, 1969), 47-53 and his "Joseph Chailley-Bert," 178-79.

7. Charles-Robert Ageron, *France coloniale ou Parti colonial?* (Paris: Presses Universitaires de France, 1978), 156-62.

8. For a discussion of the *mise en valeur* philosophy of the Union, see Persell, *The French Colonial Lobby.*

9. Chailley-Bert, *L'Emigration des femmes*, 14. Unless otherwise stated, all translations are the author's.

10. Chailley-Bert specified the minimum amount of liquid capital for each colony: 5,000 francs for New Caledonia, 10 to 15,000 francs for Tunisia and Algeria, and 50,000 francs for Annam-Tonkin. See *L'Emigration des femmes*, 18.

11. Chailley-Bert, *L'Emigration des femmes*, 19-20.

12. To recruit members for the Society, the Union put out a pamphlet for the SFEF (hereafter the pamphlet) explaining its goals, functions and achievements. The pamphlet repeated some of the information Chailley-Bert provided in his speech.

13. Chailley-Bert, *L'Emigration des femmes*, 33.

14. Chailley-Bert, *L'Emigration des femmes*, 33.

15. Chailley-Bert, *L'Emigration des femmes*, 35.

16. Pamphlet of SFEF, np.

17. Quoted in Mme Pégard, "Société française d'émigration des femmes" in *2e congrès international des œuvres et institutions féminines tenu au Palais des Congrès de l'Exposition Universelle de 1900. Compte rendu des travaux par Mme Pégard*, vol. II (Paris: Imprimerie Typographique Charles Blot, 1902), 236-44, 240.

18. Jean-Baptiste Piolet, *La France hors de France* (Paris: Félix Alcan éditeurs, 1900), 414.

19. Mme Pégard, "La Société d'émigration des femmes 'une année d'existence,'" *La Quinzaine coloniale* (January, 1898): 40-44.

20. Chailley-Bert, "La Colonisation du Tonkin," *La Quinzaine coloniale* (July 1899): 425-27, 426.

21. Mme Pégard, "Société française d'émigration des femmes," 243.

22. The issue of white pauperism in the colonies has been extensively discussed by Ann Stoler in *Carnal Knowledge.*

23. "L'Emigration dans les colonies," *La Quinzaine coloniale* (January 1905): 47-48.

24. Chailley-Bert, *L'Emigration des femmes*, 54.

25. Gilles de Gantès, "La Population française au Tonkin entre 1931 et 1938" (Mémoire de maîtrise, Paris, 1981) and "Coloniaux, gouverneurs et ministres. L'influence des Français du Viêt-Nam sur l'évolution du pays à l'époque coloniale 1902-1914" (Diss. Paris VII, 1994); and Aurélie Gfeller "Communauté allogène européenne en Indochine française 1920-1939. Clivages et rapports de force" (Mémoire de maîtrise, Lausanne, 2000).

26. For examples of such a class mapping of colonial women, see Clotilde Chivas-Baron, *La Femme française aux colonies* (Paris: Larose, 1929) and her *La Simple histoire des Gaudraix* (Paris: Flammarion, 1923); Claude Farrrère, *Les Civilisés* (Paris: Librarie Paul Ollendorff, 1905); Georges Groslier, *Le Retour à l'argile* (Paris: Kailash, 1994); and Jean d'Esme, *L'Ame de la brousse* (Paris: J. Ferenczi & Fils, 1923). For a discussion of the works of Chivas-Baron and D'Esme, see my "Portrait of the Young Woman as a *Coloniale*" in *Empire and Culture*, eds. Martin Evans and Amanda Sackur (London: Palgrave, 2004), 161-80.

27. Even though I did raise the class issue in my two articles, I still focused mostly on the experiences of middle-class women. See my "Engendering French Colonial History: The Case of Indochina," *Historical Reflections/Réflexions historiques* 25, no. 1 (1999): 95-125, and "Portrait of the Young Woman as a *Coloniale*."

28. One woman's husband was the governor of a province, another's was a member of the government council. Several women were either spouses or children of army officers, civil servants, a magistrate and a doctor. Two were the wives of a plantation owner and a director. Only one interviewee, who was the daughter of a manufacturer of railway material, described her family as not "wealthy."

29. Madeleine and Antoine Jay, *Notre Indochine 1936-1947* (Paris: Les Presses de Valmy, 1994). For other similar accounts of upper-class social life in Indochina, see Eugène Jung, *La Vie européenne au Tonkin* (Paris: Flammarion, 1901), de Gantès, "Coloniaux, gouverneurs et ministres" and *Saigon 1925-1945 De la 'Belle Colonie' à l'éclosion révolutionnaire ou la fin des dieux blancs*, ed. Philippe Franchini (Paris: Editions Autrement, 1992).

30. For a discussion of other narratives of middle-class *coloniales*, see my "Portrait of the Young Woman as a *Coloniale*."

31. Mani, "En Indochine avec le ministre," *Le Monde colonial illustré*, 99 (November 1931): 245-46.

32. CAOM, Indo, GGI, cote 3698 "Emplois réservés aux veuves et aux filles de fonctionnaires et colons."

33. For a discussion of the colonial government's monopoly of opium in Indochina, see Chantal Descours-Gatin, *Quand l'opium finançait la colonisation en Indochine: l'élaboration de la régie générale de l'opium, 1860 à 1914* (Paris: l'Harmattan, 1992).

34. CAOM, Indo, GGI, cotes 7500 "Bulletins individuels de notes du personnel des Douanes et Régies (surveillantes) 1901," "Bulletins individuels de notes du personnel des Douanes et Régies (surveillantes) 1902," 7518 "Bulletins individuels de notes du personnel des Douanes et Régies (dames comptables) 1902."

35. CAOM, Indo, GGI, cote 48657.

36. CAOM, Indo, GGI, cote 48658.

37. CAOM, Indo, GGI, cote 48659.

38. CAOM, Indo, GGI, cotes 48660 and 48666.

39. CAOM, Indo, GGI, cote 48688.

40. CAOM, Indo, GGI, cote 48691.

8

Vietnamese New Women and the Fashioning of Modernity

Judith Henchy

In September 1935 a minor scandal erupted in the Saigon area press as a result of a seemingly innocent event at the Gia Định agricultural fair. Throughout the day of the fair excitement had been building, and crowds gathered to witness the Fair's much-vaunted beauty pageant. However, come 10 pm, the appointed hour, not one contestant had put herself forward. Only after much cajoling did six reluctant contestants mount the stage before the panel of judges, which included two Frenchmen and a majority of Vietnamese. The panel voted unanimously for one contestant (it having been decided to award only a first prize under the circumstances of such limited participation). Shortly after, a rowdy discussion erupted and the verdict was challenged, with the result that a second round of voting was demanded. "Did we have to adopt the electoral rules of the French colonial council?" asked a journalist sarcastically, referring to the complicated multiple balloting of the colonial electoral system. The second round of voting pronounced a different contestant as winner, Miss Mai Huỳnh Hoa. This reversal surprised the audience, which was left in confused anger and muttering that this second choice was not even remotely beautiful.

The events of the Gia Định fair appeared in the Saigon semi-daily *Dân Quyền* (*Human Rights*), in an article which may have been written by the outspoken young female journalist, Nguyễn Thị Kiêm, a frequent social commentator on the newspaper's pages. According to French Sûreté reports, *Dân Quyền* was the brainchild of Marxist intellectual Nguyễn An Ninh, and operated under

the direction of the veteran leftist publicist Jehan Cendrieux. By sending a reporter to cover the story, *Dân Quyền's* editors clearly intended to raise awareness of women's issues and question the value of the beauty pageant. The article paid little attention to the aesthetics of the event, with only passing reference
to each woman's outfit, but it concluded by musing on the comparative meaning of physical and moral beauty, and the questionable place of beauty in the
political arena.[1] The report provoked response from a conservative commentator[2] who wrote a disquisition on the moral decline exhibited by the women par-
ticipating in this affair, who, he claimed, could only have gotten up on the stage
if they were under the influence of decadent American-European ideas. Men
would never do such a thing. Unfortunately for the unwitting *Dân Quyền*, Mai
Huỳnh Hoa turned out to be an unlikely target for its moralizing narrative. The
daughter of Indochina Communist Party (ICP) operative Mai Văn Ngọc, who
died in prison in Laos in 1933, having been arrested on his way to Thailand on
the orders of the party, and granddaughter of Cochin-China's first acclaimed
patriotic poet, Nguyễn Đình Chiểu, she was herself a poet and former political
prisoner who had spent several months in Saigon's notorious Maison Centrale
prison for her activism. Perhaps equally importantly, she was at the time the
lover, later to become the second wife, of Trotskyite intellectual Phan Văn
Hùm.[3] The Gia Định affair led to the publication of a rebuttal by Mai Huỳnh
Hoa herself, in which she countered the narrow categorizations of the conservative commentator's letter and their class-based assumptions,[4] and to a rather
uncharacteristically touching defense by Hùm in which he evoked both her an-
cestry from a good patriotic family and her moral standing as a revolutionary
heroine. He also questioned conceptions of beauty as an aesthetic marker of
cultural alterity and class-based sensitivities.

This story exemplifies the complexity of the multiple interpretations of
modernity that influenced the lives and representations of women in 1930s
Vietnam. It also demonstrates the restrictions under which the press operated at
the time; the researcher is left with much to ponder about this incident. Its dis-
cordant outcome points to the fluidity of social and political categories of which
modern women felt that they should be part. It indicates the willingness on the
part of women to engage in this act of unquestionable modernity, even though
its significations were still ill-defined and little understood. Could the *Dân
Quyền* story have been crafted as an allegory for the political process itself, with
its contested votes and discontented audience? Did the divisions in the panel of
judges break down along racial lines? As for Mai Huỳnh Hoa's participation:
why would an educated and "enlightened"[5] Stalinist participate in such a pageant? Did she participate out of mockery for the event? Unfortunately her written testaments to the newspaper do not tell us much about her motives, only that
she refuses to be bound by the narrow constraints imposed by conservative and
prejudiced interpretations of feminine modernity. Nonetheless, women's participation in this self-consciously modern performance does beg those very
questions raised in the polemic: questions about the meaning of beauty (*sắc
đẹp*) in traditional and nationalist discourses of the racialized and gendered

body, and its role in sustaining a commodified bourgeois aesthetic that emerged in the 1930s. At the same time the affair exposes the vulnerability of women as autonomous actors in the public sphere, where they may be objectified in various media interpretations as potentially or already decadent; either as vulgar mimics of Western culture, or dangerous purveyors of exotic sexuality.

This chapter explores some of the complexities demonstrated by this story of modernity, with its multiple and contradictory valences of hesitation, self-confidence, and confusion. This anxiety and uncertainty, which I see as axiomatic of this period of rapid transition, pervades media images throughout the 1930s. I explore here ways in which this anxiety might be read as a tension between common media tropes naturalizing a positivist teleology of aesthetics and technology—coopted by bourgeois commercialism as what might be called a "fetish of modernity"—and "realist" and "surrealist" images that emerge in the 1930s press to counter these tropes. Debates about culture and society, including understandings of beauty, desire and coercion, reflected an intellectual world in which bustling urban modernity was exemplified by French ideas, lifestyles, empirical sciences and technology. These attributes of "Western" progress were tempered by understandings of loss and alienation brought about by urbanization, industrialization and fast-changing technologies of transport and communications. I use the writings of commentators such as Nguyễn An Ninh, Phan Văn Hùm and Nguyễn Thị Kiêm, as well as nontextual representations made possible by new graphic and photographic technologies, to demonstrate how women in particular were implicated by media images, advertising and bourgeois fashion.

Nguyễn An Ninh, who graduated as a lawyer from the Sorbonne in the early 1920s, became a brilliant polemicist in the French language Vietnamese press, and the focus of a youth cult that inspired a generation of young Vietnamese men and women toward revolutionary political engagement. An eloquent orator, and an early devotee of Nietzsche, he was adept at manipulating the emerging mass media of the 1920s and 1930s. He was arguably the first to recognize "culture"[6] as a pliable category in the service of colonial power and bourgeois capitalism, and relentlessly satirized the shallow trappings of Western civilization cultivated by fashionable élites. Ninh and Phan Văn Hùm, trained as a philosopher at the Sorbonne in the early 1930s, seem to be at the forefront of a struggle against what they recognized as new forms of colonial cultural hegemony, enabled and staged through mass media advertising, and the bourgeois cooptation of ideas of beauty and desire.

Phan Văn Hùm's contribution to the Gia Định beauty contest polemic addressed the primary critique of the conservative commentator mentioned above: whether or not the panel of judges was qualified to evaluate beauty. Since the contestants neither claimed to represent a traditional Vietnamese form of aesthetic, nor to aspire to Western understandings of beauty, what criteria could be used to assess such beauty? Hùm's letter predates his most important contributions to a Marxist discourse on aesthetics, delivered as part of his prolonged polemic against the Art for Art's Sake movement throughout 1936. In his well-

publicized debate with Hoài Thanh,[7] Hùm argues for a Marxist popular aesthetic which the masses may understand and attain.[8] According to this view,
artistic dress and style cannot be considered to define beauty, since only the
upper classes have access to these luxuries.[9] His critique of bourgeois capitalist
use of aesthetic tropes to engender desire and false notions of freedom and
choice is paralleled by his assault on literary romanticism, which he sees as being supported by a bourgeois complacency born of such quasi-philosophical and
pseudoscientific mystical fads as Theosophy and sociology.[10]

It was often around the question of women that the contradictions of modernity crystallized. As elsewhere in the world, women were used to symbolize
the nation.[11] Narratives of the state essentialized women as guardians of the
nation's future and family tradition. At the same time, women's concerns seem
easily coopted by modernity's commodifications and mystifications: concerns
for the health and welfare of the family exposed them to an array of pharmaceu-
tical potions and quasi-medical theories which placed them at the fulcrum of
traditional beliefs and little understood scientific technologies. Such enslavement to the scientifically modern even extended to the use of radium skin whit-
ening treatments. Women became objects of alluring advertising valorizing scientific technology as quintessentially modern. Recognizing the importance of
women's influence over the modern family, the French established a journal for
women in 1918 (edited by Mai Huỳnh Hoa's aunt), which promoted family
welfare and included the popularization of ideas of science, medicine and hygiene. This project was closely related to that of the controversial "collaborator"
intellectual Phạm Quỳnh. His state-sponsored literary journal, *Nam Phong*,
which sought to popularize the romanized Vietnamese *quốc ngữ* script, also
introduced key French literary and philosophical texts to a Vietnamese audience. "Vulgarization" of science and medical practices remained a dominant
theme in the *quốc ngữ* press throughout the 1920s and 1930s; much of this production targeted a female audience.

Women in the Public Sphere

Although lacking the foreign educational opportunities of men such as Ninh and
Hùm, young women were quick to engage in the radical fervor of the early
1920s. While still regarded with suspicion and some condescension by the male
leaders of the radical movements of the early 1920s, by the time Ninh was arrested for the first time in March 1926, it was the female students in the Saigon
high schools who shamed their male compatriots at the élite Chassaloup
Laubert lycée to walk out of classes.[12] Many female students in Saigon and Hue
were expelled from school for their actions; some from the Hue schools subsequently lived with Hùm's family during the time he was a clerk with the Public
Works authority there. On the other hand, it seems that many women, like the
men, were drawn to the revolutionary movement for its excitement and romanticism. Nguyễn An Ninh's second wife, Trương Thị Sáu, describes her first

meeting with Ninh in her recollections, as reported by her daughter.[13] This memoir, which is clearly a work designed to bring her father's eclectic intellectual biography into conformity with state hagiography, describes how it was not unusual for young women to spend time helping at the offices of Ninh's radical newspaper, the *Cloche Fêlée*. Many of the young radicals returning from France in the early 1920s were still seen as good marriage prospects by fashionable families, who were seeking to secure their daughters' futures with the opportunities offered by lofty French qualifications. They soon changed their minds, however, when many of those men refused the administrative positions with the colonial authorities that were expected of them.

Reports from the male participants in the radical movement include comments on how charming the ladies are.[14] Throughout the 1920s this ambivalence toward women in the public sphere is openly expressed. Following the unsettling events of Spring 1926, however, with the arrest of Ninh and many other young leaders for contravention of press and public security laws, as well as the death of patriotic hero Phan Chu Trinh, the stakes changed for women. French propaganda, together with merciless criticism and satire from nationalists, served to undermine Confucian familial propriety, forcing many young women to make a choice between the safety but oppression of family tradition and an uncertain future with a husband who may well spend much of his life in jail.[15] Rejecting conventional marital arrangements,[16] and with their employment options limited by their antigovernment activities, many educated young women, like men, were driven to teaching in private institutions or to journalism, where their influence was considerable.

It seems that entry into the public sphere was something young Vietnamese women saw as a natural act of emancipation, partly as a result of European role models. From the mid 1920s on, the lawyer Paul Monin, a member of the Ligue pour le Droit de l'Homme and co-editor with André Malraux of two Saigon opposition newspapers in 1925-1926, *Indochine* and *Indochine Enchaînée*, had considerable influence among radical circles. His wife, who was involved in international anti-imperial and human rights activities, was regarded in Sûreté reports with no less suspicion for her influence on young women. Such external role models were reinforced throughout the 1920s, with the delegations of the Misses Pye and Drevet of the Ligue Internationale des Femmes pour la Paix et la Liberté in 1927.[17] A delegation of women and girls was formed in 1927 to greet the Comité International des femmes, supported by the wives of such moderate nationalist politicians as Dương Văn Giáo.[18] While Monin and Malraux were considered dangerous, particularly for their associations with Chinese revolutionaries, the international women's movement appeared to be less threatening to the colonial administration, and was regarded with some quizzical amusement. Women's rights held a privileged position within the register of radical discourses, and were quickly adopted by male leaders as effective subterfuge for a more dangerous political rhetoric which could have led to arrest under the prevailing oppressive press laws. This cooptation by men of the question of women's rights soon resulted in women themselves demanding a more dominant role in public discourse.

1928 saw the beginning of a proliferation of women's journals, including the influential *Phụ Nữ Tân Văn* (*Women's News*), which began publication in February 1929; many other requests for publishing authorization were denied. The propagandizing efforts of illegal radical publications and the establishment of the Indochinese Communist Party in February 1930 certainly changed the stakes yet again for men and women hoping to be active in the public sphere. In a 1976 article, David Marr has written of the submissive nature of Vietnamese women, "Women internalized submissive norms almost to the point of believing them to be natural law; only some disputatious folk songs and risqué poetry gave evidence of alternate values."[19] He argues that the establishment of the Party in February 1930, and its proclamation of the "struggle for the equality of the sexes" as one of its ten principles, was most important in promoting this issue as a popular, rather than an élite preoccupation.[20]

Revolutionaries were not alone in their attempts to engage women in national discourse, and to do so by invoking heroic and epic narratives of struggle: the conservative Phạm Quỳnh, in his effort to establish a national literary canon, promoted Nguyễn Du's late eighteenth-century epic poem, the *Tale of Kiều*, as a foundational text. Many traditional Confucian literati argued that the poem, by extolling the virtue of Kiều, the victim-turned-prostitute, destabilized Confucian morality and chastity. Local performances of a play by Phan Bội Châu (first published in 1911), showed the heroic Trưng sisters' resistance to Chinese authority and emphasized parallels between the Chinese occupation and French colonial authority. Phan Bội Châu's work inspired a play on the same theme by Nguyễn An Ninh in 1927.[21] This seditious work evoked well-known instances of humiliations suffered by nationalists at the hands of colonial authorities, and contributed to the consciousness of women as historical actors in the public sphere of the nascent nation-state. History itself had become an arena of political contestation, as its events were subject to manipulation and nuanced interpretation in the pages of various newspapers and journals. The prominent positioning of historical narrative in the press, and understandings of Social Darwinism promoted both by the media and by the imperial enterprise itself, reinforced the naturalization of this historicization. Historical positivism was thus encoded in the semiotics of the mass media.

Andrée Viollis' shocking revelations of colonial abuse in her work *Indochine SOS*, published in 1935, was covered extensively in Vietnamese vernacular publications, including the women's journal *Đàn Bà Mới* (*New Women*), and reinforced the idea of women as important contributors to the international movement for equality and justice. The call in 1936 by Nguyễn An Ninh to take up the Popular Front government's promise of a commission of inquiry into colonial conditions led to another wave of radicalization in society, with the formation of networks of political action committees under the auspices of the Indochina Congress. These committees propelled many women into the political arena, as activists in the women's sections of the village and province level committees associated with the Congress, and greatly reinforced the clandestine networks of the communist party. A year after the exchange of letters between Mai Huỳnh Hoa and *Dân Quyền* following the Gia Định fair incident, both Huỳnh Hoa and *Dân Quyền*'s prominent journalist Nguyễn Thị Kiêm were at one of the inaugural meetings of the Indochina Congress in Mỹ Tho arguing for the formation of women's sections.[22]

Although few narrative histories of these women in the public sphere have been written in English (or French), their stories are archived in the files of the Sûreté, in their vernacular autobiographies, and on the pages of the numerous journals of the 1920s and 1930s. Some vignettes from the lives of a few prominent women illustrate the range of positions held by them and the way in which they were received by society: the poet, journalist and hard-line Stalinist Mai Huỳnh Hoa, mentioned in the opening story, the activist, journalist, and poet of the New Poetry movement, Nguyễn Thị Kiêm, and the two daughters of the leader of the Constitutionalist party, Bùi Quang Chiêu exemplify this diversity. Of the latter's two daughters, Henriette was the first Vietnamese woman to graduate in France as a doctor; she returned from Paris in the 1920s and married a fashionable Vietnamese lawyer in a well-publicized media event.[23] His second daughter, Madeleine, founded the first beauty parlor in Saigon. Both women were frequent commentators in the Saigon press and obvious objects of curiosity.[24]

Representations

My objective here, however, is not to trace the biographies of these women, but to draw upon them to explore further the didactic and coercive modes of operation of the historicizing and aestheticizing tropes of the bourgeois media which had the feminine as their referent and implicated women in their forms.

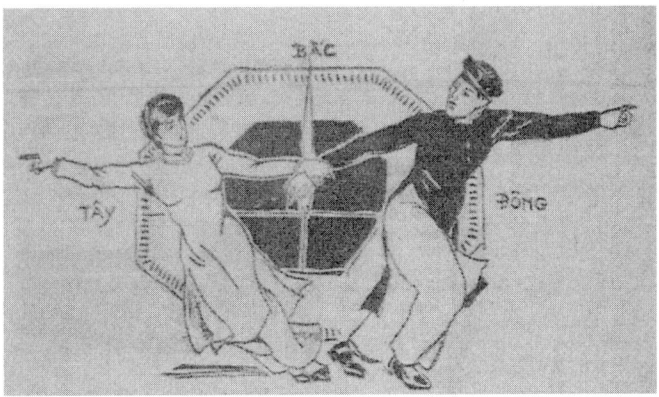

Figure 8.1: "First Auspicious Steps for the New Year." From the satirical journal *Loa* 101 (January 23, 1936).

In figure 8.1, a woman and a man take opposite directions for the future, as represented in the inaugural, auspicious steps from the house on the first day of the New Year. The woman, who is a caricature of the modern woman, is heading west, while the man, who is still wearing the traditional *khăn*, or scarf, worn to hide the hair in the period before men started cutting their hair short, is pulling her east.

Figure 8.2: The New Woman. Published in the journal *Sáng* (February 1939).

Vietnamese modernity of the 1920s and 1930s was defined by a media imaginary of desire and discomfort, as suggested by figure 8.2, which shows the modern woman concerned with fashionable pursuits, while society falls apart, a binary common in cartoon images. The late 1920s saw a transformation in the vernacular press, which increasingly adopted to the more sophisticated forms of graphic representation that were previously limited to French language organs. In contrast to David Marr's suggestion that women were quickly influenced by the establishment of the Communist Party, I question its immediate impact on the popular imagination, given the limited, clandestine and inept quality of its print propagandizing efforts prior to the liberalization of press laws under the leadership of the French Popular Front government in 1936. Although, as Hue Tam Ho Tai points out, the clandestine revolutionary publication of the Youth League, *Thanh Niên* (Youth), smuggled into Vietnam from Canton, carried radical articles on women's issues which did embolden the legal Vietnamese press to mimic the more daring discussions of these issues.[25] While moderniz-ing narratives and depictions of women as partners in progress—either as activ-ists in a socialist/Marxist agenda which circulated through the colonial territo-ries from the beginning of the 1920s, or as consumers in a bourgeois capitalist modernity—were powerful agents eroding the Confucian family, the ICP was tightly circumscribed in its propagandizing efforts.

As élite and aspiring middle-class women increasingly became targets of bourgeois advertising, the "legal"[26] communist and other nationalist publicists challenged the hegemony of French colonialism over this media imaginary of modernity. By adopting the same alluring media tropes of photographs, car-toons and graphics, a more subtle counter discourse exposing the materialist base of this modernity emerged. Unlike the "legal" press, with its professional typesetting, layout, and skillful journalism, the clandestine press of the party consisted of informally duplicated newsletters, whose didactic texts were aimed primarily at a peasant or worker audience.[27] French officials may have been justified in their claims that the recipients of these texts often found the ideas contained there alienating.

Little or no work has been done on the semiotics of the visual forms of rep-resentation included in these Vietnamese texts; consequently, my investigations of form and style are cautious. Images of bourgeois domesticity created through studio portraiture and photographic representations were much influenced by the French-trained photographer Khánh Ký.[28] Although histories of photogra-phy show that its association with representations of the dead is widespread, a "reading" of photographic representation in Vietnam is surely complicated by the ritual value of portraiture on the family altar. The introduction of coy atti-tudes and the frank and direct engagement with the camera of modern photo-graphic poses were possibly seen as a way of freeing photographic representa-tion from these confines. Nguyễn An Ninh, seen in figure 8.3, supported his education at the Sorbonne by working as an artist's model. This photograph, taken by Khánh Ký—a friend of both Ninh and Nguyễn Ái Quốc from the time of their sojourn in Paris together—became a symbol to the youth generation for whom he was an idol. It sold to the throngs of supporters outside the courtroom during his trial in 1926, and could be found adorning the living rooms of houses throughout the South in this period.[29]

Figure 8.4 shows a portrait of Ninh's second wife, Trương Thị Sáu, also taken by Khánh Ký, that is clearly a studio production. Museums in the Saigon area displaying photographs of heroic mothers who lost sons in the independ-ence wars routinely included two or three photographs of women in exactly this pose of bourgeois domesticity; in these clothes, at this table. Although arrested twice for subversive activities, Khánh Ký astutely capitalized on colonial repre-sentations, not only of a bourgeois urban elegance he sought to capture in his portraiture, but through his guided tours to the Paris Colonial Exposition, which he advertised in the Saigon newspapers throughout early 1931.[30] Trương Thị Sáu was indeed a woman of some means and obvious elegance. Her daughter's biography of Ninh, however, describes how Ninh's father demanded soon after their marriage that Trương Thị Sáu drop her fineries, as they were inappropriate attire for the wife of a revolutionary family.[31] In fact, she was to sell all her assets, including her jewelry, in order to finance her husband's revolutionary activities. A photograph taken during her husband's imprisonment in 1939, for a journal article on how the wives of the political prisoners were coping, clearly intends to project a very different image, that of the oppressed and hardworking mother.

Figure 8.3: Nguyễn An Ninh. Portrait by Khánh Ký, 1926. CAOM. Courtesy of CAOM and Daniel Hémery.

Figure 8.4: Trương Thị Sáu. From the cover of her republished memoir, *Cùng anh đi suốt cuộc đời: hồi ký của bà Nguyễn An Ninh*. (*With him throughout his life: memoir of Madam Nguyễn An Ninh*) HCM NXB Trẻ, 1999.

While European ideas of form and pose, which helped construct women's images in photographic compositions, may have had an impact on their audiences in Indochina, photographic and literary representations of women aimed at a metropolitan audience without doubt also influenced self-perceptions of women within the colonial territories. Orientalist literary and cinematographic discourses on Indochina were subjects of discussion and critique in Vietnam. Representations of the colonial expositions have been explored by Timothy Mitchell in his work on the colonial "exhibitionary order." Building on Mitchell's ideas, Panivong Norindr has examined representations of Indochina at the colonial expositions. He describes Indochinese women as being ambiguously signified as "primitive natives" and as elegant dancing girls, transported and domesticated within the safe confines of a miniaturized and disrupted geography.[32] Indeed, the archives pertaining to the staging of the colonial expositions abound with expressions of a policy aimed to domesticate women and limit them within the normative roles of weaver, basketmaker and embroiderer.

Reflections on Stillness and Motion

Attempts by Paris authorities to persuade the Indochina administration to submit examples of women's art for a colonial art exhibition failed to produce any works that the local administration considered to be of sufficient originality, women's work being only repetitive mimicry of long-established traditions.[33] It is notable that the 1932 women's fair staged by the Saigon women's journal, *Phụ Nữ Tân Văn*, used the same limiting techniques as the expositions, depicting women's work as a series of handicraft categories. The categorization of women's production as stagnant contrasts with the unlimited possibilities of progress depicted in ever-changing commercial fashions. The dual tropes of aesthetisization and historicism were visually set in motion on the pages of the popular media: progress was represented by the movements of people from village to town, by the decisive and practiced motion of sport and Western dance, and the increasing speed of travel, most particularly the private car, which was ubiquitous in advertising images in the 1930s. Both advertising and literary representations of the car posit it as an icon of a kinetic modernity and an object of women's desire.

Like the photograph, that other aesthetic artifice which enabled self-reflection—the mirror itself—is a nexus of signification in Vietnamese tradition and in modern femininity. Again like the photograph, its use is ritualized in memorialization of the dead, on family altars and shrines. Discourses on the mirror in Chinese aesthetics, ritual and mysticism are wide-ranging,[34] though interpretations of the mirror in the Vietnamese context are lacking. The Vietnamese word for mirror, *gương*, is also used to mean an example, or model, invoking notions of faithful repetition, or mimesis, and a teleology of truth or redemption. However, use of this term to signify historical texts also implies a positivist historical trajectory, a link between the present and the past through the mediation of this optical instrument that connotes a temporal and historicizing dimension.[35]

Placed on the family altar, or on a grave, the mirror is seen as a means of deflecting evil spirits, but also as a device representing a liminal space between past, present and future. Its cooptation as a modern fashion accessory and aesthetic trope complicates this role, as can be seen in figure 8.5, which shows the grave of revolutionary heroine Võ Thị Sáu on the prison island of Côn Đảo. Here the traditional ritual mirror is replaced with a fashionable powder compact, accompanied by other trappings of modern beauty that are not the traditional items of devotion to be found on the family altar. The mirror's use as an object of decorative art also seems to be adopted from an aesthetic not uncommon in late nineteenth-century Chinese portraiture. The example in figure 8.6 incorporates not only the reflection of a reflection extending from an historical infinity, but a photograph of the same image miniaturized on the adjacent chest, as if the instability of this historical framing has to be countered by the permanent impression of the photographic representation.

Figure 8.5: Võ Thị Sáu's Grave. Author's   Figure 8.6: Illustration from *Loa* 93 (November 28,
photograph (February 2002).   1935).

Like the photograph, the mirror is a site of excess signification shifting from ritual object on the family altar to cosmetic utility. Moreover, the newspapers of the 1930s began to show design elements and cartoon images which play with ideas of both enframement and reflection, often using contrasting black and white patterns and even negative images, as if in the photographic negative that Homi Bhabha has associated with the double inscription of colonial mimesis.[36] Figure 8.7 shows a cartoon entitled, "Topsy Turvy Life"; in the first caption the photographic editor calls out: "Hey, she's *white*?" The mirror image of the paper's masthead is visible in the second image, while the bemused typesetter remarks: "Even the N is back-to-front." The ironical use of this transposition in the case of skin color was not lost on the Vietnamese, at a time when racial coding, including the common use of the term *người da vàng* ("yellow-skinned people"), is being variously inscribed in terms of national particularism and a pan-Asian consciousness.

In Homi Bhabha's double inscription of mimesis, the native other is always lacking, like the refracted void of the photographic negative. The graphic tropes discussed here, however, may operate in Vietnamese imaginaries as instruments of recuperation, empowering their audience through their ironic and mocking gestures. The excess of signification of photographic images, introduced to Indochina within a matter of ten years, included representations which allowed for a new form of self-contemplation by Vietnamese subjects, as well as bringing an array of imported knowledge. These complex representations, however, are augmented in the press by simple and didactic forms, using minimalist line drawings to better display the forms of fashion items, and beauty techniques. Removing the technical form of production from the object of desire can perhaps make it seem more attainable. While the reader is captivated by the allure of the photographic representation, the form of the object is reinscribed in less complex forms; the publication of fashion designs as sewing patterns implies the ease with which even those of limited means could understand and aspire to the luxury of fashion.

Figure 8.7: This cartoon, entitled, "Topsy Turvy Life" is from the journal of the Tự Lực Văn Đoàn literary group. *Phong Hóa* 79 (December 29, 1933).

New Media Women

While many media images sought to domesticate the bourgeois woman as passive consumer, her image was exploited as evoking a world of transgression and transition, becoming an icon of modernism's complexities. As a metonym for an orientalized and colonized geography, the new woman retained her exotic charm, but was domesticated and contained within the limits of transgression that served to define a position of moral purity befitting the "mission civilisatrice," and in contrast to which the rhetorical discourse of moral decadence and decline could be posited. This *errance* placed the new woman outside traditional mores and made her a putative danger to male sobriety and a challenge to Confucian morality. Like the poor French girl of Marguerite Duras's novels, she not only transgressed social categories, but challenged racial ones. She was Europeanized, took a French official as a lover, and entered the bourgeois class as an unequal imitation of her European sisters. The dangerous and exotic femininity projected by these media images was affirmed in official reports as an object of French male desire. The endlessly debated phenomenon of prostitution hid a register of social behaviors, real and imagined, which situated the modern woman within society in ways which exposed the fragile boundary between women as public actors in a contentious "liberated" domain, and the various real and constructed images of women as vulgar imitations of Western custom. This register ranged from the common prostitutes of the *maisons de tolérance*, to *ca trù* singers—a highly specialized and difficult form of professional singing involving a female singer and two male instrumentalists—and extending to women who marry or are lovers of Western men.[37]

In this complex matrix of gender-indexed interpretations, a phenomenon that the French soon came to call the social "malaise" came to the fore. This condition referred to the superficiality of the "new" life and the ennui that it engendered in the bourgeois class. It was a phenomenon which crossed gender lines; it may well have had its real roots in the unemployment crisis of the depression, but was symbolically associated with young women and their suicidal tendencies. French analysts defined the "malaise" as a lack of moral substance, sometimes admitted by officials as having resulted from a French policy of undermining traditional institutions and learning and replacing them with nothing: very low educational enrollments, few opportunities for bright children in French language schools, and high unemployment even for those who did have an education. This psychological state was soon adopted by local commentators as the basis of a discussion of immorality, which many blamed on the decadent state of Confucian learning. Suicide became the focus of media debate and cartoon representation, and was quickly linked by revolutionaries, and proponents of Art for Life, with the dominance of literary romanticism, as well as economic conditions.[38]

The evolution of the "Annamite legal code," and its relationship to a growing understanding of personal and community "rights," further heightened awareness of women as a distinct social group. Slander and libel laws, imported by French decree, became powerful political tools, particularly within the world of the press, as a means to control or silence opponents.[39] While cartoons abounded with wives threatening to sue their husbands for failing to meet their expectations of bourgeois luxury, it is not clear to what extent women were actually able to better their social position through such juridical means. This new media woman is likely to have cut her hair short, have worn shorts for tennis and cycling, and to have swum shamelessly in scanty costume in the seas off the fashionable Đồ Sơn beach. She would have flaunted a daring outfit from the fashion house of Nguyễn Cát Tường, the designer of the Vietnamese *áo dài* who was popularly know by the literal French translation of his name, Lemur. This putative "traditional" costume was created as a result of a competition in around 1931, probably promoted by the Tự Lực Văn Đoàn, self-strengthening literature group, through its popular paper *Phong Hóa* (*Morals*). Interestingly, just as the fateful *Tale of Kiều* was adopted as a national narrative, so the first atavistic claim to a national aesthetic, in the form of a national costume, was one to be displayed by women. Lemur wrote regularly about fashion for *Phong Hóa*[40] and *Phụ Nữ Tân Văn* (Modern Ladies). The fact that Lemur not only promoted fashion as an index of moral progress, but also used his basic *áo dài* design for a range of fashion embellishments, again suggests the conflation of the aestheticization of "culture" with a positivism which served to naturalize material fashion as a register of progress.

The common depiction of feminine modernity is critiqued by male revolutionaries and satirized by several novelists of the 1930s, most notably Vũ Trọng Phụng and Nguyễn Công Hoan. Lemur is mercilessly lampooned in Vũ Trọng Phụng's novel *Số Đỏ*.[41] His tailor's shop is one fulcrum around which this satirical depiction of modernity as fetish is enacted. Lemur's diaphanous creations, ever more daring and appropriate for the modern woman's varied life style, range from the seductive lingerie essential for affairs, to the latest in funeral attire. However, the phantasmatic sexual nomenclature assigned by Vũ Trọng Phụng to the fictive Lemur designs could easily be read to disrupt this historicist teleology, with its reference to the tragic trajectory of colonial conquest: *Innocence, Conquest, Hesitation, Wait-a-Minute, Coquette, Stop-Those-Hands.*[42] The family at the center of this drama cannot wait for the patriarch to die, not only because they covet his money, but because the women want to display the latest in funeral attire to the admiring observers of Hanoi society. Vũ Trọng Phụng's novels and reportage target not only the bourgeois deceits of the élite class and its nouveau riche aspirants, but the equally superficial understandings of the new political aristocracy, including revolutionaries of all stripes. They provide vivid insights into the lives of women which were much too explicit for French press censors, often focusing on women involved in the indistinct realms of commerce, performance and leisure, which were closely associated with prostitution and opium smoking.

Conclusion

This chapter does not claim to provide any answers to the questions arising from the beauty pageant at the 1935 Gia Định fair, but it does suggest different ways of viewing them. It shows the complexity of negotiating womens' subjectivities in the public sphere. It also argues that women were promoted in bourgeois media as vehicles for the transmission of an image of normative progress which sought to naturalize technological complexity and material commodification. I have attempted here to explore the modes of operation of a media semiotics which historicized commercial aesthetics by conflating progress and fashion. I also show how this semiotics was disrupted not only by expressions of anxiety that permeated the press and its cartoon pages, but by revolutionary intellectuals, who by the 1930s were well aware of the importance of this representational dimension to class struggle, and were as adept at manipulating it as the capitalist press barons. I demonstrate ways in which political discourses, and a broader media imaginary of resistance, implicated women as performers through whom modernity's anxieties and disjunctures were enacted. While this paper takes a very broad approach to the questions raised by the textures and fabrics of a Vietnamese modernity, clearly much work is still to be done on the fashions and fads that both upheld and subverted the materialist colonial order.

Notes

1. The article states that while beauty has no value, plainness ensures a woman's morality and worth in society. Anonymous, "Dêm bế mạc cuộc đấu xảo canh nông Gia Định: cuộc thi sắc đẹp," *Dân Quyền* (September 9, 1935).

2. Diêu Hoa, "Xin hiện cho ban giám khảo thin sắc đẹp dêm 8 sept 1935 ở GiaĐịnh," *Dân Quyền* (September 11, 1935).

3. See note 18.

4. In her attack, Mai Huỳnh Hoa asks: "Am I a person who emulates Euro-American civilization? I plead ignorance, because I don't even know what you mean by the phrase. Do you actually know yourself what you mean?" "Đấp lời Diệu Hoa Tiên-sinh," *Dân Quyền* (September 13, 1935).

5. The Buddhist term for enlightenment, *giác ngô*, was regularly used to describe political and class awareness.

6. His first public speech on returning from France, in February 1923, concerned culture. "Une Culture pour les Annamites: Conférence faite par M. Ng An Ninh, Licencié en droit à la Société d'Enseignement Mutuel de Cochinchine." *La Voix Annamite*, 4 (February 2, 1923).

7. Ironically, Hoài Thanh became one of the leading proponents of the principles of Art for Life enshrined in the post 1943 cultural policies of the Việt Minh. See Kim Ninh, *A World Transformed: the Politics of Culture in Revolutionary Vietnam, 1945-1965* (Ann Arbor, University of Michigan, 2002), 23.

8. Phan Văn Hùm, "Chủ nghĩa và chủ nghĩa nghệ thuật," *Trang An* (January 6, 1936).

9. In his polemic with Hoài Thanh he argues that André Gide is not yet "enlightened" to Marxist doctrine, since he believes that the average worker could understand the beauty of the Mona Lisa. Hùm contends that in a society which provides no aesthetic training to the proletariat such an élite concept of beauty cannot be accepted.

10. Phan Văn Hùm, "Phương pháp Xã Hội học của Durkheim." *Tiến Bố* (February 23, 1936).

11. Lynn Hunt explores symbolic connections between family and the iconography of the French state in *The Family Romance of the French Revolution* (Berkeley: UC Press, 1992). Hue Tam Ho Tai discusses this phenomenon in Vietnam: "The language of family has so often been invoked by revolutionaries as to seem the natural idiom of revolutionary rhetoric." *Radicalism and the Origins of the Vietnamese Revolution* (Cambridge: Harvard University Press, 1992), 197.

12. Grèves scolaires. Service de Sûreté, 1924-1926. Centre des Archives d'Outre-Mer (Aix en Provence), hereafter CAOM. GGI 65475.

13. Nguyễn Thị Minh. *Nguyễn An Ninh: "Tôi chỉ làm cơn gió thổi"* (*Nguyễn An Ninh: "I only caused a little wind to blow"*) HCM: NXB Trẻ, 2001. This work includes much that was first published as Trường Thị Sáu's own biography: "Hồi ký." (*Memoir*) In *Con đường giải phòng*. Vol. 2. Hanoi: NXB Phụ Nữ, 1976; republished as: Trường Thị Sáu.

Cùng anh đi suốt cuộc đời: hôi ký của bà Nguyễn An Ninh. (*With him throughout his life: memoir of Madam Nguyễn An Ninh*), HCM NXB Trẻ, 1999.

14. Ninh himself speaks of his own foolish romanticism regarding the ladies in his early writings. After some 5 years in prison, the father of three children, with a wife struggling to survive in his absence, his attitudes were much changed. "Phái duy tâm với phụ nữ giải phóng," ("The Idealism Faction and Women's Liberation") *Trung Lập Báo* (March 30, 1933).

15. Discourses on the family proliferated in the early 1930s. Ninh wrote a series of articles in the Saigon papers defending the position of revolutionaries who advocated the destruction of Confucian patriarchy. He argued that reestablishing the family based on gender and economic equality and loving partnerships would strengthen the nation. Nguyễn An Ninh, "Gia đình và phụ nữ giải phóng" ("The family and the liberation of women"), *Trung Lập Báo* (March 30, 1933).

16. Many of this generation of radical men did not marry their partners. Although Trường Thị Sáu claims to have married Ninh in 1924, archival records show that they did not legally marry until 1928, just before the birth of their second child (CAOM. SPCE 381). I understand this as a refusal to recognize the legal authority of the state. Phan Văn Hùm openly referred to his commitment to free love as a principle. Despite this, he took advantage of the French legal system's acceptance of bigamy to marry Mai Huỳnh Hoa as a secondary wife, probably some time in 1936.

17. "Retour de M. Dương Văn Giáo en Cochinchine avec la Mission Mme Drevet et Miss Pye de la Ligue Internationale de Femmes pour la Paix et la Liberté." National Archives Center 2, Saigon (hereafter LT2): IIA.45/233 (2). A "Section Cochinchinoise du Comité Mondial de Lutte Contre la Guerre" was constituted in Saigon. Note périodique no 35 de la Direction de la Sûreté Générale Indochinoise (2ème trimestre 1935), 25. LT2: II.45/312 (1).

18. *Tribune Indochinoise* (November 23, 1927).

19. Marr, David. "The 1920s Women's Rights Debates in Vietnam." *Journal of Asian Studies*, 35:3 (May 1976), 371. Marr argues that the women's rights issues of the 1920s show the extent to which the French exploited the oppressive doctrines of Confucianism in regard to the family. This oppression is based on the three submissions: to father, husband and son.

20. The question of women's suffrage remained contested into the 1930s, with even those committed to equality believing that suffrage was an élite distraction from the urgent economic issues of most women.

21. Sûreté reports claimed that Ninh's text was a call to arms for his partisans, but no evidence was presented at his trial to show that the texts were found in the possession of those partisans arrested.

22. Assemblée Générale du douze Sept 1936 (My Tho). Procès Verbal. LT2: IIA.45/273(2).

23. Tran Thi Lien. "Henriette Bui; The Narrative of Vietnam's First Woman Doctor." In *Viêt-Nam Exposé: French Scholarship on Twentieth-Century Vietnamese Society*, eds. Gisele Bousquet and Pierre Brocheux (Ann Arbor, Michigan University Press, 2002), 278-309.

24. One discussion in the press contrasts the life of Henriette Bùi with that of ICP activist Nguyễn Thị Lữu. Henriette Bùi is criticized for considering the expectations of her family over those of the state, while Nguyễn Thị Lữu, a committed political activist, lacks the education and skills to be a role model for women or a leader in society. Nguyễn Thị Hường. "Từ cô Nguyễn Thị Lữu cho đến bà Henriette Bùi Quang Chiêu," *Nữ công tạp chí* (July 1937).

25. Hue Tam Ho Tai, *Radicalism*, 198-213.

26. The French defined the "legal" communists as those who consciously operated within the law, meaning mostly the press laws and the laws of association.

27. Many of the regional committees of the ICP distributed illegal tracts. See Shawn McHale. "Printing Revolution, Spreading Communism." In *Print and Power: Confucianism, Communism and Buddhism in the Making of Modern Vietnam* (University of Hawai'i Press, 2003), 102-142.

28. Khánh Ký had studios in Hanoi, Saigon and Paris at the height of his commercial success in the 1920s and early 1930s. Because of his German business connection he was under suspicion from French authorities and was implicated in the "Trotskyite plot" of 1932. CAOM: 3Slotfom/42; LT II: IIA.45/276 (3).

29. Peycam, Philippe. *Intellectuals and political commitment in Vietnam: the emergence of a public sphere in colonial Saigon (1916-1928)*. Ph.D. thesis, University of London, School of Oriental and African Studies, 1999.

30. For instance, *Trung Lập Báo* (March 27, 1931).

31. Nguyễn Thị Minh, *Nguyễn An Ninh*.

32. Panivong Norindr, *Phantasmatic Indochina: French Colonial Ideology in Architecture, Film, and Literature* (Durham, Duke University Press, 1996), 22-23.

33. "Participation du Tonkin à l'Exposition de la société des artistes français à Paris, 1928-1929." National Archives Center 1, Hanoi: RS Tonkin, R72647.

34. Julia Ch'ing, "The mirror symbol revisited: Confucian and Taoist mysticism." In *Mysticism and religious traditions*, ed. Steven T. Katz (New York: Oxford University Press, 1983), 226-46.

35. The connection between history and a reflecting crystal is contemplated by Hoài Thanh in his discussion of the fad for historical fiction in "Phong trào xem chuyện lịch sử," *Tràng An* (June 8, 1935).

36. Homi Bhabha, "Signs taken for wonders." In *The Post-Colonial Studies Reader* (London: Routledge, 1995), 29-35.

37. Phan Văn Hùm stated in an interview that the causes of prostitution are economic, and the traditional first wife in a marriage is often no more than a prostitute herself, since she engages in a relationship for money and status, not desire. His statement captures the difficulty of defining women's roles at a time of shifting values. "Vấn đề mại dâm,' *Việt Dân* (April 7, 1934).

38. For further discussion of these questions, see Nguyễn Văn Ký's *Indochine face à la modernité: le Tonkin de la fin du XIXe siècle à la Seconde Guerre mondiale*. Paris: L'Harmattan, 1995.

39. Even Mai Huỳnh Hoa in her attack on her assailant in *Dân Quyền* states that she would be happy to sue him for defamation, but that she would be equally happy to have him understand her position. Journalistic polemics in this period often resulted in court cases, as did many accusations of fiduciary mismanagement; both served as a means of silencing opposition.

40. *Phong Hóa*, which published its first issue in June 1932 and was suspended in June 1935, is compared by French Sûreté officials to a metropolitan review, specifically the *Canard Enchaîné*.

41. Translated as *Dumb Luck* by Nguyễn Nguyệt Cầm and Peter Zinoman (Ann Arbor, University of Michigan Press, 2002). See Zinoman's "Introduction" for further discussion of Vũ Trọng Phụng's class perceptions.

42. Translation from Peter Zinoman and Nguyễn Nguyệt Cầm, *Dumb Luck*, 68.

9

Camille's Breasts:
The Evolution of the Fantasy Native in Régis Wargnier's *Indochine*

Lily V. Chiu

In his book *Phantasmatic Indochina: French Colonial Ideology in Architecture, Film and Literature*, Panivong Norindr discusses the effect of the International Colonial Exposition held in Paris in 1931:

> L'Exposition Coloniale Internationale de Paris did not simply strive to give a unified and complete inventory of exotic (i.e., colonized) reality, but was also designed to "ravish" and arouse desires for the colonies. It is, therefore, a privileged point of entry into what I call the French colonial phantasmatic. By colonial phantasmatic—a term I borrow from psychoanalysis—I mean the ideological reality through which colonial fantasies as the support of desire emerged, operated, and manifested themselves.[1]

This ideological "reality," which in itself is a fantasy, is one that allows the colonizer to regard the colonies, and indeed the colonized, as objects of desire. As exotic figures of the "Other" in European art and literature, the native woman is no stranger to being regarded, indeed constructed, as the object of male Orientalist gaze/desire/consumption. Yet it is important to understand that this is a construction by the colonizer of precisely what he expects the colonized native to be. As Albert Memmi has argued, "the existence of the colonizer requires that an image of the colonized be suggested."[2] Memmi quite rightly labels this portrayal of the colonized as "mythical," which is along much the same lines as Norindr's colonial phantasmatic.

In the context of French Indochina, the natives are constructed as feminine and submissive, regardless of their gender. Their model is the generic *congaie*,[3] a Vietnamese term literally meaning daughter or girl (*con gái*), which is appropriated by the French colonials to mean mistress or "wife" (another term being *petites épouses* (little wives) as in the title of Myriam Harry's 1901 novel). Although of royal blood, and French-educated, Eliane's adopted Vietnamese daughter, Camille, is raised to be something similar to this model *congaie*: a fantasy native, giving pleasure to all who gaze upon her.[4]

However, as I argue, the character of Camille evolves throughout the film; she acquires her own gaze, and with it, a subjectivity that allows her to perform her own image. She becomes nothing more than a simulacrum: an image to be disseminated, like a postcard. But unlike the image of a postcard, the simulacrum Camille performs is one of her own choosing. In the end, she escapes both the gaze of the French colonizer as well as the viewers of the film, evolving beyond the scope of the clichéd French colonial text that is *Indochine*.

The Fantasy: Régis Wargnier's *Indochine*

In a self-congratulatory publicity move, the producers of the 1991 film *Indochine* made it widely known that its film crew and director, Régis Wargnier, were the first Westerners allowed back into Vietnam to film on location after the French and American wars of 1945-1975. The film, on the strength of its famous actors and beautiful cinematography, won the Academy Award for Best Foreign Film for that year. The story, which is revealed to be narrated by the protagonist to her adoptive (grand)son, is set around 1930, the year of the Yen Bay rebellion, and a few years afterwards. Born and raised entirely in Vietnam, Eliane Devries (Catherine Deneuve) is the unwed and childless daughter of a French colonialist, Emile. Together with her father, she owns a large rubber plantation in the southern region of Annam, near Saigon. When Eliane's good friends, the Prince and Princess N'Guyen [*sic*], die in a plane crash off Cap St. Jacques (Vũng Tàu), Eliane adopts their young daughter Camille (Linh Đan Phạm), the "Princess of An Nam." In doing so, she also gains all of Camille's lands, making their combined lands one of the largest rubber plantations in Indochina.

Eliane raises Camille as her own daughter—that is, as a French girl. She speaks French, dances waltzes, wears French clothing, and attends a French girls' school. Eliane, who enjoys considerable freedom for a woman, helps to run the plantation herself and has a love affair with a young and idealistic French naval officer, Jean-Baptiste Le Guen (Vincent Perez). However, the affair is broken up by Eliane's father, and Camille ends up falling in love with Jean-Baptiste herself. She rebels against Eliane's attempt to separate her from

Jean-Baptiste, and with the help of her arranged-marriage husband, Thanh (Eric Nguyễn), escapes to join him in the North. Once she has made it to the North, she joins a family of runaway workers and they all end up in a slave auction in Ha Long Bay, where Le Guen is now posted. When Camille discovers that the family with whom she has been traveling has been executed by the French officers for "incitement to rebellion," she shoots and kills a French officer in revenge. Jean-Baptiste helps her escape from the slave market, and the two go into hiding with Vietnamese Communists, friends of Thanh.

Meanwhile, Eliane has been searching frantically for Camille, who is wanted by the colonial police for murder. During this time, Camille becomes pregnant and gives birth to a son, Etienne; however, she becomes separated from Jean-Baptiste and Etienne, who are discovered by French officers. Later, Camille is captured along with her Communist friends, and sent to Poulo Condore prison for five years. Jean-Baptiste, after having betrayed the Communists, is murdered, and his son falls into Eliane's care. When Camille is released from prison, she refuses to return to Eliane and her son, and tells them to return to France, since the Indochina they know is dead. At the end of the film, it transpires that Eliane has been telling the story to Etienne, on the eve of the Geneva Conference in 1954, when France lost Indochina and Vietnam was divided into two. Etienne has come to meet with his mother, now a high-ranking Communist official taking part in the negotiations; in the end, however, he cannot even recognize her, and does not seek her out. Eliane, he declares, is his real mother.

Camille's Breasts

The "China doll" of the film,[5] Camille is at first the model "fantasy native" for both the French colonizers and the spectators of the movie. She is raised to be pliant, obedient, and pleasing to the eye. She speaks fluent French, so that the colonizer will not have to learn Vietnamese in order to communicate fully with her. She is, as Eliane calls her, "irresistable." Her identity (in the first half of the film) as an innocent, fragile figure is reinforced by her choice of clothing: she is almost always dressed in virginal white (the exception is when she is wearing her school uniform). This is contrasted to Eliane's dark (mostly black) wardrobe, signifying her status as an independent, worldly woman.

Camille is also the only female character in the film whose breasts are shown, in two separate episodes. The first time we see Camille's breasts is during her initial encounter with Jean-Baptiste, so that the viewer is in effect invited by the camera to share the male protagonist's gaze of desire. Camille's breasts are displayed as objects for our visual consumption, as well as for her two "lovers" in the movie, Jean-Baptiste and Eliane.[6] This exhibition evokes an entire tradition of the fetishization of "native" breasts, from National Geographic magazines to Algerian *mauresque* postcards to the Hottentot Venus and Josephine Baker. It also begs the question: why not Eliane's breasts? Catherine Deneuve is, of course, one of the great symbols of femininity in

French cinema. However, this is not a film about the desire for French women. It is about the French desire for a phantasmatic Indochina, synedochically symbolized by Camille's naked breasts.

This phantasmatic desire is latent in colonial postcards of Vietnamese women produced mostly between 1900 and 1935. Many typical postcards of indigenes include those supposedly taken during mundane daily rituals, such as "Jeune femme annamite achevant sa toilette" ("Young Annamite woman washing") by Pierre Dieulefils.[7] However, even in these most mundane scenes, such as Dieulefils's "Le repas aux champs" ("The meal in the fields"), the exoticized indigene is present.[8] This postcard features four young women and a girl having their midday meal. The four women are seated on the ground, holding bowls of rice and chopsticks, while the young girl is standing, holding a two-handled pot. All five are dressed in peasant clothing, wearing *yếm* (traditional halter-style tops made from thin fabric). The sexual allure of these tops, which are traditionally worn as undergarments, is so strong that many colonial photographers portrayed Vietnamese peasant women wearing *yếm* with nothing covering them, as in a state of *déshabille*. In this particular postcard, the *yếm* of the woman on the far right barely covers her breasts, while the *yếm* of the woman on the far left has been pushed up, exposing her breasts completely.

As Jennifer Yee points out, "In postcards of Indochina, the multiplication of young women and their availability to scopic desire conjures up the theme of the harem as a magical place of sexual plenitude."[9] The fact that this is *not* a harem, but rather a seemingly normal meal in a field, is undermined by the nakedness of the woman on the left, a gesture which categorizes *all* indigenes, no matter who they are or where they are, as sexually available. All of Indochine, this postcard suggests, is an exotic harem.

This suggestion, however, is little more than a cliché, spread about in the Metropole by colonial novels and letters home, which brag of the charms of the *congaie* and the ease with which they are bedded (as one French colonial stated in a letter home: just pretend to marry them, and when you are tired of them, sell them to a friend). The postcards sent home to France did more than reify this cliché, they were specifically created based upon it. In almost all cases, the scenes depicted in the postcards have been carefully staged by the photographer. These postcards, therefore, are not in any way a representation of "actual" or "real" life in Indochine, but rather the confirmation of an exotic fantasy. In this sense, Yee argues, "the postcard is photography in a mythic (in a Barthesian sense) form: it represents an attempt to recreate the world in conformity to the clichés of colonial exoticism."[10]

In addition to the carefully staged harem-type postcards were the pseudo-ethnographic "type" postcard, portraying types of certain ethnic groups. One of these, by the colonial photographer Ludovic Crespin and entitled "Type de jeune annamite" ("Type of young Annamite woman"), displays a young Viet-namese woman from the waist up, wearing dark peasant-styled trousers, but with bare breasts (see figure 9.1). The young woman, whose face is slightly turned away from the camera, nonetheless gazes obliquely back at the photographer. Her pose is almost exactly mimicked in the scene in *Indochine* where Camille's breasts are exposed for the second time. This scene is, as I argue, the turning point of the film. After having rebelled against Eliane for sending Jean-Baptiste away, Camille is taken to the royal palace in Hue (her "rightful" home, as a member of the royal family), in order to marry Thanh. As a Westerner, Eliane is not allowed to attend the wedding itself. The day before the wedding, however, she is permitted to see Camille, who is in a court-mandated period of isolation and purification reserved for brides-to-be. The shooting of this scene is particularly interesting: the camera rests first on Camille, naked from the waist up, gazing at herself in the mirror. The camera then pans to show the entry of Eliane, which Camille has not noticed. Then the camera cuts back to a close shot of Camille and her reflection; Camille notices Eliane's presence in the mirror and turns, covering herself up.

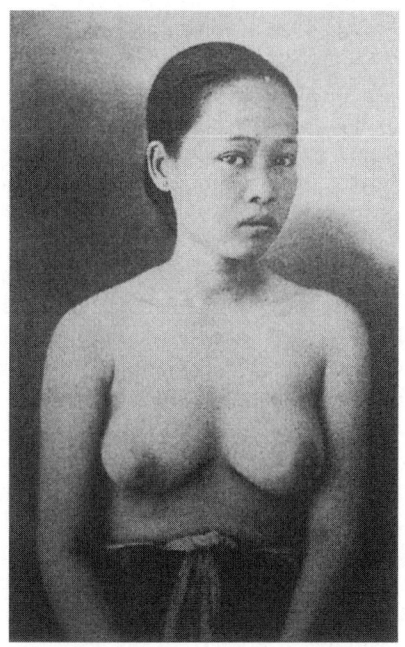

Figure 9.1: "Type de Jeune Annamite." Ludovic Crespin, c. 1910, Centre des Archives d'Outre-Mer (Aix-en-Provence).

Figure 9.2: "Annam. Les deux Reines." P. Dieulefils, Hanoi, c. 1905. From the author's collection.

This mise-en-scène presents the viewer with two different images of Camille: Camille and the mirror-image of Camille. Her naked breasts, doubled, become the objects of scopophilic consumption for three viewers: Eliane, the audience, and Camille herself. In the postcard, the native woman is caught by the single gaze of the colonial photographer, she gazes back at him, but obliquely. In this scene in *Indochine*, Camille is caught by Eliane's colonial gaze, but it becomes a shared gaze: Camille sees what Eliane sees. This is the pivotal point in the film: this is the moment in which Camille sees herself *as a Western fantasy native object*. In the mirror, Camille sees not a Lacanian totality image that can never be achieved, but rather, a constructed image of the native that is nothing more than a fantasy. She sees herself, not as what she is or wants to be, but as the French see her.

However, as Camille's gaze turns upon herself, it also turns *into and within* herself; the Camille we see from this point onwards is not the innocent, light-hearted girl of before, but an introspective, determined person. As she gazes at and into herself, Camille acquires the ability to gaze for herself. Camille's breasts, formerly objects of consumption for others alone, now become objects of consumption for herself as well; she transforms and appropriates others' gaze for her own use. Camille's acquisition of a gaze of her own is demonstrated in another scene, shortly afterwards. After running away to the North, Camille joins up with a peasant family who are making their way to Ha Long Bay in search of better work. In this particular scene, Camille and the family have reached a starving village. There, the family and Camille share the rice they have received from missionaries. As she sits to eat her rice, the camera follows Camille's gaze to take in the suffering of her fellow Vietnamese. It is here, when she is able to exercise her newly-found gaze, that Camille realizes her own status as "native"—Vietnamese. With the ability to gaze for herself, and her realization of both her identities of constructed (fantasy) native and ethnic (Vietnamese) native, Camille begins a series of performances of native identity. Significantly, these performances mimic images of different types of natives shown in colonial postcards. The first of these performances occurs soon after the mirror scene. Being a princess, Camille is engaged at court, in the presence of what we assume to be the emperor and the empress. Camille appears calm, collected, playing the role of the royal bride beautifully in a traditional silk *áo dài* (Vietnamese tunic). In fact, her beauty is remarked upon by Eliane as being the result of Camille's decision to join Jean-Baptiste: "Elle était tellement douce, tellement calme, comme si elle avait accepté sereinement son sort: épouser l'homme qui lui était destiné. En fait, elle venait secrètement de décider de sa vie. C'est pour ça qu'elle était si belle." ("She was so gentle, so calm, as if she had serenely accepted her fate: to marry the man destined for her. Actually, she had secretly made up her mind. That was why she was so beautiful.") The incongruity between her internal rebellion and her external calm suggests a performance on Camille's part: that of the obedient royal, also a popular postcard subject, as in Pierre Dieulefils's postcard of around 1905, "Annam. Les deux Reines" (see figure 9.2).

Luckily for Camille, Thanh is also playing a part, hiding his communist leanings under the guise of obedient fiancé. With his help, Camille begins her journey north, in search of her French lover. In doing so, she assumes another role: that of Vietnamese native. For the duration of the rest of the film, Camille wears only dark-colored Vietnamese clothes, the complete opposite of the white, Western clothes she had worn before. Dressed as a native and speaking Vietnamese in order to survive, Camille nonetheless still remains within the scope of colonial postcards; her peasant dress (which includes a *yếm* top), though somber, is still sexy. She could be one of the peasant native girls taking her lunch on the field in "Le repas aux champs." Furthermore, since her performance as Vietnamese native remains within the scope of colonial postcards, Camille also remains within the colonial phantasmatic imagination. In other words, she can still be considered a *congaie*, and as such, sexually available to the French colonizer (Jean-Baptiste).

The Amazing Disappearing Native

Each performance of Camille's takes her spatially further away from Saigon and symbolically out the reach of both the colonial authority of the French and the visual authority of the film. Each performance takes her closer to her ultimate disappearance from the film.[11] When Camille kills the French officer (an act ironically enabled by her revolutionary French upbringing), she disappears from French eyes and appears only to Vietnamese audiences. In order to escape detection by the colonial police, Camille and Jean-Baptiste travel with Communist friends of Thanh, disguised as a troupe of wandering folk opera performers, who were also popular subjects for colonial postcards.[12] Camille and Jean-Baptiste are both incorporated into the opera as characters, or images for the native audience. Thus Camille returns to being the object of a gaze; this time, however, it is a native gaze, not a colonial gaze.

At the same time, Camille's image is being disseminated throughout the country as "la Princesse Rouge" in a folk opera that tells the story of Camille and Jean-Baptiste's love affair, and Camille's murder of the French official. The title "la Princesse Rouge" is significant in that it claims Camille as doubly Vietnamese: hereditarily (she is a member of the Vietnamese royalty), as well as politically (she is an anticolonial Communist). Thus Camille becomes an imaginary native, or a simulacrum whose image is repeated over and over, on folk opera stages all throughout Vietnam. Her disappearance from the French (colonial authoritative) gaze is replaced by her appearance-as-image ("la Princesse Rouge") to a native (Vietnamese/Communist) gaze. Furthermore, this image is transmitted back to Eliane, who has gone to see the actress playing "la Princesse Rouge," in the vain hope that she might be Camille.

Camille's disappearance from the French gaze in the film is mirrored by her disappearance from the film itself. After she is caught by the French authorities and sent to Poulo Condore prison, she is seen only once more in the film: after being released from prison, she commands Eliane to take Etienne and return to France, telling her "ton Indochine est morte" ("your Indochina is dead"). By the end of the film, Camille's disappearance is complete. Not even her son Etienne, who has gone specifically to the Geneva Convention to meet her, can recognize her. She has evolved completely beyond the scope of the French gaze. The only way she still exists is as a colonial memory, a character in a story told by Eliane, the French colonizer.

How can we read this banishment, this disappearance from the film that is imposed upon Camille's character? One way to interpret it is as punishment for a native who refuses her identity as fantasy: she is disappeared from the French authorial text and denied a place in the (French version of) history. Another way to read Camille's disappearance places more agency in her hands. In this reading, the different performances of native identities that Camille demonstrates are key. With each performance, Camille evolves further away from the fantasy native constructed by the French colonizer. Yet each performance, up until her disappearance, remains scripted in the French imagination, present in the form of colonial postcards. It is only Camille's final incarnation, as a radical (Communist) liberation fighter, that escapes the French imagination. A postcard entitled "Type de jeune femme communiste" ("Type of young Communist woman") simply doesn't exist.

Losing Indochina, Keeping "Indochine"

Indochine is ultimately Eliane's story: she is the (colonial) authority who narrates the story and thus controls the production and dissemination of the text. More than that, "Eliane becomes the embodiment of the French colony in symbol and image, the "colonial Marianne"; simply put, she personifies Indochina." [13] *Indochine* is a story of lost love (colonial Indochina, Camille, etc.) for the French, while it is a story of war for the Vietnamese. As Madame Minh Tam (Thanh's mother) tells Eliane: "Je ne comprendrai jamais les histoires d'amour des Français. Il n'y a que folie, fureur, souffrance. Elles ressemblent à nos histoires de guerre." ("I will never understand the love stories of the French. There is nothing but madness, fury and suffering. They are like our stories of war.") For Eliane, Indochina is her home; she has lived all her life in Vietnam and even constructs her own identity as "Asiate."[14] Her pipe-dream is for Indochina to continue under the French protectorate; thus she "saves" the plantation for Camille and Etienne and further generations of Frenchified Vietnamese elite.

Camille, on the other hand, dreams of Indochina as a place where her people can live in freedom and peace. In her penultimate meeting with Eliane, Camille tells her about the emperor Minh Manh's search for the perfect burial spot. Once he had found it, he said, "Now I can die." Camille adds that, "Moi aussi, je rêve d'un liêu d'harmonie . . . mais pour y vivre" ("I also dream of a place of harmony . . . but to live there"). Eliane, not understanding the radical nature of Camille's statement, replies that such a place exists, indeed belongs to Camille and is waiting for her. While Camille is referring to the entire nation, Eliane means only the plantation, her domain. The two women have two separate dreams: Eliane's is keeping her "Indochine," that is, her private phantasmatic realm of a French-protectorate plantation; Camille's is a nationalist and/or Communist dream about regaining Vietnam.

In the end, Eliane loses Indochina but is still able to keep "Indochine," her dream, alive through her adoption and custody of Camille's son Etienne. Although she has lost all her (phantasmatic) objects of desire—Jean-Baptiste, Camille and Indochina—Eliane retains control over their substitute, Camille's French-Vietnamese métis son Etienne. It is no coincidence that Etienne is introduced into the film at the exact moment of Camille's resistance and subsequent disappearance from Eliane's gaze (directly after Camille's escape to join Jean-Baptiste). Etienne acts as both souvenir and memorial: as the son of both Camille and Jean-Baptiste, he represents a fusion of the two people Eliane loved and lost; as the "son" of Eliane, he represents Eliane's parental/protectorate power over Indochine(se). Eliane has lost the plantation, but she still keeps one souvenir of her "domain"—the native son.

Eliane's custody and protection of Etienne puts her in the position of the "good mother," a position the film itself is eager to promote for its own ideological reasons. The French were good protectors of Indochina, and they still are: just look at Eliane. In order to emphasize the positive impact France has had on Indochina, the film sets up a binary opposition between Camille and Eliane in terms of motherhood. Eliane, the "colonial Marianne," nobly adopts two orphaned (or abandoned) native children. Camille, on the other hand, is figured as a "monstrous mother"[15] who doesn't even know her son's name. She is forced to abandon her son the first time, when Jean-Baptiste was captured, but the second time she voluntarily turns him over to Eliane's care, choosing instead to join the nationalist/Communist struggle to liberate the country. In effect, Camille chooses nation over son, Communism over colonialism. This act in itself signifies monstrous motherhood to French colonial ideology. As both a French-educated native and a (French) mother, Camille is a failure. Her punishment is banishment from both her son's life and from the film itself. As Norindr argues, "Camille is denied not simply the status of mother but more problematically the status of subject on the screen."[16] In the end, even her son refuses to recognize her.

The film's ideological stake in this issue is great. The binary opposition Eliane = good mother/Camille = monstrous mother extends itself to encompass the more important binary opposition of France = good protectorate/Communism = bad protectorate. Communism, like Camille, is a monstrous mother, the film preaches. The Vietnamese are like children, and the Communists don't make good parents. They don't even know their own children's names . . . Wasn't it better when the French protected Indochina? The film *Indochine*, creating a phantasmatic nostalgia of the golden days of colonialism, leads the viewer to believe exactly that. With its complete disregard of both the Franco-Vietnamese and the American-Vietnamese wars, *Indochine* succeeds in its ideological goal of valorizing French colonization in Indochina: it is a French story of love, not a Vietnamese story of war. And those who could offer an opposing version (i.e., Camille), are silenced and "disappeared" from the filmic text.

Ironically, it is precisely Camille's banishment from the filmic text that reveals her status as phantasmatic or imaginary; as such, the imaginary native threatens to reveal the constructedness of the text itself, saying, like Rey Chow's indifferent native: "There was nothing—no secret—to be unveiled underneath my clothes. That secret is your phantasm."[17] Camille's status as an imaginary native is contingent upon the (con)text in which she is seen; in other words, Camille can exist only as an imaginary native *in a (neo)colonial text* such as *Indochine*. Looking for native subjectivity in such a text is similar to Gayatri Spivak's frustrated search for a subaltern with a voice in the colonial texts of the East India Company which she describes in her essay "Can the Subaltern Speak."[18] Camille, like Spivak's theoretical subaltern-who-can-speak, can only exist as an imaginary native in a colonial text. As an imaginary native, she has little or no power in the production of a colonial discourse (that power is reserved for Eliane). However, as an imaginary native, she is able to escape the colonizer's gaze, presenting herself as simulacrum ("the Princesse Rouge" performed over and over again) and pure image. In doing so, she demonstrates that her very presence (or lack thereof) in the colonial text reveals the fact that the colonial text itself is an imaginary construct.

The Reappearance of the *Congaie*: Contemporary Cover Art in France

The trend in neocolonial nostalgia is not only present in films such as *Indochine*, but can also be detected in the publishing industry of France today. France has been witness to a recent explosion in the publication of Vietnamese literature, both Francophone and in translation.[19] Many of these new editions and translations of Vietnamese novels and short stories are published by Editions de l'Aube, a relatively young Parisian publishing house specializing in what could be called third-world literature. The books that Editions de l'Aube publish are all mass-distributed, and can be found in any major bookstore in France. What interests me particularly is not only the text but also the images used on the covers of these books. Many of these covers feature images of Vietnamese women, such as Kim Lefèvre's *Métisse blanche* (*White métisse*) and *Retour à la saison des pluies* (*Return to the rainy season*). For both of these novels, reprinted in 2001 by Editions de l'Aube, the cover images (formerly illustrations) have been replaced by old tinted photographs of two separate Vietnamese women, both in pink *áo dài* (see figures 9.3 and 9.4).

Three other books published in 2001 by Editions de l'Aube feature either black and white or sepia-colored photographs on their covers. Two of these are collections of short stories by Nguyễn Quang Thiều, *La Fille du fleuve* (*The River Girl*) and *La Petite marchande de vermicelles* (*The Little Noodle Seller Girl*). Another is a novel by Hồ Anh Thái titled *L'Ile aux femmes* (*The Island of Women*). Of these three, *La Fille du fleuve*, shown in figure 9.5, has the raciest cover: that of a young Asian (presumably Vietnamese) woman squatting on a beach, completely naked. The photograph on *La Petite marchande*, though not so explicitly sexy, is also suggestive: a sensuous young Asian woman looks at the camera with her eyes half closed. The final cover, *L'Ile aux femmes*, shows two women washing their long black hair in a river (see figure 9.6). All of these photographs bear what I see as striking resemblances to old colonial postcards, resemblances that are perhaps deliberately manufactured to maximize their evocation of a colonial era, lost but not easily forgotten.

Figure 9.3: Cover illustration of *Retour à la saison des pluies* (Kim Lefèvre, Paris: Editions de l'Aube, 1995). Courtesy of Editions de l'Aube.

Figure 9.4: Cover illustration of *Retour à la saison des pluies* (Kim Lefèvre, Paris: Editions de l'Aube, 2001). Courtesy of Editions de l'Aube.

All of these book covers signal a trend in both publishing and advertising in France today: a shift towards colonial nostalgia that results in the production of neocolonial images such as these postcard/books. Furthermore, I see these new publications as more than just sporting postcard images on their covers. The old postcards functioned, as I argued earlier, as a reinforcement of the stereotypes created by the colonizers to imagine the native *congaie*; these stereotypical images would then be disseminated back to the Métropole as representative of some kind of colonial "reality." It becomes extremely interesting then to regard these new editions of "Vietnamese literature" published by Editions de l'Aube as a modern-day postcolonial genre of postcards. Instead of relying upon the photographer's lens to bring the "reality" of postcolonial Vietnam to the Métropole, the French can now read (through French translations) the actual literature (and by extension, experience) written by the Vietnamese themselves. It is not without significance, or even irony, that the back cover copy of *L'ile aux*

femmes refers to the film *Indochine* and includes a statement like "Un roman
. . . qui nous emporte au coeur des espérances et des contradictions des jeunes
Vietnamiens d'aujourd'hui" ("A novel . . . that takes us to the heart of the hopes
and contradictions of today's young Vietnamese"). Similarly, a quote by Alexie
Lorca on the back cover copy of *La Fille du fleuve* calls "[c]hacun de ces textes
. . . une mise en lumière du Viêt-Nam contemporain" ("each of these texts . . .
sheds light on contemporary Vietnam"). The packaging of these books suggests
that, by reading them, the reader will *know* the "real" Vietnam (or the real Vietnamese woman, as all of these books concentrate on women, both in their titles
and in their cover images), just as the recipient of a colonial postcard a century
ago could say "Aha! Now I know what a *congaie* looks like." If we take this
juxtaposition and analysis to the final step, then it should show that these texts,
like the postcards, like Camille, are only performing the stereotypes of the native Vietnamese woman, stereotypes created by the colonial order, and reinforced by the neocolonial market today.

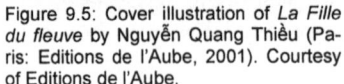

Figure 9.5: Cover illustration of *La Fille du fleuve* by Nguyễn Quang Thiều (Pa-ris: Editions de l'Aube, 2001). Courtesy of Editions de l'Aube.

Figure 9.6: Cover illustration of *L'Ile aux femmes* by Hồ Anh Thái. (Paris: Editions de l'Aube, 2001). Courtesy of Editions de l'Aube.

In conclusion, I would like to hint at a possible reason for this trend in neo-
colonialism present in France (and other ex-colonizing nations) today. I'd like
to suggest that it is in reaction to the current globalization and Europeanization

movements that the French find themselves faced with today. As Philip H. Gordon argues in his article "Liberté! Fraternité! Anxiety!"[20] the French are living in a state of great cultural anxiety in these modern days of globalization. No longer confident in a monolithic and omnipresent French Culture-with-a-capital-C, the French now turn to (colonial) nostalgia as the answer. Hence the increase in tourism to ex-colonies such as Indochine and renewed interest in the culture and literature of a country once ruled by France, a country that fueled so many phantasmatic desires and dreams in the French imagination. Camille may disappear, but the image and the ideal of the native *congaie* are forever engrained upon the French mind.

Notes

1. Panivong Norindr, *Phantasmatic Indochina: French Colonial Ideology in Architecture, Film and Literature* (Durham, NC: Duke UP, 1996), 16.

2. Albert Memmi, *Portrait du colonisé précédé de Portrait du colonisateur* (Paris: Gallimard, 1957 (1985)), 101. Translated by Howard Greenfeld, *The Colonizer and the Colonized* (Boston: Beacon Press, 1991 (1965)), 79.

3. Another way of referring to native Vietnamese of both genders was the derogatory term *annamite*. This term derives from the name of the central section of Vietnam under French colonial power: Annam (the other two sections were Tonkin in the North and Cochinchine in the South). Despite the geographic specificity of the term, most French colonials used *annamite* to refer to all native Vietnamese. The derogatory sense of the word is most likely retained from its Chinese usage: *An Nam*, literally "the pacified South" in Mandarin Chinese, was the name for Vietnam during China's thousand year-long occupation of the country, and hints at the disdain with which the Chinese viewed their southern colonized subjects.

4. Because sexual relationships between French colonials and native women were frowned upon, when it is discovered that Camille is in love with the French officer Jean-Baptiste Le Guen, the French girls at her school call her by the derogatory epithet *petite congaie*, meaning, in this context, "little whore."

5. This epithet is taken from a review of *Indochine* posted on Amazon.com, which describes Eliane's "adopted (Vietnamese) daughter [as] a China doll."

6. Eliane's homoerotic desire for Camille, crystallized in a scene in which Eliane obliges Camille to dance with her, may signify her identification with white male colonizers (such as her father Emile) who took native *congaie* mistresses.

7. "Tonkin. Femme annamite achevant sa toilette." Reprinted in Vincent Thierry, *Pierre Dieulefils, photographe-éditeur de cartes postales d'Indochine* (Aix-en-Provence: T. Vincent, 1997), 126.

8. See "Tonkin. Le repas aux champs" (Pierre Dieulefils, Hanoi, c. 1900), in Bernard Dupaigne, *Visages d'Asie* (Paris: Editions Hazan, 2000), 206.

9. Jennifer Yee, *Clichés de la femme exotique: un regard sur la littérature coloniale française entre 1871 et 1914* (Paris: L'Harmattan, 2000), 39. Author's translation.

10. Yee, *Clichés de la femme exotique*, 35.

11. Norindr uses the word "elision" in his discussion of this move in the film; however, I prefer "disappearance" for its political connotations, as well as to highlight the image-centricity of my argument.

12. See for example "Acteur de théâtre viétnamien. Hanoï (Mission Croisière Jaune 1932)" in Dupaigne, *Visages d'Asie*, 191.

13. Norindr, *Phantasmatic Indochina*, 135.

14. Norindr explains that Eliane's use of this term in the film does not have the common pejorative sense of "one who has gone native," but is rather used to mean "a French woman born in Indochina who has never left it" (*Phantasmatic Indochina*, 135).

15. I use this term in reference to both Marie-Hélène Huet and Rosi Braidotti's works on monstrous motherhood.

16. Norindr, *Phantasmatic Indochina*, 136.

17. Rey Chow, *Writing Diaspora: Tactics of Intervention in Contemporary Cultural Studies* (Bloomington, Indiana: Indiana University Press, 1993), 52.

18. Gayatri Spivak, "Can the Subaltern Speak?," *Marxism and the Interpretation of Culture*, ed. Cary Nelson and Lawrence Grossberg (Urbana, Illinois: University of Illinois Press, 1988), 271-313.

19. This publishing phenomenon is not limited to France. The United States has also experienced a similar increase in the publication of Vietnamese literature in translation as well as Vietnamese-American literature in the past decade or so.

20. Philip H. Gordon, "Liberté! Fraternité! Anxiety!," *London Financial Times*, January 20, 2002.

10

Trần Anh Hùng as Diasporic Filmmaker

Carrie Tarr

In this essay I aim to explore the way Trần Anh Hùng negotiates his position as a diasporic/exilic filmmaker and the ways in which his films can be addressed as diasporic/exilic films. Trần has been claimed both as a Franco-Vietnamese and as a Vietnamese filmmaker, and he also enjoys an international reputation.[1] I would however like to highlight here his position as a French filmmaker of Vietnamese descent, a position comparable to that of French filmmakers of Maghrebi descent, in order to emphasize both his hybridity and the potential of his work for troubling the homogeneity of French national cinema. This essay draws on Hamid Naficy's analysis of exilic filmmaking in *An Accented Cinema* and Laura U. Marks work on experimental intercultural cinema in *The Skin of the Film* to discuss aspects of Trần's work which enable them to be read as diasporic/exilic texts, specifically his nostalgic representations of the Vietnamese family, and cinematic strategies which privilege a multisensory but spatially and temporally distanced mode of viewing.[2] Firstly, however, I will situate his work in the context of other modes of postcolonial filmmaking in France in order both to underline its singularity and to argue, as veteran émigré filmmaker Lâm Lê suggested in his critical review of *L'Odeur de la papaye verte* (1993), that it expresses the desire of the "tronci" (a slang term for second-generation Vietnamese) to mediate their integration in France.[3] Trần's diasporic status derives from the arrival of his family in France from South Vietnam via Laos in 1975 when he was twelve and his subsequent education and career development in France.[4] His films set out both to reconstruct images of Vietnam that have been erased by his family's cultural dislocation and to provide audiences with alternative images of Vietnam from those dominant in French (and American) cinema. They draw on his knowledge of Vietnamese language and culture, his memories of childhood, and, in the case of his second and third feature films, the experiences of his subsequent return visits to Vietnam; they are all shot in Vietnamese and, with the exception of the short film *La Pierre de l'attente* (1991), they are set (and in the case of his second and third films, shot) in Vietnam. However, his filmmaking is informed by his professional training in France and an awareness of European and Japanese art/auteur cinema (he cites Bergman, Bresson, Kurasawa, Tarkovsky and Ozu as influences, among others); and his first three feature films have all been produced with French funding by Christophe Rossignon of Lazennec Films (who has also produced films by Mathieu Kassovitz). *L'Odeur de la papaye verte* drew on a primarily French crew and a nonprofessional "émigré" cast, while *Cyclo* (1995) featured Hong Kong star Tony Leung Chiu Wai alongside Le Van Loc (a nonprofessional Vietnamese actor) and *A la verticale de l'été* (2000) included both émigré and professional Vietnamese actors. Both *Cyclo* and *A la verticale de l'été* were shot by an international crew, the cinematographer for *A la verticale de l'été* being Mark Lee, an American of Taiwanese origin. Common to all three films is the luminous presence of Trần's actress wife Trần Nữ Yên Khê and the musical scoring of composer Tôn Thất Tiết, both of whom, like Trần himself, are French citizens of Vietnamese descent. All three films have enjoyed a successful domestic and international distribution, particularly *L'Odeur de la papaye verte*, which won the Caméra d'Or at Cannes, the César for Best First Film and was nominated for the Oscar for Best Foreign Film (as a "Vietnamese" film), while *Cyclo* won the Golden Lion at Venice.[5]

If a glance at the elements which go into the production of the films suggests the underlying hybridity, not to say internationalism, of Trần's work, what is striking in the films themselves is their attempt to deny or downplay that hybridity, and the historical events which have given rise to it. Their apparent reluctance to address hybridity and difference, in combination with an authorial style which has often been criticized as overly aestheticized, means that his work is not immediately comparable to that of other exilic/diasporic filmmakers working in (funded in) France.

First, although the foregrounding of Vietnamese characters and concerns in *L'Odeur de la papaye verte* can be seen as a response to the three French blockbusters of 1992, *Indochine* (Régis Wargnier), *L'Amant* (Jean-Jacques Annaud) and *Diên Biên Phu* (Pierre Schoendoerffer), films which project Eurocentric neocolonial fantasies of repossessing the land, people and culture of Vietnam, Trần's interest does not lie in providing a counter-history of Franco-Vietnamese relationships and/or of (the ending of) French colonialism in Vietnam, or in deconstructing the myths informing French heritage cinema.[6] He does not propose either alternative epic historical films, or an alternative self-reflexive political filmmaking practice in the manner of Lâm Lê's anticolonial film *Poussière d'empire* (1983). Rather, his films evacuate the presence of (and therefore

any political or cultural dialogue with) Western or other Southeast Asian characters. Their largely self-contained world may offer traces of past and present
Western and Asian influences (a Singer sewing machine, the sounds of curfew
sirens and jet planes, the musician's Conservatoire certificate and playing of
Chopin, Debussy and ragtime in *L'Odeur de la papaye verte*; the circulation of
the dollar, recuperated and recycled planes, a bullet-scarred hitman and the music of Radiohead in *Cyclo*; the music of the Velvet Underground, the story of
the mother's lover who died of starvation under the Japanese, a bottle of French
wine, and the atmosphere of the international hotel in Saigon in *A la verticale
de l'été*). However, while these traces may hint at the French, Japanese and
American occupations of Vietnam, or the impact of globalization on post *doi
moi* Vietnam, these concerns are not translated into the negotiation of relationships by and between characters of different origins and histories. Trần thus
avoids the type of intercultural cinema to be found in the work of filmmakers of
Algerian descent in France, whose films construct Algeria/Algerians primarily
from the point of view of second-generation immigrants (the *beur* generation),
and in relation to France/the French.

Equally, Trần's films do not engage with the question of Vietnamese immigration in France (or elsewhere) and the ways in which first or second-
generation Vietnamese immigrants negotiate their bicultural (or multicultural)
identities. French filmmakers of Maghrebi descent have typically disclaimed
and/or protested about their in-between status and lack of belonging in France,
addressing questions of ethnicity and exclusion in what often appear to be semiautobiographical realist films.[7] To my knowledge, however, the only film that
foregrounds the issue of Vietnamese immigration in France is a comedy, *Le Fils
du Mékong* (1992), by white French filmmaker François Leterrier, while issues
of hybridity and identity in postwar Vietnam are addressed in *Poussières de vie*
(1994), directed by Rachid Bouchareb, a filmmaker of Algerian descent. Significantly, Trần's only film to be set (in part) in France is his second short film,
La Pierre de l'attente, the second section of which takes place in a flat in the
13e arrondissement.[8] While the film hints at the continuing desolation caused
by the traumatic events of Vietnamese history, there are no interactions between
the Vietnamese immigrants and others.

It follows that Trần does not make autobiographical films, or inscribe himself personally within his films in the manner of Sophie Bredier, for example,
who, in *Nos traces silencieuses* (Sophie Bredier and Myriam Aziza, 2000), uses
the scars on her body to speculate about her identity and past as a Korean child
adopted by French parents. It is true that there are characters within each of
Trần's feature films who seem to be his authorial stand-ins: the musician in
L'Odeur de la papaye verte, the gangster Poet in *Cyclo* and the botanical photographer in *A la verticale de l'été*, each of whom are creative individuals
pulled between two worlds. The French-educated musician has to choose between his independent-minded, westernized girlfriend and the more traditional
subservient Mui (and chooses the latter). The Poet is torn between an attraction
to innocence and nostalgia for the past, and a drive towards cruelty and vio-

lence, a dilemma represented by his periodic nosebleeds (and which he eventually resolves by immolating—and perhaps purifying—himself in fire). The photographer is divided between two families, the legitimate one in Hanoi, the secret one in Halong Bay (a situation resolved by his wife's decision to accept his unorthodox situation in return for love and openness). Trần has described the photographer's situation as in some respects like his own,[9] and the development of this series of stand-in characters from film to film perhaps reflects Trần's own trajectory from a nostalgic return to roots, via the horrified discovery of present-day corruption and violence in Ho Chi Minh City, to the acceptance of a more complex identity in the more contemplative atmosphere of Hanoi. But if these conflicted individuals can be read as projections of Trần's changing attitudes toward Vietnam, they do not engage with the social and historical realities of his displacement, exile and hybridity.

Finally, he does not make social realist or documentary films. Though his films draw on ordinary people and everyday life in Vietnam, as do various contemporary Vietnamese films like Viet Linh's *L'Immeuble* (2000), his distance from social realism is underlined by his obsession with perfecting the look and sound of his films, evident in the fact that *L'Odeur de la papaye verte* was shot in the studio of Bry-sur-Marne, that *Cyclo* necessitated the construction of an entire block of flats in Cholon, and that in *A la verticale de l'été*, streets and walls were repainted (and even the sentences in the dialogue lengthened) to achieve the desired artistic effect. The subject matter of his films is effectively distanced by an authorial style characterized by the self-conscious use of color, composition, camera and lighting, evocative sound and music tracks, carefully paced editing and ambiguous, elliptical narratives, all markers of European art cinema.

It is clear, then, that Trần's work is not typical of other "second generation" or diasporic filmmakers in France, nor of more experimental, intercultural filmmakers, whose films "make visible colonial and racist power relations."[10] One might account for this through a consideration both of the particular legacy of France's colonial rule in Vietnam compared with that in Algeria, for example, and through the particular material constraints on Trần's filmmaking. First, for a variety of reasons, immigrants of Vietnamese descent are less subject to racism and exclusion than immigrants of Maghrebi origin. On the one hand, the French war in Indochina involved fewer indigenous French than the war in Algeria, memories of it are more distant, and it has been displaced in public awareness by the American war in Vietnam (as well as the French war in Algeria). Indeed, as Alec Hargreaves points out, Vietnamese refugees are seen as victims of the Cold War/Communist regime rather than as former colonial "natives,"[11] and are also perceived as being more middleclass and having significant business skills in comparison with unskilled laborers from the Maghreb. On the other, as Nicola Cooper has observed, Vietnamese immigrants have also seemingly been willing to invest in the neocolonial stereotype of the "good immigrant" invented by the majority French, as a way of avoiding visibility and racism. She describes the characteristics of the stereotype as "peaceful, apolitical, discreet, undemanding, not causing any fuss, industriously pursuing economic objectives, and slipping quietly unnoticed into the background."[12] Trần's first feature, as Lâm Lê's review suggests, typically avoids material that would antagonize either the majority French or the various waves of Vietnamese immigrants, all with their own political agendas. His second and third features are even further constrained by his desire to build bridges with the government of Vietnam and avoid censorship.

Arguably, however, despite his sidestepping of history and actuality, Trần's reconstructions of the sounds, images and people of Vietnam (what Jean-Pierre Jeancolas calls his "mental Vietnam"[13]) are still typical of the work of exilic postcolonial filmmakers who aim to recapture elements of their culture of origin by drawing on "stories that unfold under non-Western chronotopes."[14] Trần's declared desire to represent "the humanity of the Vietnamese"[15] and his references in interview to "the essence of the Vietnamese soul"[16] point to his desire as a diasporic filmmaker to access and control the meaning of the lost home country through film. As Hamid Naficy points out, many exilic filmmakers avoid addressing troubled contemporary realities and reconstruct the homeland through, for example, shots of an iconic timeless landscape. Trần's imagined Vietnam repeatedly draws on nostalgic, idealized representations of the rituals of everyday family life and iconic, timeless images of the Vietnamese woman. Such imagery makes the films easily available for consumption by an international art house audience, for whom Vietnam may be simply a place of exotic reverie and/or an intended tourist destination. Their "peaceful, apolitical, discreet" nature even begs the question as to whether they actually reproduce certain neocolonial stereotypes.

Trần's liminality, his geographic and cultural displacement, is marked stylistically in particular by his use of framing strategies (from behind plants, screens, windows, door frames or shutters; from the point of view of a free-floating moving camera; from unexpected angles), which invite the spectator to experience this imagined world from a distance. Distancing is also achieved through other devices: the careful use of lighting, color and composition; long, slow panning shots over the interiors; languid pacing and long takes; a paucity of dialogue; and the frequent use of nonnarrative close-ups. These devices may impede emotional involvement with the narrative and characters, but they invite the spectator to enjoy not just voyeuristic pleasures but also other sensory experiences evoked by Trần's use of image and sound.

For Laura U. Marks, "Intercultural cinema has quite specific reasons for appealing to the knowledge of the senses insofar as it aims to represent configurations of sense perception different from those of Euro-American societies, where optical visuality has been accorded a unique supremacy."[17] In her discussion of L'Odeur de la papaye verte, she suggests that the "sensuous intensity" of the film, exemplified in the rituals involved in the gathering, cutting, preparing and admiring of the green papaya (a metonym for Vietnamese cuisine and a homage to the remembered gestures of Trần's mother) awakens synaesthetic experiences of smell, touch and taste (in addition to sight and sound), that enable spectators to recall (or imagine) a mythical or forgotten past and so "embodies the exile's nostalgia."[18] Arguably, however, Trần's use of close-ups, slow pacing or long takes may also isolate sensory moments from their sociocultural and narrative context, and enable spectators to take pleasure in them for their own sake, as "art," or in order to make rhizomatic connections. Just as Trần's narratives work to evacuate history, so the spaces of his films periodically evacuate place, making the sensory moments available for consumption (or rejection) by a variety of audiences. As I will go on to show, configurations of sense perceptions, along with representations of the family not only mark him as a diasporic filmmaker but also indicate why he has enjoyed an international success.

Figure 10.1: A nostalgic sensory moment: Mui (Lu Man San) learns to prepare food in *L'Odeur de la papaye verte* (1993). Courtesy of the Ronald Grant Archive.

Trần's first three feature films are all structured by family narratives. *L'Odeur de la papaye verte* is explicitly nostalgic in its linear, if elliptical, evocation of the past (set in 1951, then dissolving to 1961), whereas *Cyclo* and *A la verticale de l'été* are set in the present and interweave simultaneous multiple narrative strands. However each film is marked by instability, separation and loss, in particular in relation to the parents' generation. In *L'Odeur de la papaye verte*, the protagonist Mui is separated as a child from her biological parents and as a young woman from her surrogate mother, the mistress in the household where she works; the mistress herself is separated from her parents and has lost her own daughter, her mother-in-law's husband is dead, and her own husband disappears (as he has before) and subsequently dies. In *Cyclo*, the parents are dead, brother and sister become separated, the Poet-gangster has been abused and then is rejected by his father, the Boss Lady loses her mentally handicapped son and has been abandoned by the child's father (and fixes on the cyclo-driver as a surrogate son). In *A la verticale de l'été*, the parents are dead, the sisters' lives are troubled by suspicions of infidelity (including on the part of their dead mother), the eldest sister and her husband are both secretly committing adultery and the husband has an alternative family elsewhere.

Nostalgia for the lost family is asserted through the incorporation of family photographs (a device typical of diasporic films), as a way of fixing the past. Photographs adorning the altars to the ancestors (the father-in-law and daughter in *L'Odeur de la papaye verte*, the parents in *A la verticale de l'été*) call attention both to their absence and to the desire for their continuity and presence. A similar function is filled by the photograph of the Poet as a child with his mother in *Cyclo*, and the photographer's photos of his lover and child in *A la verticale de l'été*, while in *Cyclo* (which is dedicated "to my father and Serge G."), the absence/presence of the cyclo-driver's dead father is constructed instead through an opening voice-over of the father's words of guidance to his son and through a dream which leaves the son feeling as though he is inhabiting his father's body.

The destruction of the parents and the fragmentation or destabilizing of the family can be seen as metonyms for the loss of family caused by Vietnam's troubled history and for the perceived loss of authority of the parents' generation brought about by the experience of exile. However, Trần counteracts this fragmentation and loss through devices which seek to restore family values, in particular through ambivalent narrative resolutions and the fetishizing of the young Vietnamese woman, devices which also evoke a sense of nostalgia and longing in relation to an imagined, absent idealized family/Vietnam.

Each film is structured in a cyclical manner, ending with the partial restoration of the family and a new beginning. In *L'Odeur de la papaye verte*, ten-year-old Mui's initiation into a life of willing domestic service is followed by her employment by the man she loves and thence to her becoming his lover and pregnant with his child (a last image pans from her smiling face to the approving figure of Confucius). In *Cyclo*, after a depiction of the daily life eked out by his honest, toiling family, a young cyclo-driver becomes forcibly embroiled in violence, murder, drugs and madness while his older sister becomes a prostitute and gets raped; however when the cyclo-driver is finally released from the criminal gang to which he had been assigned, a long, high-angle panning shot shows him reunited with his family, pedaling them through the streets of Ho Chi Minh City. *A la verticale de l'été* begins with the joyful rituals of family life, specifically preparations for the commemoration of the mother's death,

then uncovers the tensions and infidelities in the lives of the three sisters and
their menfolk before ending a month later with the anticipation of their reunion
to commemorate the death of the father. Despite the costs involved—Mui's
acceptance of traditional feminine subservience, the cyclo-driver's dependence
on his Boss Lady (and an anarchic economy), the sisters' acceptance of doubts
and compromises in their lives—the ambivalent endings of these films fore-
ground the desired restoration of a semblance of harmonious family life.

The films also compensate for the instability of the family by offering fixed
images of Vietnamese womanhood, embodied in Trần's wife, actress Trần Nữ
Yên Khê. Instead of fetishizing the landscape of the homeland, Trần fetishizes
the figure of the young Vietnamese woman, variously offering up her face,
smile, hair, feet and gestures to the voyeuristic spectator, whether as the innocent young servant woman in *L'Odeur de la papaye verte*, the reluctant sister-
prostitute in *Cyclo*, or the flirtatious but innocent youngest sister in *A la verticale de l'été*. In each case, narratives which underline women's self-sacrificing
nature, embodied in Trần Nữ Yên Khê's graceful, choreographed performances
(during which she is regularly lit as an "icon"[19]), set out to convince of the timeless, untouchable beauty and purity of the woman, even when, as in *Cyclo*, she
is subjected to unspeakable (if unvisualized) sexual abuse.

Figure 10.2: The fetishized sister-prostitute (Trần Nữ Yên Khê)
and the Poet (Tony Leung Chiu Wai) in *Cyclo* (1995).

Trần's representation of children is another way of evoking nostalgia for
the family. If the first part of *L'Odeur de la papaye verte* centres on the experiences of Mui, it also represents the disturbed young boys of the household who
make her life difficult, frightening her with a lizard, for example. (In his preface
to the screenplay of *Cyclo*, Trần recalls with some shame his own assaults on

little girls when he was a schoolboy.[20]) In *Cyclo*, childhood is evoked nostalgi-
cally, if ambivalently, in the Poet's poetry (and in the song sung by veteran mu-
sicians) as well as through a brief flashback to the Poet's childhood. But the
film is also punctuated with both diegetic and non-diegetic shots of young children, including an unattached montage of children's faces accompanying the
Poet's flashback, another of children in school singing after the Poet carries out
an execution, and shots of children in a school classroom making music accompanying the final credits.[21] *A la verticale de l'été* (which is dedicated to Trần's
wife and child) is permeated by the theme of pregnancy and parenthood, be it
imagined, incipient, real or rivaled, and includes shots of the child "Little
Mouse" which have no particular narrative function. How are these nonnarrative evocations of childhood to be read?[22] Though on the one hand they
may suggest social change and/or hopes and fears for the future, arguably, like
the timeless images of the Vietnamese woman, they also embody the diasporic
director's longing for a fantasized, lost, innocent, stable past.

Among the structures of feeling which inscribe the personal and social experiences of exile, Naficy counts not just retrospectiveness and liminality, but
also tactility, a feature which is taken up by Marks. Certainly the tactile quality
of Trần's filmmaking is very evident, as is the sensuality of his selective use of
sound, which creates an imaginary Vietnam through the natural sounds of bull-
frogs, cicadas and water, through the texture of human voices—deliberately
infrequent in *L'Odeur de la papaye verte* and *Cyclo*, and contrived to produce
harmonious rhythms in *A la verticale de l'été*—and through a haunting, hybrid
music track (created by Tôn Thất Tiết) which mixes diegetic Vietnamese popular songs and music, and nostalgic or hallucinatory western music, with non-
diegetic music using traditional Vietnamese instrumentation, and which invites
the spectator to enter a kind of dream state. The patterns and repetitions of
Trần's visual style similarly activate cultural memories as well as lending themselves to the imagination, evoking colors, textures, tastes and smells, in particular through the use of close-ups and long takes. *L'Odeur de la papaye verte*
offers close-ups of insects, animals and plant life and scenes which crystallize
rites of passage: the disturbed elder boy's torture and destruction of ants in can-
dle wax; Miu's application of lipstick. *A la verticale de l'été* offers lingering
shots of food preparation, the interior décor of the art-filled apartments, and
sensuous moments in the lives of the three sisters (the eldest sister kissing her
lover through a silk veil; the middle sister washing her husband's hands; the
youngest sister's waking rituals with her brother, to the sound of Lou Reed).
Arguably the close-ups of jackfruit and chicken skin in this film are less pleas-
urable than the close-ups of papayas in *L'Odeur de la papaye verte*, and are
linked, not with the anticipation of a fruitful future, but rather with the women's
playful revelations about their feelings of disgust towards the male sex. The
film thus opens up more of a disjunction between the surface harmony of the
imagery and an underlying "reality" (underlined by the fragmented narrative
and at times surprisingly abrupt, elliptical cutting). Nevertheless, like *L'Odeur
de la papaye verte*, *A la verticale de l'été* repeatedly invites the spectator to take

pleasure in nonnarrative moments that play on the senses, a good example being the close-up of water movement and light in the bowl given to the eldest sister by her lover.

However the effects of the close-up, slow pacing or long take may be two-fold: on the one hand they may highlight moments of significant, sensory ex-perience related to the film's narrative or setting; on the other they may (tempo-rarily) remove them from their narrative and spatial context, resulting in an at times rather abstract experience (a focus on color, texture and composition for their own sake). This element of abstraction, present to a degree in both *L'Odeur de la papaye verte* and *A la verticale de l'été*, is particularly evident in *Cyclo*, potentially Trần's most political film, which was inspired by the shock of his first visit to Ho Chi Minh City in 1991. *Cyclo*'s negative, nightmarish vision of the city as the result of *doi moi* and uncontrolled westernization (or by implication the earlier years of American intervention in Vietnam) is neverthe-less traversed by nostalgic longing for family life, an insistence on the funda-mental innocence of the cyclo-driver and his sister (enhanced by repeated close-ups of his flip-flops and her face) and sensory memory-images of Vietnamese insects, animals and plants (like the young prostitutes eating ripe papayas, the Poet cutting open a betel nut flower). However, the film's appeal to the senses also includes erotic images of the sister's prostitution (as when her stocking is cut open to reveal her toes) and surreal images of the cyclo-driver's descent into hell (a little model skeleton plunged into a goldfish tank, a struggling goldfish flapping from the cyclo-driver's mouth, the cyclo-driver's blue-painted face), which draw attention to various international influences on Trần's work. The cyclo-driver's drug-induced painting of his body with blue paint recalls *Pierrot le fou* (Jean-Luc Godard, 1965); shots of pigs being butchered in an abattoir were inspired by the paintings of Francis Bacon; the spectacle of Mr Lullaby demonstrating a killing or the Poet executing the client who raped the cyclo-driver's sister resonate with images from Tarantinoesque gangster films. *Cyclo* is thus a more hybrid film than *L'Odeur de la papaye verte* or *A la verticale de l'été*, mixing diasporic nostalgia with postmodern violence in a way that dis-tances audiences from the film's concerns with contemporary Vietnam.

Arguably, then, unlike the experimental intercultural films discussed by Marks, Trần's attempts to capture the "essence of the Vietnamese soul" result in films which sidestep or downplay contemporary historical and political realities and intercultural experiences, and betray instead the diasporic filmmaker's muted anguish and desire for the lost homeland. Rather than foregrounding the ways in which the Vietnamese family and Vietnamese womanhood have been transformed by history and by intercultural experience, Trần's films work to reassert traditional images of family and womanhood. These nostalgic, idealized representations of the family are inseparable from a sensual cinematographic style that evokes nostalgic, multisensory memory-images of the homeland typi-cal of the diasporic filmmaker. However Trần's audiovisual imagination is not bounded by memory-images, and his evident pleasure in the cinematic possi-bilities of sound and image create spaces for imagery that also circumvents the specificity of Vietnamese geography and culture.[23] In the end, his first three feature films allow for both a nostalgic and an exoticizing vision of Vietnam, comforting to Western audiences because they do not fundamentally challenge perceptions of the East. What is significant about Trần Anh Hùng's work, then, is not just the particular "phantasmatic" representation of Vietnam that it offers, but the fact that a contemporary French filmmaker of Vietnamese descent in France has been able to make films of this nature. It is hard to imagine a film-maker of Algerian descent being able to make similar films about Algeria and enjoying a similar international success.

Notes

My thanks to Tess Do and Panivong Norindr for their helpful comments on my original conference paper.

1. Vietnamese names put the family name first followed by the middle and given names. In Vietnamese, the given name, which appears last, is the name used to address someone. Following other critics writing in English, I will refer to Trần Anh Hùng by his family name, Trần.

2. Hamid Naficy, *An Accented Cinema: Exilic and Diasporic Filmmaking* (Princeton and Oxford: Princeton University Press, 2001); Laura U. Marks, *The Skin of the Film: Intercultural Cinema, Embodiment, and the Senses* (Durham: Duke University Press, 2000).

3. Lâm Lê, "La petite Cosette du delta du Mékong," *Libération*, June 9, 1993, 42-43.

4. Trần's family settled in the Parisian banlieue of Villeneuve-Le-Roi. Trần first studied philosophy, then, inspired by Lâm Lê's anticolonial film *Poussière d'empire* (1983), took up cinematography at the Louis Lumière School in Paris.

5. It should however be noted that Trần's attempt to make a film about a modern-day Christ did not receive funding, suggesting that his choice of topic may be curtailed by the expectations of producers.

6. Such myths are still in evidence, as in Marco Pico's TV film, *Leclerc: Un rêve d'Indochine* (2002).

7. Trần's fourth feature film, *Night Dogs*, an adaptation of an American novel by Kent Anderson, is based on the story of an American Vietnam vet (and set to the music of Jimi Hendrix).

8. This film draws on a Vietnamese legend according to which a fisherman, after discovering his wife is actually his sister, abandons her, leaving her and their child to wait, hopelessly, for his return (and get turned to stone). In Trần's film, the incestuous couple first meet in a camp for displaced Vietnamese (boat people), and the man (played by Lâm Lê) discovers that the woman (played by Trần Nữ Yên Khê) is actually his sister, only when they are married with a child and living in Paris. Having already lost the rest of their family at sea, the loving but illicit couple face once more the anguish of separation and loss.

9. See Geoffrey McNab, "Good Afternoon Vietnam," *Sight & Sound* 8 (2001): 27-28.

10. Marks, The Skin of the Film, xii.

11. Alec G. Hargreaves, "Ethnic difference in post-war France," in *Immigrant Narratives in Contemporary France*, eds. Susan Ireland and Patrice J. Proulx (Westport, Conn. and London: Greenwood Press, 2001), 10.

12. Nicola Cooper, *France in Indochina: Colonial Encounters* (Oxford and New York: Berg, 2001), 200.

13. Jean-Pierre Jeancolas, "*L'Odeur de la papaye verte*: Un Viêt-nam mental," *Positif* (July-August 1993): 22-23.

14. Dina Sherzer, "Introduction," in *Cinema, Colonialism, Postcolonialism: Perspectives from the French and Francophone Worlds*, ed. Dina Sherzer (Austin: University of Texas Press, 1996), 11.

15. Jacqueline Artus, "Qu'elle était verte, ma papaye," *Le Nouvel Observateur*, June 10, 1993.

16. Michel Pascal, "Cyclo Driver," *Le Point*, September 23, 1995. Trần's notions of "soul" and "authenticity" suggest a nostalgic desire for essence and fixity rather than an openness to historical and social change.

17. Marks, The Skin of the Film, xiii.

18. Marks, The Skin of the Film, 223.

19. See for example, Andrew O. Thompson, "Vicious Cycle," *American Cinematographer* 77, no. 9 (September 1996): 68.

20. Laurence Trémolot and Trần Anh Hùng, *Cyclo* (Paris: Actes Sud, 1995), 6.

21. Other examples include shots of young boys and the cyclo-driver's little sister shining shoes, boys firing a firecracker at the Boss Lady's son, and a boy inviting the cyclo-driver's sister to a meal in the aftermath of the Poet's death.

22. These scenes could point to the cyclical nature of life, as suggested by the films' narrative structures. They could also hint at the loss of innocence that will follow growing-up and/or globalization (as suggested by *Cyclo*'s final panning shot of the city). They may link, too, with the theme of the doubling and interchangeability of characters, as with Mui and her mistress's daughter, the cyclo-driver and the Boss Lady's son, the various lovers and children of *A la verticale de l'été*.

23. After *A la verticale de l'été*, Trần declared that he was looking "to go beyond cultures and work on the specific materials of film art." See Jason Wood, "A Quick Chat with Trần Anh Hùng," <http://www.kamera.co.uk/interviews/trananhhung.html> (January 27, 2004).

11

From Incest to Exile:
Linda Lê and the Incestuous Vietnamese Immigrants

Tess Do

Writing explicitly about incest, even nowadays, is something that many authors might shy away from, especially when they are women and come from an Asian background like Linda Lê, a young Franco-Vietnamese writer. Not only is incest—even more than rape or adultery—cloaked in almost total silence in the real life of Vietnamese people, there are also very few accounts of incest in Vietnamese fiction, with the best-known examples to be found in the legend of the Waiting Wife Mountain (*Hòn Vọng Phu*), the story of Betel Leaf and Areca-Nut (*Trầu Cau*), and the myth of the Hundred Eggs (*Trăm Trứng*). Yet, the degree of incest varies greatly in these stories, from the sexual in *Hòn Vọng Phu* to the emotional in *Trầu Cau* and the spiritual in *Trăm Trứng*. Furthermore, incest has never been the focus of these stories. In *Trăm Trứng* the emphasis is on the origin of the Viet people and their descendants from the same womb of Mother *Âu Cơ* who gives birth to a hundred-egg bag that hatches into a hundred sons (or fifty boys and fifty girls according to some versions), the eldest being the forefather of the Vietnamese people. In *Hòn Vọng Phu* where brother and sister mistakenly marry and have a son from their incestuous relationship, the shameful truth is never revealed to the sister although the brother knows about it and decides to leave never to come back. In fact, the whole issue of incest is swept away, to be replaced by the theme of love and faithfulness, embellished by the image of the loyal (and exemplary) wife forever waiting for her husband's return from war. In *Trầu Cau* when an elder brother leaves home to look

165

for his younger sibling, prompting his own wife to set out to look for him, what is praised here is deep brotherly and conjugal love. When all three of them die of exhaustion at the same place by the river, the younger brother turning into a limestone, the elder brother into an areca tree and the wife into a vine, what is retained is the use of betel chewed along with areca nut and lime at traditional marital ceremonies to honor the trio's love. Little is said about how the identical twins fall in love with the same girl, who decides to marry the elder brother; how they all live in the same house and how, one day, upon his early return from work, the younger brother is warmly greeted by his sister-in-law who mistakes him for her husband, a mistake that causes the younger twin's departure.

The rarity of accounts of incest in Vietnamese fiction and the suppression of any issue of incest in the interpretation of well-known legends suggest that in Vietnamese culture incestuous passion and public representation of incestuous behavior have no doubt been nipped in the bud by the ancestor-worship and Confucian and Buddhist teachings which have shaped Vietnamese thinking for thousands of years, as well as by the rigid hierarchy that dominates Vietnamese social and family life. Placed in such a context, the occurrence of incest in Lê's work is both unusual and intriguing. The incestuous nature of a relationship is manifested in a variety of ways, from the metaphorical to the explicit, and mostly among a specific group of characters, young Vietnamese immigrants. What motivates them to commit such scandalous acts and what they seek from these relationships is far more than sexual pleasure. On the one hand, being Vietnamese and knowing very well the implications of Confucian doctrine, these young immigrants openly challenge Vietnamese family hierarchies and the authority of their parents by breaking the incest taboo. On the other hand, by creating an exclusive bond with each other, be it emotionally, spiritually or sexually, solely based on their ethnic background, they withdraw into themselves and reject any integration into Western society. Incest, in this context, is not simply a theme that Lê exploits in her work but rather a figure that stands for the ambivalent feeling and desire of the young Vietnamese immigrants. No matter how lost they feel in the Western world, no matter how strongly they desire to return to the (Vietnamese) womb, these exiled characters soon realize the impossibility of their dream. Since their incestuous union is the very force that destroys the family and the parental figures, it can never recreate the womb and bring back the lost paradise of childhood.

I will start my investigation of the incestuous relationships in Lê's work by recalling that incest is a term of multiple connotations. Depending on different definitions given by the *Littré*, *Robert*, or *Larousse* dictionaries, incest has been defined in terms of juridical aspects, sexuality, marriage or love. It is interesting to compare these with the Vietnamese definition. *Loạn luân*, synonymous with *loạn dâm*, is a Sino-Vietnamese term which means "to have heterosexual relations with those of the same family blood, contrary to customs or the law." Both terms include *loạn*, which means disruption, upheaval, disorder, chaos, rebellion. With *luân* meaning moral order in society, and *dâm*, sexuality, *loạn luân* and *loạn dâm* emphasize the disruptive consequences of incest, highlighting its rebellious aspect. Such concern to point out the antisocial behavior of incest and its threat to social order, in addition to the inexistence of any other terms for it in Vietnamese, clearly indicates that incest, as conceived today by the Vietnamese, is heavily infused with Confucian thought. It defines (and condemns) sexual acts that shake the social and familial hierarchy imposed by Confucian doctrine: King—Teacher—Father for men; Father—Husband—Son for women, and filial obligation for all. Set against this moral background, the manifestations of incest among Lê's Vietnamese characters are invested with the full strength of rebellion.

Among the dozen novels Lê has written, *Les Trois Parques* is the book that describes the most spectacular case of incest between Vietnamese characters, a case that will shed light onto other incestuous relationships.[1] Unlike the other novels where the immigrants are referred to vaguely as Asians from a mysterious, far-away "Pays" (Country), *Les Trois Parques* is the only book which specifies the ethnic origin of its immigrant characters as Vietnamese and the country they come from as Vietnam. To Lê, this book bears the mark of one of the greatest losses in her life, that of her father in Vietnam in 1995. With the disappearance of her beloved father, Lê has been deprived of the reader for whom she has been writing ever since she published her first novel in 1986. In an interview with the magazine *Lire* Lê declared: "Tant que mon père était en vie, tous mes livres lui étaient adressés. Il était mon lecteur idéal, mon lecteur imaginaire" ("As long as my father was alive, all my books were addressed to him. He was my ideal reader, my imaginary reader").[2] In the sudden void that surrounds her, Lê lets herself explode with the pain and anger of an abandoned child. Using incest as one of the means of destruction she mocks and defies the parental figures who, in her eyes, have failed in their duty towards their children.

Les Trois Parques is a sarcastic, gripping tale of three young Vietnamese cousins in a Parisian suburb. Before migrating to France, one of them, Manchote, the handicapped cousin, harbored incestuous feelings for her twin brother who ended up raping her. By exposing their love and living it to the point of non-return when brother and sister join each other in sexual union, Manchote and her twin break all taboos and cross all moral boundaries. This transgression makes them the exemplary case of incest and rebellion that could be seen as a climax of all other cases where relationships are kept platonic. The twins' sexual consummation of their love is unprecedented: none of the other couples, Mortesaison and her twin brother in *Les Dits d'un idiot*, the crazy uncle and his sister, the shoemaker and the female narrator in *Calomnies* (*Slander*),[3] dares to go as far in defying the moral system and the parents' authority. Coming after both *Les Dits d'un idiot* and *Calomnies*, which also portray Asian characters, *Les Trois Parques* marks a real breaking point where passion climaxes, and both secret and hymen are broken. Manchote lost her virginity and exposes her illicit love in the same way as she reveals the name of her mysterious "Country," publicly disclosing what she considers as the shameful secret of her origins. Shame and love are intertwined in both cases, and we can see a clear parallel between the incestuous coupling of Manchote and her twin brother, and the monstrous coupling of Lê and Vietnam, the lost homeland she has been carrying inside her like the dead fetus of her twin. In this metaphor the discovery of the rotten fetus stands for the shocking revelation of the twins' incestuous relationship. In a violent outburst of sexual desire, the twin rapes his sister and literally rips her open. The deflowering of the fifteen year-old girl is described in extremely violent terms:

> Il y avait du sang par terre, du sang sur les cuisses de la cousine, du sang sur sa lèvre sucée, mordue par le fêlé, qui avait enchâssé son pieu dans l'écrin étroit, ses mains plaquées contre les fesses de son petit cœur pur et sa langue de chiot affamé fouillant dans l'oreille, les narines de sa petite chose, à qui chaque enfoncement du pal arrachait grimaces de douleur et soupirs d'extase. Ils étaient là, soudés l'un à l'autre, cuirassés contre le monde extérieur. Le dreadnought, sans peur et sans reproches, embouquait, prenait la passe, perçait jusqu'au fond du canal. Les voix derrière la porte signalaient l'approche de l'ennemi. Mais, quand la porte s'ouvrit, quand les pas s'approchèrent de l'armoire, au lieu de virer, il avait continué à s'enfoncer, sa bouche aspirant la lèvre de la jumelle. Les cris ne les avaient pas désemboîtés. Tout juste si elle avait baissé la tête, pour cacher son plaisir. Il avait fallu les frapper, tirer le fêlé en arrière pour qu'enfin les jumeaux aboutés s'arrachent l'un à l'autre. Et crac! Encore un grand amour cassé en deux. Avec du sang partout, à commencer par les cuisses de la petite vierge entée, pour la vie hantée par le scion greffé en elle.

> (There was blood on the floor, blood on the cousin's thighs, blood on her lips, sucked and bitten by the madman who had inserted his stake into the narrow case, his hands gripping the buttocks of his little sweetheart and his hungry puppy-like tongue groping in her ear and nostrils, causing her to grimace with pain and sigh in ecstasy. They were there, glued to each other, armed against the outside world. The dreadnought, fearlessly and blamelessly, was screwing, pouncing, drilling to the end of the channel. Voices behind the door signaled that the enemy was closing in. But when the door opened, when the footsteps came near the cupboard, instead of backing out, he went on plunging forward, his mouth sucking the twin sister's lip. The screams did not pull them apart. She had barely lowered her head to hide her pleasure. They had to be beaten, the madman had to be yanked backwards, so that the enjoined twins could be pulled apart. And crack! Another great love broken in two. With blood everywhere, starting with the thighs of the little virgin, who would be haunted for life by the scion grafted inside her.) [4]

At first sight, the terrible violence of this scene seems to denounce the culprits, especially the brother, and confirm the judgment of the parents who, horrified by what they have seen, rush in to break away the twins' embrace. By locking up their crazy son in a madhouse, the parents destroy the twins' bond and sentence their daughter to a solitary, loveless life where she spends the rest of her days regretting the blissful state of wholeness she once knew with her twin. The separation of the twins here recalls the first time when they were broken apart, at birth. In this perspective, what we normally see as birth is reversed into death, and the parents' interference is shown as a murderous act. Casting the parents in the unflattering role of tyrants, Lê invites us to read incest in a different way. In spite of the rape, the violence committed by the brother is not directed at his twin sister, but at the parents and the family. The incest between siblings thus becomes something much more serious than it has generally been considered by Western opinion: "Brother and sister incest is the most common type. Its consequence is less damaging because this type of incest does not cross generational boundaries and often is an extension of sex play."[5] In Lê's novels, incest reveals itself as something profoundly disturbing because it means both rebellion against and rejection of the parents. In fact, it foretells the symbolic murder of the father and announces the end of his reign as head of the family according to Confucian hierarchy. By penetrating the sister's flesh, the brother does not simply breach the incest taboo; the pressure that breaks the hymen also rocks the whole foundation of the Vietnamese family. For what, indeed, is more rebellious than this frenzied copulation where the children expose themselves, standing up and locked in embrace, in a fighting position, as little soldiers "soudés l'un à l'autre, cuirassés contre le monde extérieur" ("glued together, armed against the outside world")?[6] What is more aggressive in the parents' eyes than the furious thrusts of their son who is violating and piercing his sister's body, as if by brutalizing her flesh, he wanted to reach out and strike them? What is more provocative than this deflowering, this baptism in sweat and blood, performed by the brother, which removes the sister from the parents' supervision and authority? By marking her with "un scion greffé en elle" (TP, 182: "a scion planted inside her") and making her his possession, the brother lays claims on her body in the same way as would a father on his daughter's name. Thus, the sister's body becomes a battlefield where the son defeats the father and takes over his place. If by naming his daughter, the father imposes his paternity, then by taking his sister's virginity, the brother both leaves his stamp on her flesh and declares victory over their genitor. According to the Confucian familial hierarchy, as long as the father is alive, the unmarried daughter stays in the parental home and under his direct authority. But, after his death, authority is transferred to the eldest brother, and not to the mother. In fact, the Sino-Vietnamese term for "parents" reflects this transfer: *phụ huynh* means, word by word, "father" and "elder brother." In the Vietnamese family the elder brother is the father's substitute, replacing him when he is away and taking over his headship when he dies. Seen as such, both the Confucian concept of filial devotion and the supreme authority of the father are challenged by the son when he sexually takes possession of sister in front of his parents' very eyes. Faced with his children's incestuous mating and disobedience, the father loses his authority in the same irreversible way as his daughter loses her virginity.

In spite of the violent deflowering the daughter should not be viewed as a passive victim in the hands of her brother. On the contrary Manchote is no less aggressive and defiant than her twin. Firstly, she readily opened herself up "au premier venu" (TP, 181: "to the first man who came along") and carelessly got rid of her virginity in the pursuit of an immoral, condemnable love. Secondly, and most importantly, she dared to take that love to its sexual fulfillment and to exhibit her carnal pleasure in front of the parents' eyes, shamelessly showing everyone how she was enjoying herself. Among the three Parques (Fates), Manchote is in fact the only woman who has experienced great love and sex with, above all, a man of her own race and blood. Neither the married eldest sister nor the unmarried younger sibling who has moved from man to man, has ever known what love and pleasure are. That these women's relationships with Western men are disappointing is very interesting and significant. The younger sister, a frigid woman, has a French fiancé, but she soon tires of him. The sensual eldest sister fares no better in her love life when she married a cold-blooded German, "une brique sans défaut, bien lisse, bien droite, bien sèche" (TP, 76: "a perfect brick, very smooth, very straight, very dry"). One after the other, both sisters discover bitterly the reverse side of their men and the loneliness in their love lives, having never known the sweet taste of amorous complicity between two soulmates, as their cousin Manchote and her twin have. From an early age, brother and sister are inseparable: "ils restaient assis, collés l'un à l'autre, main dans la main, ils se chuchotaient à l'oreille et ne parlaient à personne" (TP, 211: "They sat glued together, hand in hand, they whispered in each other's ear and spoke to nobody"). In front of the family, they resist, standing side by side like real warriors "sans peur et sans reproche" (TP, 182: "fearless and beyond reproach"), sealing a lifelong alliance. Manchote and her brother are without doubt the most defiant incestuous characters in Lê's works. They adopt a much more challenging attitude than the couples who came before them. Their love survives the scandal and they do not die from shame or sorrow after being discovered. Separated from her twin, Manchote still holds on faithfully to her love. By contrast, the crazy uncle and his sister in *Calomnies*, for example, did not dare to expose or consummate their incestuous love: hiding in their room, they just read poems to each other. Far from being warriors, they were terrified children who "se sont aimés en tremblant" ("loved each other, trembling"), clinging to one another because "ils avaient peur du monde et de la malédiction dont le monde les menaçait"[7] ("they were afraid of the world and the curse it threatened them with"). Two factors can explain incest: the first is the inborn and universal need for roots, intimacy and protection; the second, the fear of the outside world and a feeling of insecurity.[8] In the case of the crazy uncle and his sister, fear has defeated them. After their separation, they did not survive the punishment of their family: with the brother locked away in a madhouse, the sister, left alone, could not bear the family's blame and accusations, and hanged herself. Years later, he too, killed himself in a fire. Unlike this defeated couple, Manchote and her twin were not afraid of the world. It was not fear, one must point out, that threw them into each other's arms, but quite the opposite. Their incestuous love, which makes them turn away from everyone else, is a choice that bears witness to their indifference and to disgust for the world around them. Manchote does not bear any resemblance to the fearful sister mentioned earlier because she was not crushed by the family's punishment. Incestuous and rebellious, she is one of Lê's most inflexible and invincible Vietnamese female characters, a true Atropos who firmly takes back control of her life.

Brother-sister incest, as it has been demonstrated through the example of Manchote and her twin, is not only a sign of rebellion against the family and Confucian values. In the context of the Vietnamese diaspora, it is also a fusion of Vietnamese blood. A refuge for the twins against the other members of the family, it becomes a barrage against the western world. In a group of foreigners, the fellow countryman understandably stands out as a close relative, justifying the Vietnamese proverb "A drop of blood means more than a pond of water." In this light, the incestuous relationships which bind the Vietnamese immigrants together reveal both their wish to regress back into their own people, and their refusal to mix with another race. Deep down, every wish to return to the source and preserve the purity of the race can be seen as profoundly incestuous. Such incest, consequently, goes beyond the union of two bodies and longs for a spiritual union. Instead of a sexual union with one's sister or brother in flesh and blood, one seeks the spiritual fusion of two souls. In *Les Dits d'un idiot*, Mortesaison's soulmate appears in the form of the mysterious brother called "le Jumeau" ("the Twin") who lives in some far away "Pays" ("Country").[9] This pair of twins, forerunners of the couple in *Les Trois parques*, represents the spiritual and platonic aspect of incestuous love, an aspect that comes before sexual fulfillment. In contrast to Manchote who has lived her incestuous love in Vietnam, Mortesaison is a young immigrant woman who has just arrived in France and whose future seems to be wide-open. However, what stops her from integrating in the new country, pushes her to live like a homeless wanderer, and forces her to run away from the French natives and their loves, is her burning desire to be among her own people. Another reason is her wish to keep herself chaste and pure for her Twin, a fellow countryman: "elle se réservait pour celui qui dans sa sentimentalité criminelle elle appelait le Jumeau, c'est avec lui qu'elle voulait se faire enterrer tête-bêche c'est comme ça qu'ils allaient fricoter ensemble" (*Les Dits*, 105: "she saved herself for the man who in her criminal sentimentality she called the Twin, it is with him that she wanted to be buried head to foot, this is how they were going to sleep together"). Because of her Twin, she ignores the sexual advances directed at her by her employer, a rich old man named Ragot who, in her eyes, fails in every way to measure up to her adored brother. Whatever Ragot can offer her, be it love, protection or financial security, in fact everything an immigrant can hope for in a new country, she flatly turns down. By rejecting the old man's love and proposal as unsatisfying, Mortesaison reveals her longing for something that Ragot, as a Frenchman, can never give her: a perfect union with a man who is, in every way, her equal and her fellow creature. Because of his age and his authority over Mortesaison,

Ragot represents par excellence the father figure against whom the young woman rebels in order to remain faithful to her Twin: she disobeys her employer's order to stay and leaves him for her brother who, she hopes, "finirait bien par quitter le Pays pour la retrouver" (*Les Dits*, 105: "would eventually leave the Country to come to join her"). Thus, like Manchote's brother, Mortesaison's Twin also removes his sister from paternal authority. Without claiming her sexually, the Twin nevertheless takes full possession of his sister's feelings. This time, the battlefield between the pseudo-father and the brother is not the sister's body but her mind and heart. With his letters and poems, the Twin counterattacks Ragot's discourses and advises, and wipes out the latter's imprint on his sister: "*il* avait toujours été là et ce que le vieux Ragot mettait dans le crâne de son élève *il* le retirait *il* quittait chaque nuit sa cachette pour reprendre possession de la demoiselle de compagnie détruisant ainsi l'œuvre accomplie le jour par le maître des lieux" (*Les Dits*, 177: "*he* was always there and what Ragot put in his pupil's head *he* removed it every night *he* left his hiding place in order to regain possession of the young lady companion destroying thus what had been achieved during the day"). Although there is no physical contact between brother and sister, Mortesaison's love for her Twin is no less intense. In her eyes, the Twin incarnates the soul of the faraway homeland she sorely misses. His letters reach her like incessant calls, silently blaming her for having gone abroad, and tirelessly pursuing her in her exile. This is how we should read the Twin's letters. Going beyond the writer's text, they become the voice of the homeland, a voice that echoes in Mortesaison's heart and sticks on her skin, like a stench, that of the river by her brother's house. It seems that Mortesaison's fate is sealed: her face is described as that of a child who has aged too soon and her appearance that of a "veuve" (*Les Dits*, 24: "widow"). No doubt when her Twin dies, she will be his widow. But above all, as long as she lives in a foreign land, in exile and uprooted, "pas de famille pas d'amis pas de logis" (*Les Dits*, 55: "with no family no friends no home") she will always be the widow of her Country and countrymen. Just as her name, Mortesaison, indicates, she will live among the dead, in the heart of the dead season, because she has run away from the living people around her and taken refuge in the company of her twin's letters. Holding onto them, she shows how much she wanted to maintain this fraternal bond with him, and how clearly she has heard the call of the homeland. Through her love for her brother, she attempts to reach her Country and reconcile herself with her origins. That the Twin is described as "le visiteur caché de la nuit" (*Les Dits*, 177: "the hidden guest of the night") and the trigger of Mortesaison's sentimental feelings, places him in the realm of the subconscious and the emotions. For the same reason, the Twin is only a name: a bodiless character, he only exists on paper, in letters, and in the stench of the river. If, on the one hand, his immateriality makes him the very incarnation of the beloved-but-lost homeland, on the other hand, his twinning with Mortesaison also lets him act as her double, her conscience, and her Vietnamese ego who has been suppressed in exile.

Nostalgia for this other half, either lost or buried within oneself, endows sibling incest with a narcissistic scope where love for the other is also a form of self-love. The unity of each twin couple is the most striking manifestation of this narcissism. The incestuous relationship that binds Manchote and Mortesaison with their respective twin/lover reaches such a degree of intensity that their burning desire for unity is transformed into a desire for a complete symbiotic fusion, for in no other coupling can they find a union that binds together two perfectly equal beings. Quasi-identical in their genetic codes, inseparable from the very first moment of conception, brother-sister twins recall most vividly the fantastic image of an androgynous being. Both male and female, the latter represents unity and wholeness before the separation of the sexes, and from the mother's body. Brother-sister incest is therefore an attempt at regression to the womb and to childhood, with the hope of recreating the lost unity. In a union that brings together heart and body, the twins seek to prolong their primal bond and come back to a lost paradise where they were united in blissful innocence without attracting any condemnation. Lê, in fact, is also looking for this lost paradise which, in her mind, is closely related to her early childhood in Vietnam. This paradise, however, is fraught with signs of its own destruction, just as behind their apparent unity, the twins already carry the seed of their separation. Vietnam, as a twin brother, represents in Lê's eyes both unity and loss: land of dreams, ancestors' land undivided, on the one hand; land of war and death, country cut in two at the seventeenth parallel, on the other. Separated from her homeland by war and exile, Lê visualizes her broken ties with Vietnam in the metaphor of her dead twin: "Ma patrie, je la porte comme ce jeune paysan portait le foetus de son jumeau. C'est un lien monstrueux. Un lien où le pays natal, le jumeau donc, est couvé et étouffé, reconnu et nié. Et finalement porté comme on porte un enfant mort" ("My homeland, I carry it in the way that that young peasant carried the fetus of his twin. It's a monstrous bond. A bond where the homeland, the twin, is cocooned and suffocated, recognized and denied. And finally carried as one does a dead child").[10] Incestuous or monstrous ties, this is how Lê defines her relation to her birth country. In her works, incest has all the aspects of exile, separation, loss, regret, and loneliness, and all the longing of the exiled, return, reunion, belonging, wholeness. The return to the homeland (one might say motherland) or the psychological regression to the mother's womb, however, proves to be not only impossible but also fatal for the exiled twins. Manchote, Mortesaison, and the crazy uncle never return to their twins nor to their homeland. Their loss and separation are definitive and their painful search for unity only leads them to madness and death which, in a certain way, could be considered as an ultimate refuge.

In a wider and more general perspective, incest in Lê's works extends beyond the sexual encounters between twins to account for the spiritual bond among the Vietnamese people. The Vietnamese myth of origin makes the shift from blood relatives to fellow countrymen all the more evident. Born of the same womb, descendants of the same mythical parents—the Father Dragon *Lạc Long Quân* and the Mother Fairy *Âu Cơ*—all Vietnamese, without exception, consider each other as children of the same family. Using the very metaphorical term *đồng bào*, meaning "from the same womb," to indicate their compatriots, the Vietnamese reinforce the family bond among themselves. This bond is further supported by the kinship terms they use to address one another because, as Bửu Khải explained: "Vietnamese people are rarely emotionally neutral: they prefer to establish as soon as possible some kind of relationship which can show feeling and emotion; they can hardly keep the listener at a distance, they prefer to consider the listener as an uncle, an aunt, a brother, or a sister."[11] Therefore, "elder brother" and "younger sister/brother," respectively *anh* and *em* in Vietnamese, are the common terms of address used between siblings and people from the same generation. Since most love relationships tend to happen among men and women of the same age group, by extension, "brother" and "sister" are also used between (heterosexual) lovers and spouses. Consequently, this confused way of addressing each other, which blurs the boundaries between siblings, countrymen, and lovers, brings out the incestuous overtone in these relationships. In this perspective, the mutual attraction between the protagonist and the Vietnamese shoemaker in *Calomnies* can be seen as incestuous. No matter whether they are related to or know each other before their chance meeting, both immigrants already share a close bond, a bond based on race, look, and language, that set them apart from the rest of the French natives. Because of these external signs, the protagonist was recognized by the shoemaker as a compatriot, a "sister" in the larger Vietnamese family. This recognition allows him to come up to her without any invitation or permission and, much to her annoyance, address her in their mother tongue. In the middle of a Parisian park, among French natives, this language which is neither spoken nor understood by anyone except the protagonist and the shoemaker immediately establishes complicity between them and sets up a barrier against the rest of the French people. This linguistic connection is probably what annoys the protagonist most because no matter what kinship term her countryman uses to call her, it would be loaded with emotion, imposing on her a familiarity that is solely based on their ethnic background. The protagonist's curt reply (very likely in French) betrays her discomfort in being "claimed" and, to some extent, "possessed" by a man from her country. In the same way as Mortesaison's twin brother removes his sister from the supervision of the old Ragot, the shoemaker, by establishing an ethnic connection with the protagonist, has unsettled her friendship with a Frenchman, Ricin. As he is not Vietnamese, Ricin feels excluded from this blood community which naturally embraces the two immigrants. Like old Ragot, Ricin sees that his (French) influence on his friend is slipping away as she becomes more and more attracted to the shoemaker. If, up until now, under Ricin's gaze, the protagonist has considered herself to be fully French, the unexpected encounter with another man's gaze, that of a countryman, has totally shattered her French identity. Alarmed at the change in his friend, Ricin tries to "recuperate" the protagonist by stopping her from reaching out to her origin and her past. He warns her of her growing attraction toward the shoemaker and enumerates the dangers of her cultural crossing: "Tu veux savoir comment c'est d'être la poupée du cordonnier d'un homme de ton pays. Si tu tombes dans le piège il fera de toi une poupée coupable, il te forcera à rentrer au Pays, à réapprendre la langue natale, il te mettra dans la tête que tu as trahi le Pays, que tu dois écrire dans ta langue" ("You want to know how it feels to be the shoemaker's doll, to be the doll of a man from your own country. If you fall into the trap he will make a guilty doll out of you, he will force you to return to the Country, to relearn the mother tongue, he will put in your head that you have betrayed the Country, that you must write in your own language.")[12] This is, in fact, exactly what happens. The protagonist has become totally obsessed by the shoemaker even though he never talks to her again after their first encounter. She is no longer angry at him for having approached her and reminding her of their shared origins for she has realized that there will be no escape for either of them, and that it is useless for her to continue to deny their common past: "Elle se mit à croire à la loi selon laquelle ceux qui répandent autour d'eux une odeur de folie attirent les détraqués. C'est toujours la maladie qui vous ramène à la famille" ("she started to believe in the law that says that those who smell of madness will attract nutters. It is always illness that brings you back to the family").[13]

Recognizing her cultural identity, the protagonist ignores Ricin's warning and sets out to rediscover her past. No longer running away from the shoemaker's attention, she is now the one who is stalking him, watching him, analyzing his every move. By learning more about him, she learns more about herself and her identity. By looking through his eyes, she sees what he saw, and what she really is: a Vietnamese woman. By accepting his gaze, she is reconciled with her Vietnamese self. Brother and sister of the Vietnamese diaspora are thus joined in what we may call a culturally incestuous union. Although no sexual contact has occurred between the protagonist and the shoemaker, the cultural ties that bind them together can be seen as incestuous because they are based on their Vietnamese blood. In their symbiotic union, there will be no place for Ricin. The rejection of the latter (and of his culture) is made very clear in the last scene where the protagonist breaks away from the Frenchman. Leaving Ricin at the crossroad, she follows the shoemaker's dog, confident that it would lead her to its (and her) master. For who will know the way home better than this elder brother? Who will guide her steps back home better than him? Shoemaker, is he not the one who repairs broken and unfitting shoes so that people can continue their journey? In her article "Pieds nus" ("Bare Feet") published in *La Part d'exil*,[14] Lê uses the same metaphor of the unfitting shoes to represent her impossible dream of return. Recalling the story of a little girl who has lost her slippers during the exodus and who had to put on somebody else's shoes, Lê establishes a parallel between the little girl and the exiled writer: "J'ai mis des chaussures qui ne sont pas à moi. Je serai toujours celle qui porte des chaussures dépareillées et ces chaussures ne la ramèneront pas à la maison" ("I have put on shoes that do not belong to me. I will always be the girl who wears odd shoes and these shoes will not bring her home.")[15]

By portraying relationships that are sexually, spiritually and culturally incestuous, Lê's works expose the close link between incest and exile and raise the question of identity among Vietnamese immigrants. Through accounts of brother-sister incest, she reveals not only rejection of the parents but also a failure of integration as her Vietnamese characters reject and defy all authority, be it Vietnamese or French. By retreating back to their own people, they show their refusal of French culture and society. Yet, paradoxically, their regression into themselves also disrupts the Confucian familial order and rocks the whole foundation of the Vietnamese moral system, which is based on worshipping ancestors and filial duty. With the removal of both French and Vietnamese parental figures, Lê's rebellious, incestuous siblings are left with a vacuum that they cannot fill. In the same way Lê's voluntary retreat into herself after her father's death brought her face to face with a terrible inner emptiness where "le ciel était désert, le monde sans Dieu"[16] ("the sky was deserted, the world without God"). If by cloistering herself Lê comes a step closer to her origin, this recognition of her Vietnamese identity only brings her to the border of insanity. As with her twin characters, incest does not bring back any wholeness but only leads to madness and death. Orphans without a homeland, these exiled children hold on to each other for comfort and companionship. But whether or not they will find their way back and whether or not they can construct a new home is another question.

Notes

1. Linda Lê, *Les Trois Parques* (Paris: Christian Bourgois, 1997).
2. Catherine Argand, "Linda Lê: Entretien," *Lire*, April 1999, 30. All translations in this chapter are the author's.
3. Linda Lê, *Calomnies* (Paris: Christian Bourgois, 1993). *Slander*, trans. Esther Allen (Lincoln: Nebraska University Press, 1995).
4. Lê, *Les Trois Parques*, 181-82.
5. Blair and Rita Justice, *The Broken Taboo: Sex in the Family* (New York: Human Sciences Press, 1979), 192.
6. Lê, *Les Trois Parques*, 182. Further references included parenthetically, preceded by TP.
7. Lê, *Calomnies*, 87.
8. Justice and Justice, *The Broken Taboo*, 28.
9. Linda Lê, *Les Dits d'un idiot* (Paris: Christian Bourgois, 1995), 68 and 55. Further references included parenthetically, preceded by *Les Dits*.
10. Linda Lê, *Tu écriras sur le bonheur* (Paris: Presses Universitaires, 1999), 330.
11. Bửu Khải, "How to say 'You' in Vietnamese" in *Vietnamese Studies in a Multicultural World*, ed. Nguyen Xuan Thu (Melbourne: Vietnamese Language & Culture Publications, 1994), 82.
12. Lê, *Calomnies*, 70.
13. Lê, *Calomnies*, 20.

14. Lê, "Pieds nus," in *La Part d'exil*, ed. Lê Hữu Khóa (Provence: Publications de l'Université de Provence, 1995), 56-58.

15. Lê, "Pieds nus," *La Part d'exil*, 58.

16. Argand, "Linda Lê: Entretien," *Lire*: 30.

12

"Cholen, la capitale chinoise de l'Indochine française"[1]: Rereading Marguerite Duras's (Indo)Chinese Novels

Julia Waters

While the French colonization of "Indochina" lasted less than a century, China's imperialist claims to the region date back more than two millennia.[2] The Chinese language, economy, culture and institutions have had a profound influence on the national identities of the countries of the Indochinese peninsula, as has a long history of often violent resistance to Chinese domination. Within Vietnam, the Chinese constitute an important, long-established and influential ethnic minority which, despite centuries of cultural exchange and intermarriage, maintains a quite distinct identity from that of other ethnic groups. French colonial attitudes toward the Chinese reflected the specificity of their position in Indochina: while the French feared the threat that the Chinese, as former colonizers, might pose to their own colonial presence, they also exploited the Chinese control of trade in Indochina, using Chinese merchants as go-betweens—"indispensable enemies"—in their negotiations with the indigenous population.[3] Such was the tenacity of Chinese cultural and economic hegemony that, Brocheux and Hémery argue, "Indochina only became French with the reluctant consent of China."[4] Similarly, Dorgelès reflected on France's only superficial domination of the colony, with the ironic observation that, "L'Indochine n'est toujours qu'une colonie chinoise gérée par les Français" ("Indochina is still no more than a Chinese colony managed by the French").[5]

179

Although, over the past decade, critical attention has begun to be drawn to the colonial thematics of Marguerite Duras's literary representations of French Indochina, critics have consistently neglected to take into account the very particular position of the Chinese in the colony and the ways in which Duras's novels reflect this. This oversight has persisted despite the fact that the primary focus of critical interest and dissent has been Duras's portrayal in *L'Amant* (*The Lover*) and *L'Amant de la Chine du Nord* (*The North China Lover*)[6] of the "scandalous" affair between the poor, young, white heroine and her rich, older, Chinese lover. Some critics have argued that Duras's portrayal of this interracial relationship disrupts colonial constructions of gender and racial difference.[7] Others have asserted that Duras's inversion of conventional gender roles of male activity and female passivity, in the depiction of the young girl's power over her lover, in fact reinforces the racial hierarchies of European superiority and native inferiority that underpinned colonial ideology.[8] In either case, however, critics have overlooked or underplayed the importance, in Duras's works, of the fact that the young girl's lover is Chinese. Some critics simply deny the lover's Chinese origins altogether, referring to him as if he were an indigenous "Indochinese."[9] Others mention the fact that the lover is Chinese, but nonetheless conflate his ethnicity with more general forms of Oriental or Asian "Otherness."[10] Jane Winston refers explicitly to the fact that Duras's female characters "have sex only with *colons* or Chinese men" and explores the influence of the perceived "Chinese Threat" on the ideology of the colonial education system within which Duras was schooled.[11] She does not, however, make it part of her project to examine in detail the specifically Chinese references in Duras's "Indochinese" novels.

Countering this general critical oversight, the aim of this chapter is to examine the important place allotted to China and the Chinese in Duras's representations of colonial Indochina, in her semiautobiographical novels, *L'Amant* and *L'Amant de la Chine du Nord*. The fact that the lover is Chinese and *not* Indochinese problematizes prevalent readings of Duras's texts in terms of a binary opposition between European Self and "native" Other, between colonizer and colonized. While Indochinese characters remain largely secondary, voiceless and undefined in Duras's novels, the Chinese lover is granted a quite different, central status. Vigilance to the lover's national and cultural origins, repeatedly and categorically signaled as Chinese in both novels is, I argue, crucial to a full understanding of Duras's portrayal of the couple's interracial affair and of colonial Indochina in general.

In *L'Amant*, revelation of the identity and nationality of the lover is at first suspended. When the couple first meet, the initial "shock value" comes, within the context of colonial Indochina, from the fact that, "Ce n'est pas un blanc" (25) ("He's not a white man" (16)). Very soon, however, the specificity of the lover's racial difference is emphatically highlighted, first, as he introduces himself: "Il dit qu'il est chinois, que sa famille vient de la Chine du Nord, de Fou-Chouen" (44) ("He says he's Chinese, that his family's from North China, from Fushun" (33)), and then, as the narrator correspondingly and very precisely positions him within the colonial ethnic and class system: "Chinois. Il est de cette minorité financière d'origine chinoise qui tient tout l'immobilier populaire de la colonie" (44) ("Chinese. He belongs to the small group of financiers of Chinese origin who own all the working class housing in the colony" (33)).

The girl is portrayed as being fascinated by the man's essential difference, his "inconnue nouveauté" (50) ("strange novelty" (38)). Importantly, this novelty comes not just from the fact that he is not white, but that he is not Indochinese either. The poverty of the girl's family places them at the bottom of the colonial ladder, and brings them into a day-to-day interaction with the Indochinese locals that higher echelons of French colonial society would not experience. She speaks fluent Vietnamese and eats only local food. Her constant immersion in Indochinese culture is seen to have had such a profound influence on the girl's identity that, "elle est devenue une jeune fille de ce pays de l'Indochine" (120) ("[it has] turned her into a girl of Indo-China" (103)).[12] However shocking and transgressive an interracial relationship between a white girl and a "native" man may have been to French colonial society, there is nothing novel or different about the Indochinese locals to "la petite blanche" ("the white girl") of Duras's text. The native Indochinese are a part of her everyday experiences. The novelty of her lover, and the cause of her fascination, is, precisely, that he is Chinese.

As has already been briefly discussed, the Chinese were an important minority in colonial Indochina, with a commercial, cultural and linguistic identity that was perceived to be quite different from that of the indigenous Indochinese peoples. Their separation from the rest of Indochinese and French social structures is symbolized, in Duras's work, by the Chinese district of Cholon, where the lover has his garçonnière. So distinct is Cholon from the rest of Saigon, that it is described as a town in its own right, even constituting a Chinese capital in striking opposition to the French colonial capital: "Cholen, la capitale chinoise de l'Indochine française" (119) ("Cholon, the Chinese capital of French Indochina"). When the white girl first has sex with her lover, her crossing of cultural boundaries, away from both French and Indochinese societies, and towards the alterity of China, is reflected in the location's geographic separation: "C'est à Cholen. C'est à l'opposé des boulevards qui relient la ville chinoise au centre de Saïgon" (46) ("It's in Cholon. It's at the other end of the avenues that link the Chinese town to the centre of Saigon").[13]

When the lovers are inside the garçonnière, the sounds of the street outside, which invade their intimate space, are quintessentially Chinese sounds and, as such, disorientating and alien to the "petite blanche" ("the white girl"): "Les claquements des sabots de bois cognent la tête, les voix sont stridentes, le chinois est une langue qui se crie comme j'imagine toujours les langues des déserts, c'est une langue *incroyablement étrangère*" (52, my emphasis) ("The clatter of wooden clogs is ear-splitting, the voices strident, Chinese is a language that's shouted the way I always imagine desert languages are, it's a language that's *incredibly foreign*" (41)). While the radical alterity of the Chinese district is a source of fascination for the young girl, its separation from the reas-

suring normality of the Indochinese and poor white *milieux* with which she is
accustomed is also a source of fear. Such feelings of attraction and repulsion,
desire and horror are underlined in the following description, which likens
Cholon to the girl's violent, dysfunctional family: "C'est un lieu irrespirable, il
côtoie la mort, un lieu de violence, de douleur, de désespoir, de déshonneur. Et
tel est le lieu de Cholen. De l'autre côté du fleuve. Une fois le fleuve traversé."
(93); ("It's a place that's intolerable, bordering on death, a place of violence,
pain, despair, dishonor. And so is Cholon. On the other bank of the river. As
soon as you've crossed to the other side" (78)). The reference here to Cholon as
a place of dishonor and, elsewhere, as a "quartier mal famé" (109) ("disreputa-
ble quarter" (93)), is consonant with contemporary images of Cholon as an area
of ill repute, full of brothels and opium dens, and with colonial-era stereotypes
of the Chinese as violent, frightening and indecipherable in their fundamental
difference from Europeans. The parallel set up between Cholon and the girl's
"white trash" family implicitly emphasizes their common violence and deprav-
ity and thus begins to undermine the assumption of difference that underlines
the colonial racial hierarchy.

This implicitly unfounded sense of European superiority is reflected, but
similarly complicated, elsewhere in *L'Amant* in the girl's attitude toward her
Chinese lover. When asked by her mother about the reality of her relationship,
she hypocritically uses colonialism's racialist ideology in her own defense:
"Comment veux-tu, je dis, avec un Chinois, comment veux-tu que je fasse ça
avec un Chinois?" (74); ("How could I, I say, with a Chinese, how could I do
that with a Chinese?"(60-61)).[14] Yet the racism underlying the relationship between the young white girl and her Chinese lover is not simply unidirectional,
based on colonialist beliefs in France's superiority over "inferior races." The
Chinese lover's father refuses to countenance the idea of his son's shameful
marriage to "la petite prostituée blanche" (45) ("the little white whore" (35)). In
a little remarked passage, the lover himself states that it would be a "déshonneur" ("dishonor") for him to marry her, his term mirroring the girl's description of the Chinese area of Cholon. Importantly, the reason he goes on to give
for his aversion to the idea of marrying her is that he is Chinese: "Il dit que lui
ne pourrait pas en supporter l'idée (de ce déshonneur) dans le cas du mariage. Je
le regarde. Il me regarde à son tour, il s'excuse avec fierté. Il dit: je suis un
Chinois." (56); ("He says he himself couldn't bear the thought (of this dishonor)
if it were a question of marriage. I look at him. He looks back, apologizes,
proudly. He says: I'm a Chinese."(44-45)). The lover's pride here in his Chinese origins, his implicit affirmation of his own cultural superiority in refusing
to consider marrying the white girl, and his self-assertive meeting of her gaze,
cast him in a very different role from that of the weakened, feminized, subservient lover that he frequently assumes in the bedroom, and which has been the
object of much critical attention. The love affair between the young French girl
and the Chinese man in many ways represents the meeting of equals and oppo-
sites, with corresponding feelings of mutual fascination and fear. Indeed, given
the young girl's poverty, her family's sordid disaffection, and her close associa-

tion with the *indigènes*, the shock of their affair is not so much that she transgresses *French* colonial norms and racial hierarchies, but that, by asserting control over her rich, powerful and proud lover, she manages to disrupt *Chinese*
racial and social hierarchies.

L'Amant de la Chine du Nord, written seven years after *L'Amant*, reworks
much of its predecessor's largely autobiographical material, but with certain
striking additions and changes in emphasis, notably the insistent foregrounding
of the lover's Chinese origins and culture. As if in response to the public's and
critics' oversight when reading *L'Amant*, Duras is at pains from the start to
stress the Chinese dimension of her later novel. In the very first paragraph of
her preface, Duras mentions some of the proposed titles for the book, but states
that: "Pour finir on a eu le choix entre deux titres plus vastes, plus vrais:
L'Amant de la Chine du Nord ou *La Chine du Nord*" (11) ("In the end, I had a
choice of two broader, truer titles: *The North China Lover* or *North China*"(1)),
so emphasizing the importance or even veracity of the lover's birthplace, over
the setting of the novel in Indochina or, indeed, over his role as lover. The
change in emphasis from *L'Amant* is explicitly underlined in the sequel's intertextual reworking of the couple's first meeting on the Mekong ferry: "De la
limousine noire est sorti un autre Chinois de la Mandchourie. Il est un peu dif-
férent de celui du livre." (35) ("Out of the black limousine stepped another Chinese from Manchuria. He is slightly different from the one in the book").[15] Not
only is this lover more handsome and confident than in the earlier version but,
as this quotation and the book's title stress, he is more emphatically and specifically Chinese.

In their first meeting, a clear distinction is established between the North
Chinese lover's racial purity, signaled by the text's insistence on his whiteness
(an insistence not present in *L'Amant*) and the girl's ambiguous "French-but-
not-quite" status:

> Elle . . . première en français tout le temps partout et détestant la
> France, inconsolable du pays natal et d'enfance. . . .
> Lui, c'est un Chinois. Un Chinois grand. Il a la peau blanche des
> Chinois du Nord.   (36)

> (She . . . always first in French at all her schools, yet disgusted by
> France, and mourning the country of her birth and youth. . . .
> Him, he's Chinese. A tall Chinese. He has the white skin of the
> North Chinese. (26))

In *L'Amant de la Chine du Nord*, there is far more elaboration of the young
girl's in-between identity than in *L'Amant* and, in contrast to the lover's repeated geographic and ethnic labeling, far less reference to her as "la petite
blanche" ("the little white girl"). On the same page as the lover is referred to
three times as "le Chinois" ("the Chinese"), the girl's physical appearance is
portrayed as racially ambiguous: "Cette gracilité du corps la donnerait comme
une métisse, mais non, les yeux sont trop clairs" (39) ("Her slenderness sug-

gests a half-caste, but no, her eyes are too light" (29)). The perceived superiority attached, within colonial racialist ideology, to the girl's French origins is undermined by her "impure," non-European appearance and her at least partial absorption of influences from her Indochinese surroundings. On several occasions, she refers to the fact that she was "née en Indochine" (38; 49) ("born in Indochina" (28; 39)) and she even has to learn about French culture, which is alien to her, from her mother. When she is looked at in the street, it is by "des métis surtout. Jamais des Français" ("Mostly half-castes. Never any French") and, importantly, "Jamais non plus de Chinois" (45) ("Never any Chinese either" (79)). Such insistence on the young girl's racial ambiguity and on the Chinese lover's whiteness problematizes prevalent critical readings of Duras's works in terms of their disruption, or reaffirmation, of the colonial opposition between white European Self and "native" Other. As in *L'Amant*, the girl's subversive power lies, I would argue, more in her ability, in colonial terms, to "contaminate" and weaken the racially pure Chinese Other than in an assertion of her inalienable superiority as *colon*.

As is repeatedly emphasized throughout *L'Amant de la Chine du Nord*, the lover comes not just from China, but from Manchuria in northern China, and hence from the region geographically furthest, and culturally and ethnically most different, from Indochina. The lover's very specific, distinct identity is underlined in his own observation that: "ici les Chinois de l'Indochine, ils viennent tous du Yunan" (90) ("Here, the Chinese in Indochina, all come from Yunnan").[16] This statement concludes a long passage (86-90 (77-81)), in which the Chinese lover tells the girl, and by extension the readers, about his childhood in northern China, about his family's emigration to escape persecution, and about his father's consequent business success in Indochina. Sections of this story, which is almost entirely new material, not previously included in *L'Amant*, read rather like a lesson in Chinese history, complete with dates of wars and reigns, and the names of successive leaders. It is as if, through the mouthpiece of the central male character, Duras seeks to explain to the reader the specificity of his identity and hence his essential difference from both French colonial and indigenous Indochinese societies. The detail and empathy with which the lover's personal, family history of suffering and exile is woven into the events of Chinese history in many ways reflect the treatment of the girl's mother's parallel story of emigration and suffering at the hands of a corrupt colonial regime. Unlike the Indochinese characters of Duras's novels, the Chinese lover is granted a personal prehistory and a degree of individuality on a par with that of the young girl herself.

Strikingly, as he recounts Chinese history and his own family's story, the lover is portrayed as becoming ever more Chinese, distancing himself from the French language in which he talks and the culture with which it is associated: "Il est redevenu complètement chinois" (88) ("he has become totally Chinese again" (79)); "J'oublie le français quand je parle de la Chine" (89) ("I forget my French when I talk about China" (81)); "Elle écoute la voix, cette autre langue française parlée par la Chine" (89) ("She listens to his voice, that other French spoken by China" (80)). The lover's story, the history with which it is inextricably linked, and ultimately the identity that he has derived from them—linguistically, he becomes China as he speaks—are thus portrayed as radically other to both France and to Indochina.

Respect and fascination for the lover's Chinese heritage are, however, again tempered by the mutual fear that underlies the couple's interracial relationship. Both the girl and the lover are repeatedly described as being frightened of one another,[17] predominantly on account of their racial and cultural differences and of the colonial-era prejudices that inure to these differences. The following exchange between the couple is revelatory of both general and more specific fears underlying colonial segregationist ideology:

> Il demande de quoi elle a peur cette société.
> Elle dit:
> —De la syphilis. De la peste. De la gale. Du choléra. Des Chinois.
> —Pourquoi les Chinois?
> —Ils ne sont pas colonisés les Chinois . . . On peut pas les attraper pour les coloniser, on le regrette d'ailleurs. (114)

> (He asks her what they're afraid of.
> She says:
> "Syphilis. Plague. Mange. Cholera. The Chinese."
> "Why the Chinese?"
> "The Chinese—they haven't been colonized. . . . You can't catch them to colonize them, and that upsets people." (105))

Conflated within the young girl's ironic words are general colonialist fears of contamination from interbreeding or from *les maladies indigènes* (native diseases), and a more specific fear of China, based on the threat that it is seen to pose as an alternative colonial power *and* as a strong, cultural and economic counter-influence to the French in Indochina.[18] References to the Chinese Empire recur in conversations between the young French girl and her lover—"Le Chinois raconte, les yeux sur elle seule, la petite Blanche, une histoire de la Chine impériale" (103) ("The Chinese tells her a story of imperial China, his eyes on her alone, the little white girl." (94)); "C'est la route des invasions chinoises" (107) ("Those places, they're also the Chinese invasion routes."(97))—and the ambiguous feelings of mutual fascination and fear, love and hate, alienation and respect that underlie their relationship in many ways reflect French colonial-era attitudes toward China.[19]

Such attitudes to the Chinese can be detected in Duras's propagandist text, *L'Empire français* (*The French Empire*) (1940), which she co-wrote with Philippe Roques, under her birth surname of Donnadieu, while working at the Ministère des Colonies in Paris, and which is a nonfictional precursor to her literary career.[20] In the introduction to *L'Empire français*, the "Chinese Threat" is invoked to justify the French colonization of Indochina: "Il s'agit pour la France d'arrêter les exigences de Pékin" (47) ("For France, it is a matter of halting Peking's demands.") Elsewhere, references to the historical domination of the area by China and to the contemporary threat that it is perceived to continue to pose are slightly more veiled: "Si l'Indochine . . . était livrée à son propre sort, elle pourrait très difficilement vivre par elle-même et ne saurait se défendre des convoitises de ses voisins en mal de conquête." (209) ("If Indochina were left to its own devices, it would have problems surviving on its own and would not know how to defend itself from the greed of its neighbors, bent on conquest.")[21]; "la domination chinoise . . . durera deux siècles et imprégnera fortement les Annamites" (110) ("Chinese domination was to last for two centuries and would have a profound influence on the Annamites"). Consistently, China is portrayed as both a historical and a contemporary rival to France, its equal in power and culture, but radically and frighteningly other.

In L'Empire français, the perceived racial purity of the Chinese is contrasted with the ethnic diversity of Indochina and its peoples: "L'Indochine . . . n'est, au point de vue ethnique, qu'un mélange de races et de civilisations" (103) ("Ethnically, Indochina is merely a mix of races and civilisations"); "Les Annamites . . . ne sont, en fait, qu'un mélange de plusieurs groupes de races" (109) ("The Annamites are, in fact, merely a mix of several racial groups"). The dismissive "ne . . . que" ("merely") construction in each of these sentences is revelatory of colonial-era perceptions of miscegenation as synonymous with bastardization, contamination and regression. As if resulting from their racial mixing, the various Indochinese peoples are repeatedly referred to as "indolents," "calmes" and "sédentaires" ("indolent, peaceful and sedentary"). The ethnic Chinese, in contrast, are seen as "pleins d'allant et d'énergie" ("full of vigor and energy") and, consequently, as commercially and financially successful. Even within a text whose unambiguous purpose is to sing the praises of French imperialism, the Chinese are portrayed as separate, different and essentially uncolonizable.

Critics have frequently interpreted the interracial relationship between the young white girl and her Chinese lover, in Duras's novels, in terms of the positive associations granted to notions of transgression, subversion and métissage at the time of their writing, in the 1980s and 1990s, and in so doing, have overlooked the ways in which it may also reflect the negative connotations of those notions during the era in which the works are set. Read in association with the precursor text, L'Empire français, Duras's virtual silencing of indigenous voices in her Indochinese novels, her portrayal of the young girl's cultural and even physical métissage, and her insistence on the Chinese lover's alterity and whiteness paint a rather different picture of interracial relations in colonial Indochina than has previously been recognized. While, on one level, L'Amant and L'Amant de la Chine du Nord revel in the protagonist's marginal status, on the edge of both colon and Indochinese society, on another level, they also repeat colonial racialist distinctions, whereby the girl's ambiguous métissage renders her inferior to the French of the colonial elite and also, arguably, to her "pure" Chinese lover. The lover's Chinese identity means that he is positioned outside French colonial hierarchies and colonizer-colonized oppositions: not because his status is somehow "in-between" or métis, but because his racial purity places him in a different system altogether—a separate, Chinese system. The Chinese lover is portrayed as being more white than the young white girl. Their interracial relationship represents the girl's encounter with an Otherness so radical that it is *beyond* colonial racial hierarchies, and she thus transgresses not only French colonial boundaries but also the boundaries of an entirely different social and cultural system.

The following conversation, toward the end of *L'Amant de la Chine du Nord*, in which the young girl asks her lover about the source of his family's wealth, can be seen to reflect French colonial-era malaise at the insidious Chinese counterinfluence in Indochina:

> Elle lui demande s'il a des rizières, lui. Non, jamais les Chinois, il dit. Elle demande quel commerce ils font, les Chinois. Il dit: Celui de l'or, de l'opium beaucoup. . . . Il dit qu'il y a aussi les "compartiments" et les opérations boursières. Que la Bourse chinoise, elle est présente *partout dans le monde entier*. Que *partout aussi, dans le monde entier* maintenant on mange la cuisine chinoise. (213, my emphasis)

> (She asks him if he has rice paddies. No, the Chinese never do, he says. She asks what business they do, the Chinese. He says: gold, a lot of opium. . . . He says there are also the cubicles and the stock market. It's *everywhere in the whole world*, the Chinese stock exchange. Also *everywhere in the whole world* now, people are eating Chinese food (207-8)).

Echoing the sentiments expressed in the Dorgelès quotation at the start of this chapter, the Chinese family's fortune becomes representative, in Duras's portrayal of French Indochina, of a much broader Chinese economic and cultural hegemony. Despite French colonization and attempts to suppress the "Chinese Threat," the Chinese are portrayed here as continuing, economically and culturally, to dominate Indochina and, by extension, the rest of the world, as reflected in the repetition of the phrase "partout dans le monde entier" ("everywhere in the whole world").

Several critics have read the girl's departure at the end of *L'Amant* and *L'Amant de la Chine du Nord* as either a reversal or a reinscription of a key topos of colonial literature, whereby the European man deserts his native lover, his "*con gai*." Read in relation to colonial-era fears of the perceived threat from the Chinese, however, the departure of the whole family in *L'Amant de la Chine du Nord* can be seen to represent the end of French colonial rule and the implicit re-imposition of Chinese hegemony in Indochina. In Duras's (Indo)Chinese novels, the French leave but the Chinese—the historical colonizers of Indochina and imperial rivals to the French—remain. Whereas the young girl reluctantly leaves her "pays natal et d'enfance" ("the country of her birth and youth"), the Chinese lover stays behind and marries "l'autre femme de l'histoire" (191) ("the other woman in the story"), the racially-pure Chinese woman, chosen for him by his family. As the lover tells the young girl, his fiancée's skin is "blanche . . . comme la peau des femmes du Nord. Elle est plus blanche que toi" (210), ("Her skin is white . . . like the skin of women from the north. She is whiter than you." (204)). While their interracial relationship may have allowed the young girl privileged access to the radical alterity of her Chinese lover, in the end she is expelled and her place taken by a whiter, purer, Chinese woman. Rather than view this individual and more general shift in power relations with fear or regret, however, Duras's narratives seem to portray the end of French rule and the re-imposition of Chinese domination as the natural outcome of a mutually enriching, but ultimately doomed, meeting of profoundly different cultures. The departure of the French does not signal the return of Indochina to the indigenous population but, rather, its inevitable and unspoken handing back to its former colonizers.

By overlooking the specifically Chinese dimensions of Duras's (Indo)Chinese narratives, critics have tended to read them in terms of an oversimplified opposition between colonizer and colonized, between European Self and native Other. Duras's portrayal of the interracial relationship between the young white girl and her Chinese lover does indeed transgress colonial, societal and traditional gender boundaries. Yet to view her works solely in these terms, without due consideration for their colonial context, results in an only partial analysis of their racial and interracial complexities. The fact that the lover, in *L'Amant* and *L'Amant de la Chine du Nord*, is categorically Chinese, rather than "Indochinese," sets him apart from the otherwise faceless, voiceless indigenous locals of Duras's novels. China's status as an imperial power in its own right establishes the lover's credentials as a worthy match and adversary for the young white girl of French origin. Indeed, read in relation to its 1930s colonial context, the North China lover's racial purity ultimately renders him superior to the "petite prostituée blanche" ("the little white whore"), who has been *métissée*, or even contaminated, by exposure to the alterity of Indochina. Far from being weakened and emasculated by his love for the young white girl, the Chinese lover proves to be the purer and, thus, ultimately, the stronger of the two. Tellingly, at the end of *L'Amant de la Chine du Nord*, when the French family are selling up and preparing to leave, the narrator observes, as if in passing, that: "Les lits des chambres sont encore là, ils portent des étiquettes *écrites en chinois.*" (200, my emphasis) ("The beds are in the bedrooms, they've got tags on them *with writing in Chinese.*" (194)) Symbolically, the threat has become reality: China has taken over France's place in Indochina. Cholon has, indeed, become "la capitale chinoise de l'Indochine française" ("the Chinese capital of French Indo-china").

Notes

1. "Cholon, the Chinese capital of French Indochina." Marguerite Duras, *L'Amant* (Paris: Minuit, 1984), 119.
2. While French incursions into the region began with the capture of Saigon in 1860, the "Indochinese Union," comprising Cochin-China, Annam, Tonkin and Cambodia was not created until 1887. The French definitively withdrew from Indochina in 1954, after their defeat at Dien Bien Phu. As early as the first century B.C, under the Han dynasty, the northern region of modern-day Vietnam was incorporated into the Chinese empire as the province of Giao Chi. Chinese domination continued almost uninterrupted, save for intermittent periods of resistance and insurrection, until 1428, when the Chinese finally recognized Emperor Le Loi's calls for Vietnam's independence. Nonetheless, Chinese interests in Vietnam—political, military, economic and cultural—remained strong right up until the 1885 Tien Tsin treaty, when China formally recognized the French protectorate of Vietnam.
3. This description of the Chinese as "nos ennemis indispensables" is cited in Pierre Brocheux and Daniel Hémery, *Indochine: la colonisation ambiguë 1858-1954* (Paris: La Découverte, 2001), 194. This important study discusses at length the central role that the ethnic Chinese played in the Indochinese economy, arguing that a "truly symbiotic Franco-Chinese capitalism" (163) existed in the colony.
4. Brocheux and Hémery, *Indochine*, 18.
5. Roland Dorgelès, *Sur la route mandarine* (Paris: Albin Michel, 1925). The quotation is taken from the 1995 re-edition (Paris/Pondicherry: Editions Kailash), 99. The translation is my own.
6. Marguerite Duras, *L'Amant* (Paris: Minuit, 1984); *L'Amant de la Chine du Nord* (Paris: Gallimard, 1991). English translations, unless otherwise stated, are from *The Lover*, trans. Barbara Bray (London: Bloomsbury Publishing, 1993 edition), and *The North China Lover* (*L'Amant de la Chine du Nord*), trans. Leigh Hafrey (London: Flamingo, 1994).
7. See, for instance: Christine Holmlund, "Disrupting Limits of Difference," *Quarterly Review of Film and Video*, 13, no. 1-3 (1991): 1-22; Yvonne Y. Hsieh, "L'évolution du discours (anti-) colonialiste dans *Un barrage contre le Pacifique, L'Amant* et *L'Amant de la Chine du Nord* de Marguerite Duras," *Dalhousie French Studies* 35 (1996): 55-65.
8. See, for instance Pascale Bécel, "From The Sea Wall to The Lover: Prostitution and Exotic Parody," *Studies in Twentieth-Century Literature* 21, no. 2 (1997): 417-32; Marie-Paule Ha, "Durasie: Women, Natives, and Other," in *Revisioning Duras*, ed. James S. Williams (Liverpool: University of Liverpool Press, 2000), 95-111.
9. While Panivong Norindr does mention the lover's father's exploitation of poor Indochinese, he nonetheless refers to the scandal caused by "a liaison between a white female colonizer and a male 'native'" (*Phantasmatic Indochina: French Colonial Ideology in Architecture, Film, and Literature* (Durham, NC: Duke University Press, 1996), 126); Francine Dugast-Portes comments that the lover "is one of the few natives to be individualized and evoked at length" ("L'Exotisme dans l'œuvre de Marguerite Duras" in *Le Roman colonial* (Paris: L'Harmattan, 1990), 147-57); Marie-Paule Ha refers to Duras's "othering of the indigenous people" ("Durasie: Women, Natives, and Other," 93).
10. Yvonne Hsieh states that the lover "is not a real native" but then, contradictorily, sees the young European girl's seduction of "an older native" as evidence of Duras's denial of racial

difference ("L'évolution du discours (anti-)colonialiste," 59); Suzanne Chester argues that Duras's portrayal of the lover as an Asian "Other" conforms to one of Orientalist literature's exoticizing topoi ("Writing the Subject: Exoticism/Eroticism in Marguerite Duras's *The Lover* and *The Sea Wall*," in *Decolonizing the Subject*, eds. Sidonie Smith and Julia Watson (Minneapolis: University of Minnesota Press, 1992), 436-57; Pascale Bécel argues that Duras's reversal of gender roles in fact reinscribes colonialist racial hierarchies, but then indiscriminately refers to the lover as representative of the Orient, China, Indochina, the Asian continent, or of a general "Other culture" ("From *The Sea Wall* to *The Lover*"); despite her study's central focus on the ambiguous forms of métissage in Duras's work, Catherine Bouthors-Paillart views the central love affair as an example of métissage between "the white race" and "the yellow race" (*Duras la métisse: métissage fantasmatique et linguistique dans l'œuvre de Marguerite Duras* (Geneva: Droz, 2002)).

11. Jane Bradley Winston, *Postcolonial Duras: Cultural Memory in Postwar France* (New York/Basingstoke: Palgrave, 2001), 98.

12. Although the hyphenated spelling, Indo-China, originally adopted by geographers in the early nineteenth century, was, under French colonization, rapidly and generally replaced by the spelling "Indochina," Bray maintains the original spelling throughout her translation. See Brocheux and Hémery, *Indochine*, 10-12, for a discussion of the adoption and evolution of the name.

13. I have substituted my own translation here for Bray's version—"It's in Cholon. Opposite the boulevards linking the Chinese part of the city to the centre of Saigon" (36)—which does not render the original's sense of Cholon's being distant from Saigon and constituting a separate town in its own right.

14. Similarly, when the girl leaves Indochina for France, her refusal to be seen to cry seems to attest to her at least partial internalization of colonial racist reasoning: "Elle l'avait fait sans montrer ses larmes, parce qu'il était chinois et qu'on ne devait pas pleurer ce genre d'amants." (135) ("She'd wept without letting anyone see her tears, because he was Chinese and one oughtn't to weep for that kind of lover." (116)).

15. This is my own translation. Hafrey's translation places less emphasis on the fact that the man is Chinese than in Duras's French original: "The man who gets out of the black limousine is other than the one in the book, but still Manchurian. He is a little different from the one in the book" (26).

16. I have substituted my own translation here for Hafrey's erroneous version, "the Chinese in Indochina, they're all from Hunan" (81). Hafrey's confusion of Yunnan, in southwest China, adjoining Laos and Vietnam, with the province of Hunan, in southern central China, is indicative of a more general critical ignorance of the geographic and ethnic specificities that underpin Duras's representations of Indochina.

17. The lover's fear of the girl is shown, for instance, in his trembling hands when they first meet. Elsewhere, "elle voit qu'il a peur" (69) ("she sees he's afraid" (61)); "la peur le reprend" (75) ("suddenly he feels timid" (64)). The girl's fear of her lover is throughout more explicitly linked to race: "—Toi, tu as peur du Chinois?—Comme ça . . . un peu." (58) ("Are you afraid of the Chinese?" "I guess a little." (49)); she says she is afraid of "Des gens. De toi. De toi, le Chinois" (106) ("The people. You. You, the Chinese." (97)); and she even fantasizes that he will murder her: "—Comment tu m'aurais tuée à Long-Hai?—Comme un

Chinois. Avec de la cruauté en plus de la mort." (110) ("How would you have killed me at Long-Hai?" "Like a Chinese. With cruelty on top of the killing." (100)).

18. It is perhaps worth noting the persistence of such racial stereotypes in recent media coverage of Chinese illegal immigrants, of SARS or of "bird flu."

19. Jane Winston refers at some length to the perceived "Chinese Threat" and its effects on colonial racialist ideology and education policies in *Postcolonial Duras*.

20. Philippe Roques and Marguerite Donnadieu, *L'Empire français* (Paris: Gallimard, 1940). All translations of this text are my own.

21. Such statements take on an additional resonance when one considers that *L'Empire français* was written and published just weeks before the German Occupation of France, at a time when Japan was also threatening to invade Indochina—a threat which it soon carried out. For more information on the background to, and nature of, the Franco-Japanese wartime cohabitation of Indochina, see: Brocheux and Hémery, *Indochine*, or Eric T. Jennings, *Vichy in the Tropics: Pétain's National Revolution in Madagascar, Guadeloupe, and Indochina, 1940-1944* (Stanford: Stanford University Press, 2001).

13

Playing Hardball:
Linda Lê's *Les Trois Parques*

Jane Bradley Winston

The prose art . . . deals with discourse that is still warm from the
struggle and hostility, as yet unresolved and still fraught with hostile
intentions and accents; prose art finds discourse in this state and subjects it to the dynamic-unity of its own style.
—Mikhail Bahktin, *Dialogic Imagination*

To write is to search through the ruins of the burned for the arm bone
that matches the leg bone.
—Alejandra Pizarnik, *Extraccíon de la piedra de locura*

Critics have amply remarked on the autobiographical aspect of Linda Lê's
writing. Reviewing her 1993 novel *Calomnies* (Slander),[1] Ook Chung notes its
"share of autobiography"[2]; analyzing the short story "Vinh L.," Leakthina Ollier
calls Lê's writing "autofiction" and wonders if the eponymous hero isn't "also
elle (she), the author Linda L. . . . or Linda Lê."[3] This interpretation of Lê's
project is shaped by the apparent resonance between the issues, concerns, and
topoi to which she returns over and again in her oeuvre and the details which,
under the weight of critical repetition, we have come to believe we know of her
life history. Thus, her textual concern with issues of exile, alienation, and displacement resonates with her trajectory from Vietnam, where she was born in
1963, to France, where she arrived fourteen years later as one of the "boat people." Similarly, the description by *Calomnies*' masculine narrator of his female

counterpart as a "métèque écrivant en français" ("a dirty foreigner, who writes in French"[4]) echoes Lê's descriptions of her own linguistic and cultural situation between the Vietnamese culture and language that she did not ever fully master and French culture and language, with which she considers herself more conversant but not in a position of full access or mastery.[5]

But if Lê agrees that her scriptural point of departure is often autobiography, she nuances that account by describing *Calomnies*, for instance, as "an autobiography that is out of joint, off its rails."[6] This derailing can be understood, I suspect, in terms of the contradictory demands inherent in Lê's project. On one hand, she explicitly rejects the conformity she finds in the practice of "exploiting the figure of the exiled writer who exploits the clientele of the exile, the notion of a *métèque* who narrates exotic tales."[7] On the other, she clearly works through issues related to her life history in her work. Ollier, in fact, has described "Vinh L." as "an attempt to inscribe her own story."[8] As a response to both demands, blurring leads and dislocating axes permits Lê to maintain her analysis close to home while also broadening its social, cultural, and historical horizons.

Sociohistorical broadening is particularly pronounced in *Les Trois Parques*, whose semantic components, including the guilt Lê identifies "as the origin of writing, for me," direct the reader in at least two directions simultaneously— toward an autobiographical set of meanings and toward "the guilt of writing itself." Lê casts the writer as a vampire and a cannibal who consumes and speaks for "that which is mute"; "steals and uses other peoples' pain for his raw material." Like Genêt, she considers writing "the recourse of the person who has betrayed."[9] But she also addresses personal forms of guilt when expressing "the guilt and betrayal of a writer who rejects her heritage" or describing herself as a "traitor to her roots."[10] Moreover, her creative work gestures toward a guilt specifically attached to the figure of the father left behind in Vietnam. Whereas *Calomnies* is a search for identity and the father, by *Lettre morte* the narrator finds herself left with nothing of her deceased father but the pile of his un-opened letters to her. Written in a language she cannot decipher, they represent not communication or access to him, but the now irremediable impossibility of communication across diasporic borders. In fact when Chung calls *Calomnies* a failed redemption, his words apply to Lê's oeuvre, whose narrators continue to eat their own hearts, a posture graphically represented by Edvard Munch's 1889 woodcut "The Heart," used on *Calomnies*' 1993 jacket cover.

Rather than given over exclusively to loss and guilt, Lê's writing also engages in what Chung describes as a bitter and relentless "settling of scores." Borrowing a phrase from *Calomnies*, Chung calls her a "murderer in lace"; using Breton's description of Frida Kahlo's visual art, he figures her writing, too, as "a ribbon around a bomb."[11] Indeed, taking the novel as her battleground, Lê situates herself in a literary tradition that emerged in conscious opposition to the poetic genres. As Bahktin argued, the novel emerged from a "dialogic" process, as a response to the authoritative, absolute, and "undialogized" word of the poetic genres and of the higher socioideological levels. It was born as the consciously polemic and oppositional response to that word, from the playing with official language that took place in popular places (such as street fairs and buffoon spectacles) and popular genres (such as the fabliaux, folk sayings, and anecdotes). In contrast to the poetic word, the novelistic word has lost its privilege, been relativized, made aware of the existence of other meanings for the same thing. While the poetic word seeks univocality, the novel, built on concrete social speech diversity, seeks an abundance of embodied points of view. In Bahktin's words, it aspires to a "historical and concrete plenitude of actual sociohistorical languages that in a given era have entered into interaction, and belong to a single evolving contradictory unity."[12] The novel is a place where the centralizing and decentralizing verbal and ideological forces collide, a place of competition and struggle, a site of unresolved contradiction.

Lê at first approached the French language and literary traditions with what she describes as an admixture of intimidation, respect, and submission. She subsequently dismissed her first books on those grounds.[13] By *Les Trois Parques*, she challenges and unsettles both traditions from within, using, among other techniques, a complex "citational practice" that has the form of an insistent referencing of poetic, literary, and mythological traditions.[14] She builds her textual meanings in dialogue with those developed in the cited materials themselves and those attached to the social, cultural, and historical contexts of their production. In the process, she appropriates the cited materials and/or contexts, compelling them to carry meanings and serve intentions of her own. To understand the meaning of a word, Bahktin believed, one must examine its *use*: "the actual and always self-interested *use* to which this meaning is put and the way it is expressed by the speaker, a use determined by the speaker's social position (profession, social class, etc.) and by the concrete situation." Stated in other words: "*Who* speaks and under what conditions he speaks: this is what determines the word's actual meaning."[15] The conditions shaping *Les Trois Parques* include those of postcolonial era exile, displacement, and loss. The self-interested *uses* to which Lê puts her meanings include a settling of accounts, but they also include a desire and an effort to write herself into the literary and historical traditions. As we will see, one of the more unsettling aspects of her project is the fact that she sets out to further the novelistic challenge to the poetic word while, at the same time, writing herself into a community of poets, thus writing her place into what would seem to be the target of her own novelistic utterance's attack.

Les Trois Parques is Lê's "hardest" text: its treatment of its subject and the reader are her most unrelenting; its narrative, her most difficult of access. I do not align this novel with "hardball" to suggest that it is a game or that its author is playing one, but rather to capture the resolute hardness of Lê's approach to such crucial issues as diaspora and exile, human relations and human motivations. I have also made that alignment to capture the performative effect of Lê's approach: the creation of a narrative in which the writer and her readers are disoriented and destabilized; put at risk and in play, as Marguerite Duras contended true art must do. The following pages represent merely one "pass" through this novel's dense, compact, argot-, neologism-, and reference-rich fabric. That pass is structured by a somewhat ex-centric approach which, rather than engaging directly with the narrative, approaches it indirectly, through key elements in its citational fabric. It examines some of the most important citations structuring the broad architectonics of this novel, paying particular mind to the "frames" surrounding the narrative proper, from which it takes its bearings and to which it does not cease referring.

Frames

The first frame, which is constructed in the title *Les Trois Parques*, "displaces" the reader to the Greek and Roman mythological worlds in which the three Fates (*Morae*; *Parcae*) decided human destiny. Sometimes described as the daughters of Nyx (Night) and sisters of the Ceres (the goddesses of death), they were more often identified as the daughters of Zeus and Themis and the sisters of the Horae.[16] Their role was to assign a destiny to each individual at birth and to assure that it was carried out. Each Fate had her own task: Klotho, the spinner, "spun the thread of life"; Lakhesis, the disposer of lots, assigned a destiny to each individual at birth; Atropos, the inevitable, "cut the thread at death."[17] Each Fate was also aligned with a particular phase in the "female life cycle" under patriarchy and a specific discursive practice. Thus, Klotho, the "maiden," was said to sing "of things that are," Lakhesis, the "mother," to sing "of things that were," and Atropos, the "crone," to sing "about the things that will be."[18] In the *Illiad*, the Fates are in control of the broad patterns of fate, issuing dictates even Zeus cannot modify "without consequences too disastrous to contemplate."[19] In his *Life of Apollonius Tyana*, Flavius Philostratus also underscores this incontrovertible aspect of each person's fate:

> The threads which the Fates spin are so unchangeable, that even if they decreed to someone a kingdom which at the moment belonged to another, and even if that other slew the man of destiny, to save himself from ever being deprived of his throne, nevertheless the dead man would come to life again in order to fulfill the decree of the Fates.[20]

"To scorn Fate," Edith Hamilton further warns, is "to bring Nemesis, the certain consequence of defying Fate."[21] In calling her novel *Les Trois Parques*, Lê not only casts an ominous pall over it: she enshrouds it in death. As Parada puts it: "Fate mainly means Death and all circumstances leading to death."[22]

Below this title, and standing out against its somber black background, is a photograph of a famous statue. This statue comes from the western pediment of the Temple of Zeus at Olympia, whose larger composition depicts the Combat of the Centaurs and the Lapiths. As the story goes, the Lapiths invited the centaurs to the wedding of their King Pirithous, only to have the centaurs ravish the bride and other young Lapith women. A battle ensued in which the Lapiths defeated the centaurs and drove them from their land. Their victory, which was often depicted in the classical tradition, was widely taken to "symbolize the triumph of civilization over barbarity."[23] The portion of the western pediment featured on the cover of *Les Trois Parques* is known by the name "scenes of combat and rapture." It depicts a Lapith woman trying to disengage herself from the arms of a centaur; that is, from the hold of barbarity. Positioned under the sign of Death on Lê's cover, this image marks—or *names*—the novel's narrative as a combat on the level of gender, men *versus* women, and on that of the Western colonial categories, savages *versus* civilized.

The epigraph used in *Les Trois Parques* develops a third citational and connotative frame. This epigraph is drawn from a poetry collection by Alejandra Pizarnik, *Extracción de la piedra de locura* (*Extraction of the Stone of Madness*), whose title poem examines the origins of the speaker's own madness.[24] The verses forming Lê's epigraph open with an invitation: "Viens à l'aube, brave ami, viens à l'aube" ("come at dawn, brave friend, come at dawn"). They then gesture toward a collective pronoun—a "we"—whose components (I and you) recognized each other at some point in the past and "made each other disappear." The third stanza establishes "I" as witness to its own birth and its own death; a birth that coincided with meeting "you"; a death coextensive with the disappearance of "us." The final stanza recalls a "separation" and promises to engage an unending "quest" for an already lost object. Pizarnik's choice of verb tenses—the imperfect and the conditional—establishes that quest as possible but improbable: "Et moi," it reads: "j'allais marcher à travers tous les déserts du monde et même mort je continuerais à te chercher toi, qui as été le lieu d'amour" ("And me, I was going to walk across all the deserts of the world and even dead I would continue to look for you, you who were the place of love").[25] Thus, on a rudimentary reading, these lines from Pizarnik enhance the opening frame of *Les Trois Parques* by adding to it connotations of love, separation, loss, and quest.

Pizarnik's title also refers us to a painting by the sixteenth-century Flemish painter Hieronymus Bosch, *The Stone Operation*, also known as *The Cure of Folly* and *The Extraction of the Stone of Madness*. This painting dates to 1480-1485, the beginning of Western colonial exploration. Its subject is a metaphor and, some contend, a medical practice. In Flemish literature and folklore of Bosch's time, cutting the stone out of someone's skull served as a metaphor for curing his madness or folly. Although medical and art historians often argue that this operation was performed in fiction not fact, at least one historian, Laurinda Dixon, contends that surgical textbooks of the era described and graphically illustrated a procedure called *trepanation,* in which holes were made in the skull to cure headaches or madness.[26] The website for the German epilepsy museum Kork lends support to Dixon's view by declaring the operation performed until the mid-eighteenth century on epileptics,[27] and she herself points out that human skulls bearing surgical marks consistent with this intervention have been found.[28] In any case, Bosch uses this subject to comment negatively on human stupidity and treachery. His operating scene includes and castigates four figures—a patient, the man performing the operation, a monk, and a nun. Flemish script decorating the circular image's parameters reads: "Master, hurry up and cut the stone out. My name is Lubbert Das." These words name the patient Lubbert, a common name in Flemish literature and folklore that "always signified fool or simpleton."[29] The man performing the operation is also marked: the funnel on his head, a symbol of "deception" and "infidelity," establishes him as a "dangerous charlatan."[30] Finally both the monk encouraging the victim and the nun watching, unconcerned, figure and indict the corruption of the Roman Catholic clergy a few decades before the beginnings of the Protestant Reformation.[31]

Bosch's critique has specific and general targets. His representation's circular shape recalls a mirror[32] and registers the period belief that God was watching humans on earth. Often used in Bosch's time to "remind [viewers] of the earth in harmony with humanity and with the cosmos,"[33] that circular shape combines with the "overall arrangement [to] emphasize the general purport, didactic and moral, of the scene represented."[34] Most critics interpret the tableau as a general indictment of stupidity and deception, but Dixon reads it as a specific indictment of the "charlatan alchemist, who appears with regularity in scientific treatises of the time."[35] Noting that the flower being extracted from the patient's head (like the flower sitting on a nearby table) has gilded leaves, she rejects the common view that this is a tulip and reads it in terms of the golden flower of chemistry. As she explains, the goal of chemists at the time was to find a transmuted healing substance that was referred to as the philosopher's stone and took other figural forms, including the "flower of wisdom."[36] On this reading, Bosch's indictment of the charlatan takes an unexpected direction: not toward the cure, but toward its losses. I proposed in an earlier version of this chapter that figuring the stone as a flower suggests that "madness" is a sign of renaissance or a thing of beauty. Since then, I have discovered one critic's association of Bosch's tableau and these lines by the poet Jan van Stijevoort

> The hidden stone ripens fast,
> Then laid bare like a turnip
> Can easily be cut out at last,
> But even then the danger isn't past
> That man lives best who's fain to live half mad, half sane.[37]

In this light, Bosch's tableau adds to Lê's frame connotations related to the definition and deployment of the category of madness. Is it an illness or a healing substance? Is it a cause of stupidity or a means of knowledge? In dialogue with the novelistic "word" of a female writer in exile, these connotations gesture in the direction of crucial issues (common to Lê and all of the poets in whose community this novel establishes her), including exile and cultural difference, the curing of madness as an effacing of cultural (and gender) difference, the relation between the authorities promoting and performing the extraction and the victim, the possibility that they may be "cannibalizing" him, picking from his/her brain the cure for their (cultural) ills.

Finally, *Les Trois Parques'* epigraph brings with it its own literary contexts and those of its author. A child of displacement and exile, Pizarnik was born near Buenos Aires to Russian Jewish parents fleeing anti-Semitism. By her university years, she, too, evinced strong interest in French literature. Indeed, some critics situate her writing in the lineage of Mallarmé, Lautréamont, Rimbaud, and Artaud. To Melanie Nicholson, however, Pizarnik's "particular articulation of the value of evil in literature was more clearly articulated by . . . Bataille."[38] In the light of her understanding of Pizarnik, the Argentine poet's work introduces into Lê's opening frame connotations of scriptural guilt, a concern with transgression, including lesbianism, with the breakdown of the integral subject, with evil enlisted in the struggle defined by Bataille as being against "those intentions of Good which are based on rational calculations,"[39] with death ("as a presence, a companion, the supreme object of desire"[40]), and with suicide, which Pizarnik committed in 1972, while on weekend leave from a psychiatric clinic. The conditions of her death reiterate and reinforce the framing connotations addressed in Bosch's tableau on the subject of madness and the cure. At the same time, Lê's citing of Pizarnik frames *Les Trois Parques* with connotations of cannibalism, thematized in these lines from the prose poem "Extraction of the Stone of Madness": "You know they have humiliated you even when they showed you the sun. You know that you'll never know how to defend yourself, that you only want to present them with the trophy, I mean the corpse, let them eat it and drink it."[41] If these lines offer one image of the posture of the writing subject as she embarks on her quest, "Night Singer," the poem that opens the collection *Extraction of the Stone of Madness*, offers another: "Exposed to every undoing, she sings by the side of a lost child that is she herself . . . her voice corrodes the distance that opens between thirst and the hand that gropes for the glass. She sings."[42]

Linda Lê begins her narrative proper by aligning its protagonists—a Vietnamese man and his two Viet Kieu daughters—with those in Shakespeare's *King Lear,* a play that broke with the received tradition of its time to give the older King Leir tale a tragic denouement ruled by violence, hazard, and death. The relation between Lê's narrative and *King Lear* is one of similarity, distance, and difference; the relation she enlists *King Lear* to establish between her protagonists is one of separation, loss, and quest. The father, exhausted and broken, awaits death "comme le roi Lear dans sa hutte" (TP, 9: "like King Lear in his hut"). Unlike Lear however, he asks for nothing. Meanwhile in Paris, his two daughters have other plans: "jou[ant] les Cordélia" (TP, 9: "playing Cordelia"), they will bring the father they have not seen since leaving Vietnam twenty years ago to visit them in Paris. When the novel opens, they have already sent the invitation. From this point on, the novel takes the form of a quest to reunite separated entities. In the course of the novel, the initial father-daughters (familial) entity is joined by, most importantly, Vietnam (figured as an S with a line through it), and the Vietnamese and Viet Kieu communities. In all cases, the quest can be perceived as a search for re-unification—of a nation, a people, a family, of lovers, of a character, and a tradition.

True to Pizarnik's epigraph, this familial quest takes the form of a search for a lost *lieu d'amour*, or place of love. The father is aligned with two such places: his garden and the beach at Vung Tàu, from which his daughters once departed and where he now catches the fish he feeds his friend, a disabused priest called only *le couineur* (the squeaker or squealer). The oldest (and pregnant) daughter, most often called *le gros ventre* (fat stomach), is linked most closely to tradition, marriage, pregnancy, and to her maternal grandmother, to that grandmother's recipes and to the use of the Vietnamese language. This sister is associated with three places of love: (1) the authentic Norman inn in which she was married, from which her Vietnamese cultural traditions were excluded, and where her grandmother's phantom sewed havoc; (2) the conjugal bed characterized by a tomb-like cold and shared with a Western husband and Buddhist adept who, like a cement wall, separates her from the shining sun, and (3) her shiny new kitchen, where the flame of tradition burns, where ennui, repetition, and the grandmother's traditions rule, especially the culinary ones. This sister wants her father to come to Paris so that he can see her "filant droit dans la direction du bonheur parfait" (TP, 25: "moving straight in the direction of perfect happiness").[43] Her sister, called *les Belles Gambettes, la nymphe, la banquise,* and *la glacière* (beautiful legs, the nymph, the iceberg, and icebox)— is also aligned with three ersatz *lieux d'amour*: her studio rue Glacière, the bed she shares with the deadbeat lover she is just breaking with, and her older sister's garden. Characterized by an impotent melancholy, a tendency to build castles in the fog of her daydreams, and by the dust that has accumulated in her heart, this sister still has hopes for love, and she places them all on her father's visit.

Two additional female figures compete to control the protagonists' destinies: the phantom of the maternal grandmother who took the girls from the father's home twenty years ago and raised their cousin after her "fall," and that cousin herself, *La Manchote* (one-handed woman) who was discovered fornicating with her twin brother and banished to Paris to live with that same grandmother. Subsequently, and for reasons not revealed until near the end of the narrative, the cousin lost her hand. These competitors are distinct from one another in their approach to food. The grandmother is true to her *sobriquets*: called *Lady Rapace, Lady Chacal, le chacal* (Rapacious Lady, Lady Jackal, the jackal), she is voracious and carnivorous. In contrast, *La Manchote*—who is called *la pythie, la pythonisse à la main coupée,* and *L'Albatros* (prophetess, fortune-teller with the cut hand, and the Albatross[44]) and accused of playing *Les Cassandre, Les Antigone* (Cassandra, Antigone)—not only refuses to eat, but spits on all food prepared from the grandmother's recipes. As one of her fellow characters puts it, this *Jeûnesse* (fasting woman) "ne mangeait rien, sinon son cœur, *amer, amer, amer, mais elle aimait ça, parce que c'était amer, et parce que c'était son cœur*" (TP, 171, italics Lê's: "*didn't eat anything, except her bitter, bitter, bitter heart, but she liked that, because it was bitter, and because it was her heart*").

This description is, of course, cited from the well-known third poem in Stephen Crane's *Black Riders*, which, read in its entirety, draws out more broadly the contours of *La Manchote*:

> In the desert
> I saw a creature, naked, bestial,
> Who, squatting upon the ground,
> Held his heart in his hands,
> And ate of it.
> I said: "Is it good, friend?"
> "It is bitter—bitter," he answered:
> "But I like it
> Because it is bitter,
> And because it is my heart.[45]

Citing Crane, Lê introduces into her narrative the name of yet another displaced poet who wrote in exile and died young. Born in Newark (New Jersey), Crane traveled broadly before settling in Sussex, England, where he died in 1900 at age 29. Citing Crane, she also aligns her novel with his poetry, which was widely perceived in his day as too avant-garde, heretical, and darkly ironic to merit serious attention. Finally, this alignment invites us to suspect that Lê's aims in *Les Trois Parques* may well have been, as Crane said his were in *The Black Riders*, "to give my ideas of life as a whole, as far as I know it."[46]

What, then, can one say about "life as a whole" as represented in this novel by Linda Lê? First, that in that universe, God sits behind a shield of blue vellum playing the part of a *Chevillard* (a butcher who sells wholesale), *a Dépeceur* (a carver of meat), *un Lâcheur* (an unreliable fellow who leaves you in the lurch), *un Grand Sourd* (a Big Deaf Man), *un Inspecteur des Charniers* (an Inspector of Ossuaries), watching (or not) as his marionettes slide around on "une piste glissante" (TP, 8: "a slippery slope"). On that slope, a combat rages between the dynamics of love and those of cannibalism. That combat is figured in various guises: as giving *versus* taking, as retaining *versus* spending to name but two. One eats *or* one loves. One saves letters *or* one uses them to fan the flames. To one side, the grandmother figures the logics of cannibalism—eating the other, figuratively or not, consciously or not, for one's own gain. To the other, *La Manchote* figures the logics of love and passion, of the gift, of risk, of madness. More broadly in Lê's narrative, this battle pits those who, from the conquest on, have promoted their cannibalistic ways against those who, like the father and the cousin, prefer flowers to food; passion to eating. As the reader has known from the beginning, this combat's outcome is fated in advance: there will be no reunion, no reconciliation. Father and daughters, *La Manchote* and her brother, the Vietnamese people, Vietnam: all will remain separated and will continue to search, even after their death, for the lost object, the lost *lieu d'amour*.

Elements of its initial framing re-emerge in the final pages of *Les Trois Parques*. The effect of that re-emergence is a coming into view of a circular frame—the slippery slope? the world's stage?—that recalls the one used in

Bosch's tableau, and which was said, we recall, to signify a general purport, God watching human beings, and cosmic harmony. Lê uses that frame at least as critically, bitterly, and darkly ironically as Bosch. Thus, as the Vietnamese father prepares for his trip to Paris, he leafs through an old poetry anthology looking for lines to memorize. The lines he chooses come from Victor Hugo's "Demain dès l'aube" ("Tomorrow, at Dawn"), a poem composed for his deceased daughter. Repeated several times, the father's lines articulate a response to the invitation issued in Pizarnik's epigraphic poem ("Come at dawn, brave friend, come at dawn") and that other invitation, also issued before the narrative opens, to the Vietnamese father by his older daughter. The lines he picks to memorize come, as we know, from a poem of passion, infinite sadness, tragedy, and expenditure; a poem that depicts a father walking day and night, through forest and mountain, his eyes on his thoughts, blind to the outside world, alone and unknown, his back curved and his hands crossed, so that he may arrive at his beloved daughter's tomb and lay on it "un bouquet de houx et de bruyère en fleur" ("a bouquet of holly and flowering heather"). As these lines reinforce the father's alignment with love and expenditure, they second his friend's hope of one day seeing the father's daughters (whom that friend believes "planted" their father in Vietnam), laying flowers on his grave.

That same friend—a priest who lost his faith and runs a church-based racket—suggests other verses to the father for memorization. These famous lines "le vol de gerfauts hors du charnier natal" ("the flight of gerfauts out of the native mass grave") come from the poem "Les Conquérants" ("Conquerers") by José-Mariá de Heredia (1842-1905).[47] Their citation adds to Lê's narrative the "word" of yet another displaced poet. Born in Cuba to an aristocratic father and a French bourgeois mother, Heredia reputedly did in Paris what Lê vehemently refuses to do: cultivated his difference and played the exoticism card. However that may be, Heredia's poem returns us to the era in which Bosch painted and the European conquest began, to depict the conquistadores as a flock of gyrfalcons leaving "drunk on an heroic and brutal dream" from Christopher Columbus's port, Palos. It indicts the conquistadores' rapacious and cannibalistic greed for the "fabulous metal" of Cipango, an island that medieval legend located to the east of Asia and identified with Japan. Citing this poem, the priest issues a caution: the father's love and his quest (his trip to rejoin his daughters) are situated in a postcolonial era (and a) cannibalistic universe of which one must beware.

Woven of all of the strings of her narrative and its frame, Lê's denouement is orchestral. Everything, we believe for a moment, is at risk and in play. As we finally hear the cautionary tale the grandmother had told her granddaughters about witches, love, and lost hands, possibilities, along with witches and phantoms, appear to abound in the sister's kitchen. There, amorous witches cry warm tears into dishes of sugar and spice, and nubile princesses of the sort we imagine the heroines could be, fly out of them to dance on the walls. As they do, the older sister prepares dishes from both Vietnamese and French traditions—"cervelle d'agneau" (lamb's brains, an ironic figuring of West-East relations) for her Western husband and *crevettes à la grand-mere* (shrimp, grand-mothers' style) for the Vietnamese immigrant sisters and cousin to nibble on before he gets home. Lest we become too hopeful, however, the text cautions us that even witches cannot change fate (TP, 238). As the pages of a book lying open in front of *La Manchote* warn: *"Nous sommes les pièces du jeu que joue le Ciel, On s'amuse avec nous sur l'échiquier de l'être, Et puis nous retournons, un par un, dans la boîte du Néant"* (TP, 235-36, emphasis Lê's: *"We are pieces of the game God plays, He amuses himself with us on the checker board of being, And then we return, one by one, into the box of Nothingness"*). Drawn from the *Rubaiyat*, this citation establishes both *La Manchote* and Lê's novelistic word in relation to the twelfth-century poet, Omar Khayyam and his bitterness, his painful serenity, his critique of religious orthodoxy and of the interference of orthodox clerics in the good-liver's life, his carpe diem praise of good living today (wine, beauty) on the grounds that we may not (indeed will not) have tomorrow.[48]

The ending of *Les Trois Parques* comes suddenly: as the father works out on his stationary bicycle in hopes of cutting a good figure (in fact, of looking like his daughter's favorite actor) when he arrives in France, he falls off the bike, dead, a red hole in the place of his heart. Thus he is cut down at the height of his passion, at the precise moment when his friend, the priest, has come to the view that the father's faith in his upcoming reunification with his daughters has transformed him into a true believer. This conjuncture brings into view the outlines of a worldview that recalls the one developed in *The Black Riders*. Crane's perception of the human condition is especially well-articulated in the final poem in that collection, called simply #68:

> A spirit sped
> Through spaces of night;
> And as he sped, he called:
> "God! God!"
> He went through valleys
> Of black death-slime,
> Ever calling:
> "God! God!"
> Their echoes
> From crevice and cavern
> Mocked him
> "God! God! God!"
> Fleetly into the plains of space
> He went, ever calling:
> "God! God!"
> Eventually, then, he screamed:
> Mad in denial:
> "Ah, there is no God!"
> A swift hand,
> A sword from the sky,
> Smote him,
> And he was dead.[49]

In dialogue with Crane, *Les Trois Parques* significantly augments its darkly ironic meanings. In its terms, it makes no difference whatsoever that one loses faith or finds it: one will be and is cut down in any case, in what appears to be a stunning reassertion of the power of the Fates.

But it would be mistaken to conclude that all that *Les Trois Parques* produces is a bitter and profoundly hopeless universe. Indeed, what is perhaps its most significant "product" sits in the narrative's epilogue, outside of the text itself, as if expelled from the narrative. In this epilogue, the novelist appears to inform her readers of the real material and existential consequences to the writing of *Les Trois Parques*. Upon its completion, these closing lines inform us, Lê suffered "trois mois de stupeur et de confusion" ("three months of stupor and confusion"), which she withstood only thanks to the help of friends and a physician. This image of the author "closes" a scriptural journey that was undertaken, we recall, from postures established through Pizarnik: that of a writer unable to defend herself, a writer seeking only to yield her cadaver, a vulnerable and exposed writer sitting beside a lost child who is herself, and who sings (that is, in the common figuring, who writes poetry). This image closes that journey by revealing Linda Lê, once again, or always already, in the posture of Crane's self-cannibalizing creature: having played with fire and been burned, it suggests, she too sits, like *La Manchote*, eating her bitter heart, but liking it because it is bitter, and because it is her heart.

Notes

1. Linda Lê, *Calomnies* (Paris: Christian Bourgois, 1993); *Slander*, trans. Esther Allen, (Lincoln: Nebraska University Press, 1995).

2. Ook Chung, "Linda Lê, 'Tueuse en dentelles'" *Liberté* 212 (1994): 156. All translations are the author's own unless otherwise stated.

3. Leakthina Chau-Pech Ollier, "Consuming Culture: Linda Lê's Autofiction," in *Of Vietnam: Identities in Dialogue*, eds. Jane Bradley Winston and Leakthina Chau-Pech Ollier (New York: Palgrave, 2001), 250.

4. Linda Lê, *Calomnies*, 12; *Slander*, 4.

5. Chau-Pech Ollier, "Consuming Culture," 242. On Lê's characterization of her own position, see also Jack Yeager, "Culture, Citizenship, Nation: The Narrative Texts of Linda Lê," in *Post-colonial Cultures in France*, eds. Alec G. Hargreaves and Mark McKinney (New York: Routledge, 1997), 257, 261, 267.

6. Chung, "Linda Lê," 156.

7. Chau-Pech Ollier, "Consuming Culture," 242; Chung, "Linda Lê," 159.

8. Chau-Pech Ollier, "Consuming Culture," 245.

9. Chung, "Linda Lê," 156 and 158.

10. Jack Yeager, "Culture, Citizenship, Nation," 261.

11. Chung, "Linda Lê," 155-56.

12. Mikhail Bahktin, *The Dialogic Imagination*, trans. Caryl Emerson and Michael Holquist (Austin: University of Texas Press, 1981), 412.

13. Jack Yeager, "Culture, Citizenship, Nation," 263-64. Those first books were *Un si tendre vampire* (Paris: Table Ronde, 1987) and *Fuir* (Paris: Table Ronde, 1988).

14. Lê's citational practice may recall the contemporary musical "sampling," in which citations to earlier compositions are deployed to stimulate, contribute to, and enrich a new artistic composition. However it is not analogous to Bahktin's "sample," which merely presents someone else's language. Because it fails to bring with it a second linguistic consciousness, the sample is not a linguistic hybrid. Lê's citations can be understood in terms of Bahktin's "image," which contains within itself a second language intention and is thus double-voiced.

15. Bahktin, *The Dialogic Imagination*, 401.

16. George Hanes and G. A. Harrer, *A Handbook of Classical Mythology* (London: Allen and Unwin, 1931), 171.

17. Edith Hamilton, *Mythology: Timeless Tales of Gods and Heroes* (New York: Mentor, 1965), 43.

18. Carlos Parada, "Moerae," Greek Mythology Link, http://homepage.mac.com/cparada/GML/MOERAE.html (February 21, 2004).

19. Timothy Gantz, *Early Greek Mythology* (Baltimore: Johns Hopkins University Press, 1993), 60.

20. Cited in Carlos Parada, "Moerae."

21. Hamilton, *Mythology*, 331.

22. Carlos Parada, "Moerae."

23. *Petit Robert II*, eds. A. Rey and J. Rey-Debove (Paris: Le Robert, 1988), 357.

24. Melanie Nicholson, *Evil, Madness, and the Occult in Argentine Poetry* (Gainsville: University of Florida Press, 2002), 76.

25. Lê, *Les Trois Parques*, 8. Further references included parenthetically, preceded by TP.

26. Laurinda S. Dixon, *Bosch* (London/New York: Phaidon, 2003), 56.

27. German Epilepsie Museum website, <http://www.epilepsiemuseum.de> (February 21, 2004).

28. Dixon, *Bosch*, 56.

29. Robert L. Delevoy, *Bosch: Critical and Biographical Study*, trans. Stuart Gibson (Lausanne: Editions Skira, 1960), 27.

30. Delevoy, *Bosch*, 27.

31. Dixon, *Bosch*, 62.

32. Walter S. Gibson, *Hieronymus Bosch* (New York/Toronto: Oxford University Press, 1973), 40.

33. German Epilepsie Museum website.

34. Delevoy, *Bosch*, 24.

35. Dixon, *Bosch*, 59.

36. Dixon, *Bosch*, 61.

37. Cited in Delevoy, *Bosch*, 27.

38. Nicholson, *Evil, Madness, and the Occult*, 74.

39. Georges Bataille, *Literature and Evil*, trans. Alastair Hamilton (New York: Marion Boyers, 1985), 24. Cited in Nicholson, *Evil, Madness, and the Occult*, 82.

40. Nicholson, *Evil, Madness, and the Occult*, 66.

41. Frank Graziano, *Alejandra Pizarnik: A Profile* (Durango, CO: Logbridge-Rhodes, 1987), 58.

42. Nicholson, *Evil, Madness, and the Occult*, 73.

43. The verb "filer" also means to spin, suggesting a rapprochement of the two sisters and their cousin to the titular Fates.

44. French literary references to this bird include two noted in Le Petit Robert: Pierre Loti's phrase "The big heavy albatross, of dirty coloring, with their stupid sheep-like air" and Baudelaire's poem by that name. *Le Petit Robert I*, 45.

45. Joseph Katz, ed., *The Poems of Stephen Crane* (New York: Cooper Square Publishers, 1966), 5. Consistent with what appears to be her tendency to draw citations from literary referents circulating during the period of her writing's conceptualization and/or execution, these lines from Crane also refer us to the 1990 novel in which Joyce Carol Oates examines black-white race relations in 1950s and 1960s America, *Because it is Bitter, and Because it is my Heart* (New York: E. P. Dutton, 1990).

46. Katz, ed., *The Poems of Stephen Crane*, xvii.

47. Anne Bernet claims that these words "resonate in everyone's memory." This would have been especially the case in 1993, when Lê was perhaps conceiving or beginning to write *Les Trois Parques*, since this same Heredia line was being picked up and recirculated in France and Francophone Canada, where France Boisvert published *Comme un vol de gerfaut* (Montréal: Editions Noroît, 1993). Anne Bernet, "Heredia ou la Bretagne en technicolor," http://www.freewebs.com/provinciales/h01/ljh0128.html (February 21, 2004).

48. I thank William D. Paden for drawing my attention to this reference and Nasrin Qader for her insights into Khayyam.

49. Katz, ed., *The Poems of Stephen Crane*, 72.

14

Jean Hougron's Indochina:
Fantasy and Disillusionment

Jack A. Yeager

For the last twenty-five years, I have been exploring the literary production in French from Vietnam. In my earliest work I launched this examination by focusing on authors who were ethnically Vietnamese but wrote in French.[1] Yet other literary texts complicate this approach: what does it mean for a text to be "from Vietnam"? Since the appearance of my first book in 1987, I have looked at this complexity in a number of distinct ways: for instance, by studying authors—like Linda Lê[2]—born in Vietnam of Vietnamese heritage but who may consider themselves to be French, or Marguerite Duras, born in Vietnam of French parents but often writing on Southeast Asia. The traditional distinctions between Vietnamese Francophone texts as I defined them some twenty years ago, texts from today's Vietnamese diaspora, and so-called colonial texts, may not be as fruitful as they appear at first glance. Instead, Sara Suleri proposes a new theoretical framework in her book *The Rhetoric of English India* (1992), a textual confrontation that aims to interrogate the colonizer/colonized dichotomy which, in her reading, ends in a critical impasse.[3] Suleri's question is also mine: should we be thinking of so-called colonial writers in the multiple contexts of *métissage*, marginality and displacement, in much the same way we might so-called Francophone writers?

My larger project has juxtaposed texts from the best-known and most-studied authors from Vietnam who write in French. In addition to those I have already examined elsewhere—Phạm Văn Ký, Linda Lê, and Marguerite Duras[4]—I add a fourth author, who was widely recognized in the 1950s, Jean Hougron. His seven-novel cycle, *La Nuit Indochinoise*, was popular in France and elsewhere (most of them were translated and published in English, for instance). The novels went through several press runs and the cycle won the Grand Prix du Roman de l'Académie française in 1953, even before all the novels had appeared. One of these texts, *Mort en fraude*, was made into a film directed by Marcel Camus and released in 1956.[5] In this essay I would like to examine Hougron's representations of Indochina by looking at two of his narrative texts, *Les Asiates* (1954) and *Mort en fraude* (1953).

At first glance, Hougron's biography would seem to present him as a quintessentially colonial writer. Born in Normandy in 1923, he lived in Cherbourg, then in Dreux where he taught science and English. In 1946, he studied law, and shortly afterwards he worked for an import-export company in Marseille. In 1947 he left for Indochina. There, he worked as a truck driver, a tobacco planter, and a beer salesman as well as a teacher in Laos, Cambodia, southern China, and Thailand. In September 1949, he returned to Saigon where he worked for Radio France-Asie until 1951, the year of his repatriation to France. The first of his cycles of novels set in Southeast Asia, "La Nuit Indochinoise," appeared in 1950, the last in 1958.[6] In 1965, Jean Hougron was awarded the Prix Populiste. In the 1980s, he began writing science fiction novels. His *Le Naguen* (1980) won the Grand Prix de la Science-Fiction in 1981. He still lives in France, and a web search will reveal an astonishing number of links to Jean Hougron (nearly 2000, in fact) and many sites centered on him.[7]

Les Asiates recounts the story of three generations of the extended Bressan family in Saigon covering some forty years, from 1907 to 1947. A family tree at the beginning of the text suggests the epic sweep of this novel of some 600 pages. It is essentially a family story against the political backdrop of colonialism, the struggles for independence, and open conflict in Indochina. Structurally, the chapters move back and forth between 1947 and earlier years in chronological order. Reading the novel, then, becomes an exercise in understanding the upheavals of 1947 through the lens of the past as the earlier chapters gradually approach the narrative "present," only to align at the end of the novel.

At the outset, the young Bressan couple imagines their destination, inspired by a map they have purchased before their departure. A predictably exotic Indochina—captured in the Vietnamese spelling of Sai-Gon (283) circled in red—lures them. This same map, described in the opening pages four decades later, tattered and discolored, its geographical boundaries no longer distinguishable, transforms the exotic attraction of Indochina into the deterioration and dissolution of French colonial power in Southeast Asia. "C'était une vieille carte qui avait dû être très vivement coloriée autrefois: bleu pour la mer, blanc et rose allant jusqu'au brun pour les plaines et les montagnes, bleu encore pour les fleuves et les rivières. La Mère l'avait achetée à Marseille, dans une boutique du Vieux-Port, juste avant d'embarquer sur le voilier qui les emmenait à la colonie" (283: "It was an old map which must have been brightly colored in bygone days: blue for the sea, white and pink turning to brown for the plains and the mountains, blue again for the rivers and tributaries. The Mother had bought it in Marseille in a shop at the Old Port just before boarding the sailboat which took them to the colony").[8] During the sea voyage, she and her husband contemplate the map; after their arrival, she would look at it when bored, "et rêvait, comme éblouie" (283: "and dreamed, as if bedazzled"). Even in its degraded state forty years later, "Sai-Gon" remains highlighted, but its Vietnamese spelling now signals emerging indigenous control. This outcome is reflected in the gradual shift in the pages of the novel from "annamite" to "vietnamien" (352, 452-53, 676, for example: "Annamite" to "Vietnamese") as history runs its course in *Les Asiates*. The père Bressan, "intoxiqué [d'Asie]" (623: "intoxicated by Asia"), tries to realize his fantasy of pleasure in the exploitation of indigenous women, imitating Vietnamese men in taking concubines and fathering many children. His relentless pursuit of pleasure leads to his own degradation and the neglect of his family. Yet, in the end, he cannot adapt; the exotic fantasy is shattered.

In the novel, the characters' fantasies emerge from their racist and sexist views of Vietnamese society and culture. Both turn on the register of sameness marked by words such as "toujours," "uniforme," "se ressembler" (293, 337, 383, 391, 501, 503, 506, 514, 557, 559, 579, 597, for example) ("always, uniform/unchanging, to resemble") and frequent cultural generalizations. White male characters in *Les Asiates* are quick to judge and categorize, often using phrases like "comme tous les" or "comme toutes les" ("like all"). In this way, certain characters flatten difference and distance the other into an anonymous mass.

But these same characters experience a contradictory impulse, when they emerge as "asiates."[9] We see this term used for the first time in the novel to describe the patriarch:

> A vrai dire, s'il a refusé ce premier congé [pour rentrer en France], c'est parce qu'il n'avait pas envie de quitter l'Indochine. Retourner dans la métropole ne lui sourit pas, même pour un bref séjour. Il y a d'ailleurs longtemps qu'il ne pense plus à la France, et au bureau il se désintéresse si bien des projets de retour de ses collègues qu'ils l'ont surnommé "l'Asiate," le Blanc converti à l'Asie. (339)

> (To tell the truth, if he refused to take this first vacation [to return to France], it was because he didn't want to leave Indochina. Returning to the metropole didn't appeal to him, even for a brief stay. Besides, for a long time he didn't even think about France anymore, and at the office he was so uninterested in his colleagues' plans to return home that they nicknamed him the Asiate, the white man converted to Asia.)

For Henri, Bressan's son born in Indochina by his French wife Françoise, the impulse is even stronger: he speaks Vietnamese, considers Indochina his home ("C'est mon pays," 600: "It's my home"), and has no desire to leave. Even

Françoise, Bressan's French wife, adapts to the point of admitting to herself that: "elle n'a pas envie de quitter ce pays" (432: "she had no desire to leave this country").

In *Les Asiates*, these cultural "métis" find their counterparts in characters of mixed race, and the novel identifies each and every one of them in apposition, deliberately and self-consciously, heightening a sense of racial difference in this text.[10] Some of the characters are the children of Bressan himself: Chu, the son of the head servant at the Résidence (Nam); and Solange, Maurice and Alice by Pauline, identified as the father's first concubine and herself *métisse*. Others born and raised in the family compound are "de père inconnu" ("of an unknown father"), offspring of Pauline or Sao, the second concubine. But even the most minor and nameless métis characters are so identified in this novel. The composite portrait which emerges is both contradictory and alluring. Some biracial characters may show physical beauty: for Françoise, thinking of Solange, Pauline's daughter, "Ces enfants de métisses sont souvent superbes" (432: "Those mixed-race children are often beautiful"). At seven, Solange has "d'étranges yeux très bleus dans son visage doré" (525: "strange blue eyes in her golden face." She is physically beautiful, and yet somehow indefinable. Georges, Solange's half brother, thinks of himself as French, misunderstanding why he would earn less in a French company: "Ils étaient français comme les autres" (333: "They were French like the others"), he says to a friend at work who disabuses him of the notion "en bon métis aigri" (333: "like a good little embittered métis").

Characters in the novel, whether biracial or not, conclude that the physical appearance of *métissage* determines character. Alice, Pauline's third child by Bressan, may display "mines vinaigrées de petite métisse arrogante" (369: "sour expressions of an arrogant little *métisse*") according to her French half-brother Henri. They are overly sensitive: "Les Eurasiens . . . se montrent trop susceptibles" (334: "Eurasians . . . are too touchy"), says a French character with some disdain. And they are not to be trusted: Georges's status as métis explains his suspect behavior for the police (604). Revolutionaries find Georges a possible recruit: "C'est vrai que les métis, c'est encore plus agressif que les Blancs. Ils faut qu'ils se fassent pardonner leur mélange" (481: "It's true that the métis are even more aggressive than the whites. They need to be forgiven for their mixed blood"). Chu, himself métis, Nam's son by Bressan, is skeptical: "Les comités de province n'ont jamais réussi à recruter les métis, qui font presque tous cause commune avec les Français" (628-29: "The provincial committees have never succeeded in recruiting people of mixed race who almost all share common cause with the French"). For Nam, Pauline is "une de ces innombrables petites métisses qui cherchent fortune dans cette ville [Saïgon]" (424: "one of those innumerable little *métisses* who are seeking their fortune in this city [Saigon]"). Nam distrusts those of mixed race (420) while being the mother of a biracial child. Just as we have seen more recently in the texts of Kim Lefèvre, the métis raises doubts and creates an epistemological panic, portrayed as ultimately unknowable, characters at the border zone.[11]

Many of the biracial characters envy the French (Alphonse, 643) and dream of one day going to France to live (Hiem, 449). Returning from mass, Alice, for example, "loves Sunday":

> Il arrive au bout de la semaine comme un merveilleux dessert à la fin d'un médiocre repas. C'est cela: un gros gâteau d'anniversaire fragile et somptueux, givré de sucre. Elle se dit qu'en France les dimanches de printemps doivent être semblables. Elle rêve de la France, d'une rue de province assoupie, de volets à demi clos sur des bonheurs paisibles. (482)

> (It comes at the end of the week like a marvelous dessert at the end of a mediocre meal. That's it: a big birthday cake, delicate and sumptuous, frosted with sugar. She tells herself that in France Sundays in the spring must be similar. She dreams of France, of a drowsy, provincial street, shutters half-closed on peaceful happiness).

At one point she imagines "Une forêt d'Europe, de France," "Pas une forêt d'Asie" (494: "A forest in Europe, in France." "Not an Asian forest"). She dreams of marrying her friend Alphonse, also métis, and moving to France.

The pull of France is strongest on Pauline. Bressan exploits Pauline's sensitivities expertly when he mistakes her for a Parisian friend on a Saigon street, a clever pickup line (392-93). The young *métisse* school girl dreams of marrying the Frenchman who will take her to Paris, a city she imagines through the novels she has read and the films she has seen (393). Pauline detests her mother, "une vieille Tonkinoise . . . la bouche ensanglantée de chiqueuse de bétel" (394: "An old woman from Tonkin . . . her mouth reddened like a woman who chews betel nuts"). Abandoned by Pauline's French father when she was only six months old, the mother lives in "une cabane de 'nhaquê' [Pauline's words]" (394: "a hick's shack"). In *Les Asiates* Pauline will affect to speak only French (499), try to pass as white, fooling no one (568-69), have only disdain for other métis including her own children, be horrified that Alice wants to marry Alphonse (666), and consider taking a *métisse* as servant (666).

The character of Pauline recalls others from Vietnamese Francophone novels who dream the French dream, unaffected yet by what Memmi would call in his *Portrait du colonisé* the "prise de conscience" of their own self-worth. In some sense they are subject to the reverse phantasm of their French counterparts, easily fostered in the vulnerable colonized. That the American novelist Monique Truong would write about the "saison de l'amour" ("the season of love") in Paris in the editorial pages of *The New York Times*[12] surely reveals the ongoing power of what one might call phantasmatic France.

The theme of the sprawling *Les Asiates* finds interesting echoes in Hougron's *Mort en fraude*, a shorter, more concentrated, but more complex novel. It tells the story of a young office worker, Paul Horcier, sent to Indochina by his company. Owing a debt to his sister, he agrees to transport a large sum of American dollars for a third party. Having paid this first debt, however, Horcier will contract many others. The money is stolen during the sea voyage. Once arrived in Saigon, he attempts to explain the loss to the criminals to whom he was to deliver the cash. They will hear none of it, giving him a deadline to turn over the loot. When he fails to do so, they try to kill him, and Horcier is on the run. He succeeds in escaping, ending up in a narrow street in Cholon where he hides in an apartment belonging to Anh, a young woman identified as Eurasian. She will take him to her native village, Vinh Bao, far from Saigon, on the condition that he give her all the money he has left. They leave the next morning by bus, then continue on foot for several days. In Vinh Bao Horcier is hidden with Anh's family: her grandfather educated in Franco-Vietnamese schools, her mother, her younger brother, and very young twins. Living in an isolated village in a contested zone in the south during the 1946-1954 war transforms the protagonist from a naïf into a *révolté*. Seeing the misery of the starving villagers, he is determined to feed them, heal their diseases, and cultivate the rice fields again, despite the threats of the Viet Minh who take the harvest. Horcier ends up thinking that the French will be able to retake the province, an idea that takes him and Anh back to Saigon. Their own relationship, her disdain and distrust growing into mutual respect, suggests a future together. But the traffickers find Horcier in Saigon. The novel closes with his murder.

Once again, faraway Indochina is a predictable exotic space at the beginning of *Mort en fraude*. On the boat to Southeast Asia, Horcier asks many questions of those who know life in Indochina. What he learns both corrects and reinforces stereotypes of colonial life: "Les histoires qu'il entendait différaient de ce qu'il avait lu dans les livres, bien sûr. C'était plus prosaïque, mais il n'arrivait pas à être déçu. L'argent, une vie facile, une belle maison, des serviteurs indigènes, et une voiture" (17; *Fugitive*, 18: "The stories he heard were very different from the ones he had read in books, of course. They were more prosaic, but he refused to let himself be disillusioned. Money, an easy life, a fine house, native servants, a car"). Moreover, he imagines a heroic return to France after his time in Indochina. At first sight, then, this imaginary Indochina seems to exemplify Panivong Norindr's phantasmatic reading of Duras, Malraux, Wargnier, and others,[13] a far-off Indochina, quickly conjured with an array of stereotypical conventions in the opening pages of *Mort en fraude*.

Horcier's first few hours in Saigon hardly disabuse him of these stereotypes. Upon leaving the customs area at the docks, he sees:

> la rue. Tout l'exotisme de la ville sautait d'un seul jet au visage: Indiens enturbannés, Annamites aux socques de bois crépitantes, enfants dorés à demi nus et surtout cette odeur de marché oriental, de poivre, d'épices et de poussière surchauffée qui assaillait l'odorat. Des mots étranges, modulés, criés, gémis, l'éclaboussaient au passage et lorsqu'il levait les yeux, c'était le ciel d'Asie, les palmes, presque noires par contraste, de la végétation tropicale et l'éclatante blancheur des immeubles européens. (19)

(the streets. The whole exotic character of the town hit him like a blow in the face: bearded, turbaned Indians, Annamites with creaking wooden pattens, golden-yellow half-naked children, and above all the odor of the Eastern markets—pepper, spices, and sun-baked dust—pervading everything. Strange modulated words, cries and groans caught his ear, and when he raised his eyes he could see palms that were almost black against the Asiatic sky, tropical vegetation, and the dazzling whiteness of the European buildings. *Fugitive*, 22.)

After Horcier's first encounter with the traffickers, his feelings of danger transform the city into a "forêt épaisse" (21; *Fugitive*, 25: "dense jungle"). The labyrinth of narrow streets in Cholon hides him from his pursuers. The potential for these transformations of the colonial space are present in the initial street scene that assaults Horcier's senses. This space, as Hougron depicts it, is thus one of adventure, but also of corruption and upended values. As in a film noir, Horcier will be condemned by a single moral failing.

Horcier's penetration of Cholon's labyrinth and its buildings to end up in an obscure room at night figures his coming transformation as he is initiated into Vietnamese culture and into the politics of the war between the French and the Vietnamese. The first step in his education is the clearly symbolically charged encounter with Anh in her bedroom, the space Horcier allows himself to enter. However, Anh, not the privileged Horcier, is the one in control: she gives him orders and treats him with contempt and disdain, an apparent power reversal (26-28; *Fugitive*, 34-36). Horcier's naïveté and ignorance weaken his position. Anh's power is grounded on her inside knowledge and perhaps even more importantly, on her situation as seemingly privileged *métisse*. Under Anh's tutelage, then, Horcier will do an apprenticeship in Vietnamese culture.

His education will be doubled by that of the omniscient, third-person narrator in this esthetically conventional novel. Horcier and his double know little about Vietnamese culture. Neither knows the precise names of things, and neither can distinguish the Chinese from the Vietnamese. We see the first signs of transformation during the trip on foot to Vinh Bao. When Horcier has trouble following Anh on the narrow dikes between the rice fields, he exasperatedly takes off his shoes and throws them into the swamp. After many weeks in Vinh Bao, Horcier witnesses the execution of an elderly villager by a Viet Minh soldier, furthering his transformation: "C'est peut-être à ce moment-là que Horcier commença à se révolter" (79; *Fugitive*, 120: "It was perhaps at this moment that Horcier began to revolt"). When Anh falls ill with malaria, Horcier criticizes the villagers' passivity (81; *Fugitive*, 123). Near this point in the novel, the narrator's descriptions become more precise and better informed, the vocabulary more specific. The narrator begins to explain Vietnamese words (85; *Fugitive*, 130), seems more culturally sensitive (89; *Fugitive*, 136). As the narrator begins to show what he has learned, so does the main character. He can guess the meanings of words from context in the same way as the non-Vietnamese, Francophone reader (93-94, 98; *Fugitive*, 143, 151). Later on, the narrator, like Horcier, will know the names of trees, flowers and birds (142; *Fugitive*, 224-25). By its end, the novel has described many Vietnamese cultural practices, ethnographic aspects that recall the narrative texts of the Vietnamese Francophone corpus, for the implied metropolitan reader.

The narrator also begins to show knowledge of Vietnamese syntax in the French sentences spoken by Anh's brother, who has begun studying the language, first with his Francophone grandfather, then with the protagonist. We note the uninflected neutral verb form, for example, or the mark of possession and adjectival placement (75 *passim*; *Fugitive*, 112 *passim*). Even a Vietnamese word used pejoratively in French such as "nhà quê" (peasant) recovers its primary meaning (78; *Fugitive*, 118). Finally, Anh notices Horcier's linguistic progress: "Vous comprenez très bien l'annamite [*sic*] maintenant" (97; *Fugitive*, 150: "You seem to understand Annamese very well now"). Later, the narrator translates a Vietnamese sentence spoken by Anh into French (147; *Fugitive*, 233).

Despite his new knowledge, however, Horcier cannot mask a certain lack of cultural sensitivity. For example, he cannot comprehend the resignation of the villagers to their fate (98; *Fugitive*, 151). He believes himself capable of changing everything, of challenging the village's acceptance of its apparent destiny. For him it was "[trop] facile . . . de se soumettre sans tenter jamais de détourner le sort" (99; *Fugitive*, 153: "Easy . . . to submit without ever trying to avert your fate"), which explains why Horcier wants to start cultivating the fallow rice fields once again. He thus begins to give orders, to say "Il faudra" ("You must"), too often. His goal is to take care of those who are sick in the village, to give them food to eat and share everything.

The reaction of Anh's mother to Horcier's self-appointed mission is instructive. Her hate, described as "mystical," of someone who knew a French man, reminds us of the colonizer's arrogance and superior attitude. The village chief tells Horcier: "Vous avez fait pour nous tout ce que vous avez pu. Vous avez essayé de faire de nos paysans des hommes comme les autres" (139; *Fugitive*, 219: "You've done everything you could for us. You've tried to make men of our peasants"). He seems to be saying that Horcier has failed in his personal "mission civilisatrice." One might well read his "failure" as successful indigenous resistance to France. The entire colonial period is then summarized in the reaction of the mother, an abandoned woman, a "con gái."

> La mère contemplait Horcier et une haine mystique faisait resplendir ses yeux très noirs. Horcier pensa au père de Anh. Un Français probablement. Pourquoi avait-il abandonné la mère? Mais surtout, qu'avait-il bien pu lui faire pour qu'elle haïsse les hommes blancs avec une telle violence? Car ce n'est pas lui qu'elle détestait, mais toute sa race et ce qu'elle avait apporté à son peuple. (99-100)

> (The mother stared at Horcier and a mystical hatred made her very black eyes glow like coals. Horcier wondered who Anh's father was. Probably a Frenchman. Why had he abandoned the mother? But,

above all, what could he have done to her to make her hate white men so violently, for it was not only him she detested but his whole race and all the misery it had brought to her people. *Fugitive*, 153).

Later in the novel, when Horcier and Anh attempt to rent a hotel room in a nearby town, the French protagonist learns firsthand what it means to be the "con gái" of a French man. The European hotel manager sees them at the reception desk and immediately says: "La chambre, c'est pour vous seul. Pas de 'congai' ici" (148: *Fugitive*, 234: "The room's for you only. No *congaïes* here!"). The protagonist's angry reaction marks the culmination of his transformation:

> Il pensait à tous les Blancs qu'il avait vus depuis qu'il était arrivé dans ce pays. Il y pensait comme à des étrangers, à des êtres d'une autre race que la sienne. Là-bas, à Vinh-Bao, les paysans se faisaient une certaine idée de l'homme blanc. Il l'avait jugée stupide, telle-ment inexacte surtout et aujourd'hui qu'il était aussi démuni que le dernier paysan du delta, il apercevait une autre vérité. Il y avait l'image que les hommes blancs se font d'eux-mêmes en toute sincé-rité, et il y avait une autre image, pas plus vraie peut-être, mais bien plus quotidienne, celle que l'indigène se fait de l'homme blanc. De-vant cette image-là, il n'y avait que deux attitudes: la révolte ou la soumission. Mais, de toute façon, il y avait la haine. Il pensa: "On ne peut juger un peuple sur quelques hommes." (149)

> (He thought of all the whites he had seen since he arrived in this country. He thought of them as foreigners, as beings of a race other than his own. Back at Vinh-Bao the peasants had formed a certain idea of the white man. He had considered it stupid and, above all, very inaccurate, but now that he was as poor as the lowest coolie from the delta he perceived another truth. There was the picture the white men made of themselves in all sincerity and then there was another picture, perhaps no truer but far more mundane, which the natives made of them. Faced by that picture, there were only two patterns of behavior: revolt or submission. But in either case there was hatred. One can't judge a race by a few men, he thought. *Fugitive*, 235-36).

This moment of the main character's *prise de conscience* is also that of the reader, the final lesson of this novel published in 1953, a moment when France was about to lose its colony. It implies the resolve of the Vietnamese to free themselves from colonialism, one of the worst kinds of fraud.

The exterior voyage of the protagonist, physical and geographical, is dou-bled by an interior voyage, psychological and transformative. One might say that Horcier, the colonizer upon his arrival in Indochina, is changed into Memmi's "colonial," presented in the first chapter of *Portrait du colonisé* enti-tled "Le colonial existe-t-il?" As is well-known, the "colonial," aware of the true nature of power relations in the colony, becomes a de facto "colonizer" upon arrival. A colonial can only remain so by leaving the colony and the privileges that mere presence confers.[14] Horcier's coming to consciousness becomes a critique of colonialism, much like that of Marguerite Duras in *Un barrage contre le Pacifique*, for example. According to this schema, certain colonizers exploit not only the indigenous colonized but also the less fortunate colonizers, powerless at the bottom of the colonial hierarchy. Memmi suggests the colonial must leave the colony, a way, perhaps, of explaining Horcier's death at the end of the novel. He cannot survive the *métissage* and the displacement of his Indochina adventure.

In *Les Asiates* and *Mort en fraude*, then, Jean Hougron feeds the fantasies of Indochina in his readers, then disillusions them, actively disabusing them of the colonial myth—readers who devoured his novels in France in the 1950s and 1960s, during the war of liberation, the end of French Indochina and afterward. In 2004, Hougron's cycle of novels, largely forgotten on library shelves, was republished by Laffont. Is this yet another sign of a resurgent phantasmatic Indochina saturated with nostalgia, epitomized by Régis Wargnier's film *Indochine*? In parallel Hougron presents in some of his Vietnamese and métis characters the impulse of a phantasmatic France in colonial Southeast Asia. A closer critical reading of Hougron reveals, however, that this writer of French origin who spent several years in colonial Indochina, in fact seeks to overturn colonial fantasies in *Les Asiates* and *Mort en fraude*, texts written while the war for Vietnamese independence was in full swing. As Jane Winston has so convincingly shown with Duras,[15] perhaps Hougron, too, fits the category of transnational, Francophone novelist, beyond the hexagon. In the twenty-first century what will the consequences of such global perspectives be for traditional linguistic and cultural categories that define fields of study and university departments and disciplines?

Notes

I am grateful to the late John Smail for his critique of my earliest work on Jean Hougron in the 1970s. This chapter has grown out of two recent convention papers, one which focused on *Mort en fraude* at the Conseil International d'Etudes Francophones annual meeting in Abidjan in 2002, and a second which extended my analysis to *Les Asiates* at the conference on Indochina organized at the University of Newcastle (U.K.) in 2003. I would like to thank the organizers of those conferences and the participants for their questions and comments. Thanks, as well, to Jennifer Yee for her criticism. And as always, my gratitude to Timothy Cook.

1. See *The Vietnamese Novel in French: A Literary Response to Colonialism* (Hanover and London: University Press of New England, 1987).
2. See her *Calomnies* (Paris: Christian Bourgois, 1993) or *Les Trois Parques* (Paris: Christian Bourgois, 1997), for example. When her first books were published in the late 1980s, she said she considered herself to be French and Western.

3. Sara Suleri, *The Rhetoric of English India* (Chicago: University of Chicago Press, 1992).

4. See, most recently: "Writing from Exile: Pham Van Ky's Imagined Returns to Viet Nam," *Michigan Quarterly Review* 43: 4 (Fall 2004), 691-704, a special issue on Vietnamese diasporic writing edited by Barbara Tran and Rebekah Linh Collins; "Le défi de Linda Lê," forthcoming in *Le Viêt-nam au féminin*, eds. Gisèle Bousquet and Nora Taylor (Paris: Les Indes Savantes, 2005); and "Colonialism and Power in Marguerite Duras's *L'Amant*" in *Of Vietnam: Identities in Dialogue*, eds. Jane Bradley Winston and Leakthina Chau-Pech Ollier (New York: Palgrave, 2001), 224-35. In addition, I would signal two new important studies of Vietnamese Francophone literature: Karl Ashoka Britto, *Disorientation: France, Vietnam, and the Ambivalence of Interculturality* (Hong Kong: Hong Kong University Press, 2004); and Nathalie Huỳnh Châu Nguyễn, *Vietnamese Voices: Gender, Cultural Identity in the Vietnamese Francophone Novel* (Dekalb: Southeast Asia Publications, Northern Illinois University Monograph Series on Southeast Asia, No. 6, 2004).

5. The film starred Daniel Gélin and Anne Méchard. The movie poster can be viewed online at the following address: www.carnetsduvietnam.com/cinema-vietnamien/mortenfraude.htm (August 2004).

6. The novels in order are: *Tu récolteras la tempête* (1950), *Rage blanche* (1951), *Soleil au ventre* (1952), *Mort en fraude* (1953), *Les Portes de l'aventure* (1954), *Les Asiates* (1954), and *La Terre du barbare* (1958). All were published in Paris by Domat.

7. This biographical information comes from the bookcovers of his novels.

8. This and all subsequent references to Hougron's novels are from Volume II of the Laffont compendium edition reedited in 2004 (*La Nuit indochinoise*, Paris: Robert Laffont, 1989). Translations from *Les Asiates*, included in parentheses after the original, are my own, and I take full responsibility for their shortcomings. This novel is the only one in the cycle not yet translated into English. For *Mort en fraude* I used the English translation by Mervyn Savill (1955, *The Fugitive*, London: Hurst and Blackett). Quotations from and references to Savill's translation are indicated by the abbreviation *Fugitive* in parentheses included after the original French.

9. According to the *Grand Robert* (2001), the word "asiate" first appeared in 1879, as a regressive form of "asiatique," a word dating from the sixteenth century. Defined as a "personne originaire de l'Asie" as in "les yeux bridés d'un Asiate," this source cites adjectival uses: "le christianisme asiate (1879, Renan)"; "'un gang de disquaires asiates' (*Le Point*, 29 mars 1981)"; and "'Elle a le teint asiate' (*F Magazine*, 7 août 1981)." The *Grand Robert* indicates that "asiate" has "un sens vague, souvent péjoratif ou ironique." The *Dictionnaire historique de la langue française* (1993) also indicates that the word appears "dans un contexte raciste et ne s'emploie que péjorativement." The *Dictionnaire universel francophone* also concurs that the word is used pejoratively. One wonders why the word acquired its ironic rather than racist use in the years between 1993 and 2001.

10. Tellingly, the Italian translation of *Les Asiates* by Roberto Ortolani is entitled *Sangue misto* (Milan: A. Valardi, 1988).

11. See her *Métisse blanche* (Paris: Barrault, 1989).

12. August 22, 2003, A-25.

13. See his *Phantasmatic Indochina* (Durham, NC: Duke University Press, 1996).

14. See Albert Memmi, *Portrait du colonisé* (Paris: Gallimard, 1985), 29-42. Originally published by Corréa in 1957.

15. See her *Postcolonial Duras* (New York: Palgrave, 2001).

Selected Bibliography
Of Works in English and French

Ageron, Charles-Robert. *France coloniale ou Parti colonial?* Paris: Presses Universitaires de France, 1978.

Ajalbert, Jean. *Raffin Su-su.* Paris: Publications littéraires et politiques, 1911. Reprinted in *Raffin Su-su suivi de Sao Van Di.* Paris/Pondicherry: Kailash, 1995.

———. *Les Nuages sur l'Indochine.* Paris: Louis-Michaud, 1912.

Aldrich, Robert. *Greater France: A History of French Overseas Expansion.* London: Macmillan, 1996.

———. "Vestiges of the Colonial Empire: The Jardin Colonial in Paris." In *The Sphinx in the Tuileries*, edited by Robert Aldrich and Martyn Lyons. Sydney: Department of Economic History, 1999.

Appiah, Kwame Anthony. *In My Father's House: Africa in the Philosophy of Culture.* New York: Methuen, 1992.

Aragon, Isabelle. "Le Temple du Souvenir Indochinois de Nogent-sur-Marne." Mémoire du D. E. A. de Vietnamien, Université de Paris III, 1983.

Argand, Catherine. "Linda Lê: Entretien." *Lire* (April 1999): http://www.lire.fr/entretien.asp/idC=35595/idTC=4/idR=201/idG=. (October 1, 2004).

Audoin-Rouzeau, Stephane. *Men at War, 1914-1918: National Sentiment and Trench Journalism in France during the Great War.* Oxford: Berg, 1992.

Bahktin, Mikhail. *The Dialogic Imagination.* Translated by Caryl Emerson and Michael Holquist. Austin: University of Texas Press, 1981.

Baille, Frédéric. *Souvenirs d'Annam 1886-1890.* Paris: Plon, 1890.

Bataille, Georges. *Literature and Evil.* Translated by Alastair Hamilton. New York: Marion Boyers, 1985.

Bécel, Pascale. "From *The Sea Wall* to *The Lover*: Prostitution and Exotic Parody." *Studies in Twentieth-Century Literature* 21, no. 2 (1997): 417-32.

Belval, Challan de. *Au Tonkin, 1884-1885: Notes, Souvenirs et Impressions.* Paris: Plon, 1904.

Bernet, Anne. "Heredia ou la Bretagne en Technicolor." http://www.freewebs.com/provinciales/h01/ljh0128.html (October 1, 2004).

Betts, Raymond F. *Assimilation and Association in French Colonial Theory 1890-1914*. New York: Columbia University Press, 1961.

Bhabha, Homi. *The Location of Culture*. New York: Routledge, 1994.

Boissière, Jules. *Fumeurs d'Opium*. Paris: Flammarion, 1895. Reprinted Paris/ Pondicherry: Kailash, 1993.

Boisvert, France. *Comme un vol de gerfauts*. Quebec: Editions Noroît, 1993.

Booth, Anne. "Living Standards and the Distribution of Income in Colonial Indonesia." *Journal of Southeast Asian Studies* 19, no. 2 (1988): 310-40.

Borel, Marius. *Souvenirs d'un vieux colonialiste*. Rodez: Imprimerie Subervie, 1963.

Bouillevaux, C-E. *L'Annam et le Cambodge: Voyages et Notices Historiques*. Paris: Victor Palmé, 1874.

Bousquet, Gisèle, and Pierre Brocheux, eds. *Viêt-Nam Exposé: French Scholarship on Twentieth-Century Vietnamese Society*. Ann Arbor: Michigan University Press, 2002.

Bouthors-Paillart, Catherine. *Duras la métisse: métissage fantasmatique et linguistique dans l'œuvre de Marguerite Duras*. Geneva: Droz, 2002.

Brocheux, Pierre and Daniel Hémery. *Indochine, la colonisation ambiguë 1858-1954*. Paris: La Découverte, 2001.

Certeau, Michel de. *The Practice of Everyday Life*. Translated by Steven Rendell. Berkeley: University of California Press, 1984.

Césaire, Aimé. *Cahier d'un retour au pays natal*. Paris: Editions Présence Africaine, 1983 (first edition 1939).

Chafer, Tony and Amanda Sackur, eds. *Promoting the Colonial Idea: Propaganda and Visions of Empire in France*. London: Palgrave, 2002.

Chailley-Bert, Joseph and le Comte d'Haussonville. *L'Emigration des femmes aux colonies. Allocution de M. le Comte d'Haussonville et discours de M. J. Chailley-Bert à la conférence donnée le 12 janvier 1897 par l'Union coloniale française*. Paris: Armand Colin, 1897.

Chailley-Bert, Joseph. "La Colonisation du Tonkin." *La Quinzaine coloniale* (July 1899): 425-27.

Chatterjee, Partha. *The Nation and its Fragments: Colonial and Postcolonial Histories*. Princeton: Princeton University Press, 1993.

Chester, Suzanne. "Writing the Subject: Exoticism/Eroticism in Marguerite Duras's *The Lover* and *The Sea Wall*." In *Decolonizing the Subject*, edited by Sidonie Smith and Julia Watson, 436-57. Minneapolis: University of Minnesota Press, 1992.

Chivas-Baron, Clotilde. *La Simple histoire des Gaudraix: Roman des mœurs coloniales*. Paris: Flammarion, 1923.

———. *La Femme française aux colonies*. Paris: Larose, 1929.

Chow, Rey. *Writing Diaspora: Tactics of Intervention in Contemporary Cultural Studies*. Bloomington: Indiana University Press, 1993.

———. *Primitive Passions: Visuality, Sexuality, Ethnography, and Contemporary Chinese Cinema*. New York: Columbia University Press, 1995.

Chung, Ook. "Linda Lê, 'Tueuse en dentelles.'" *Liberté* 212 (1994): 155-61.

Claudel, Paul. *Œuvres complètes de Paul Claudel: Tome 4, Extrême-Orient*. Paris: Gallimard, 1952.

Coatalem, Jean-Luc. *Suite indochinoise*. Paris: Le Dilettante, 1999.

Cooper, Nicola. "Urban Planning and Architecture in Colonial Indochina." *French Cultural Studies* 11.1, no. 31 (February 2000): 75-99.

————. "(En)gendering Indochina: Feminisation and Female Figurings in French Colonial Discourses." *Women's Studies International Forum* 23, no. 6 (December 2000): 749-59.

————. "Heroes and Martyrs: the Changing Mythical status of the French Army during the Franco-Indochinese War." In *France at War in the Twentieth Century: Myth, Metaphor, Propaganda*, edited by Valerie Holman and Debra Kelly, 126-41. Oxford: Berghahn, 2000.

————. *France in Indochina: Colonial Encounters*. Oxford/New York: Berg, 2001.

————. "Investigating Indochina: Travel Journalism and France's Civilising Mission." In *Cultural Encounters: European Travel Writing in the 1930s*, edited by Charles Burdett and Derek D. Duncan, 173-85. Oxford: Berghahn, 2002.

————. "French Indochina." In *The Literature of Travel and Exploration: An Encyclopedia*, 468-69. London: Fitzroy Dearborn, 2002.

Copin, Henri. *L'Indochine dans la Littérature Française des années vingt à 1954: Exotisme et altérité*. Paris: L'Harmattan, 1996.

————. *L'Indochine des romans*. Paris/Pondicherry: Kailash Editions, 2000.

Daguerches, Henry. *Le Kilomètre 83*. Paris: Calmann-Lévy, 1913. Reprinted in *Indochine: Un rêve d'Asie*, edited by Alain Quella-Villéger, 104-246. Paris: Omnibus, 1995.

Dalloz, Jacques. "Les Vietnamiens dans la franc-maçonnerie coloniale." *Revue française d'histoire d'outre-mer* 85 (1998): 103-118.

Delaporte, Louis. *Voyage au Cambodge: L'architecture Khmer*. Paris: Librairie Delagrave, 1880.

Del Testa, David W. "'Imperial Corridor': Association, Transportation, and Power in French Colonial Indochina." *Science, Technology, and Society* 4, no. 2 (1999): 319-54.

————. "Some preliminary findings on the relationship of railroads to the economies of Tonkin and Annam Protectorates, French Indochina, 1919-1937." *Research on Vietnam's Quantitative History*, edited by Jean-Pascal Bassino, 63-96. Tokyo: Hitotsubashi University, 2000.

————. "'Paint the Trains Red': Labor, Nationalism, and the Railroads in French colonial Indochina, 1898-1945." Ph.D. thesis, University of California, 2001.

————. "Workers, Culture, and the Railroads in French Colonial Indochina, 1905-1936." *French Colonial History* 2 (2001): 181-98.

D'Esme, Jean. *L'Ame de la brousse*. Paris: J. Ferenczi & Fils, 1923.

Descours-Gatin, Chantal. *Quand l'opium finançait la colonisation en Indochine: l'élaboration de la régie générale de l'opium, 1860 à 1914*. Paris: L'Harmattan, 1992.

Devi, Mahasweta. *Imaginary Maps*. Translated and introduced by Gayatri Chakravorty Spivak. New York: Routledge, 1995.

Do, Tess. "Nourriture ou pourriture: une exploration de l'impact post-colonial du patrimoine français parmi les immigrants vietnamiens dans les romans de Linda Lê." In *Food and Lifestyles in Oceania*, Actes du Colloque CORAIL 2002, edited by Sonia Lacabanne, 141-55. Noumea: 2003.

————. "Entre salut et damnation: métaphores chez Linda Lê." *French Cultural Studies* 15, no. 2 (2004): 142-57.

Dorgelès, Roland. *Sur la route mandarine*. Paris: Albin Michel, 1925. Reprinted Paris/Pondicherry: Editions Kailash, 1997.

Dorsenne, Jean. *Loin des blancs*. Paris: Fayard, 1933.

Doumer, Paul. *Indochine française (souvenirs)*. Paris: Editions Vuibert et Nony, 1905.
Dugast-Portes. Francine. "L'Exotisme dans l'œuvre de Marguerite Duras." In *Le Roman colonial*, 147-57. Paris: L'Harmattan, 1990.
Dương Văn Giáo. "L'Indochine pendant la Guerre de 1914-1918." Ph.D. thesis, Université de Paris, 1925.
Dupaigne, Bernard. *Visages d'Asie*. Paris: Editions Hazan, 2000.
Durand, Maurice. *Imagerie populaire vietnamienne*, Publications de l'Ecole française d'Extrême-Orient 47. Paris: Ecole française d'Extrême Orient, 1960.
Duras, Marguerite (Pseudonym Marguerite Donnadieu) and Philippe Roques. *L'Empire français*. Paris: Gallimard, 1940.
Duras, Marguerite. *Un barrage contre le Pacifique*. Paris: Gallimard, 1950. Translated as *The Sea Wall*, by Herma Briffault, 1952 (several re-editions).
———. *L'Eden cinéma*. Paris: Mercure de France, 1977. Translated in *Marguerite Duras: Four Plays*, by Barbara Bray. London: Oberon Books, 1992.
———. *L'Amant*. Paris: Minuit, 1984. Translated as *The Lover*, by Barbara Bray. London: Bloomsbury Publishing, 1993.
———. *L'Amant de la Chine du Nord*. Paris: Gallimard, 1991. Translated as *The North China Lover*, by Leigh Hafrey. London: Flamingo, 1994.
Durtain, Luc. *Dieux Blancs, Hommes Jaunes*. Paris: Ernest Flammarion, 1930.
Edwards, Penny. "Womanizing Indochina: Fiction, Nation and Cohabitation in Colonial Cambodia, 1890-1930." In *Domesticating the Empire: Race, Gender and Family Life in French and Dutch Colonialism*, edited by Julia Ann Clancy-Smith and Frances Gouda, 108-30. Charlottesville: University of Virginia Press, 1998.
———. "Restyling Colonial Cambodia (1860-1954): French Dressing, Indigenous Custom and National Costume." In *Fashion Theory: The Journal of Dress, Body and Culture* 5, no. 3 (November 2001): 1-28.
———. "'Propa-Gender': Marianne, Joan of Arc and the Export of French Gender Ideology to Colonial Cambodia (1863-1954)." In *Promoting the Colonial Idea: Propaganda and Visions of Empire in France*, edited by Tony Chafer and Amanda Sackur, 116-30. London: Palgrave, 2002.
———. "On Home Ground: Settling Land and Domesticating Difference in the 'Non-Settler'' colonies of Burma and Cambodia." *Journal of Colonialism and Colonial History* 4:3 (2003). http://muse.jhu.edu/journals/journal_of_colonialism_and_colonial_history/v004/4.3edwards.html.
———. "Cambodian Religion and Colonial Elites." In *Cambodian Religion: New Studies*, edited by John Marston and Elizabeth Guthrie. Honolulu: Hawai'i University Press, 2004, forthcoming.
Fanon, Frantz. *Peau noire, masques blancs*. Paris: Seuil, 1952. Translated as *Black Skin, White Masks*, by Charles Lam Markmann. New York: Grove Press, 1967.
———. *Les Damnés de la terre*. Paris: Maspéro, 1961. Translated as *The Wretched of the Earth*, by Constance Farrington. New York: Grove Press, 1963.
Farrère, Claude. *Les Civilisés*. Paris: Librairie Paul Ollendorff, 1905. Reprinted Paris/Pondicherry: Kailash Editions, 1993; in *Indochine: Un rêve d'Asie*, edited by Alain Quella-Villéger, 247-408. Paris: Omnibus, 1995.
———. *L'Inde Perdue*. Paris: Flammarion, 1935. Reprinted Paris/Pondicherry: Kailash Editions, 1998.
Fournier, Christiane. *Perspectives occidentales sur l'Indochine*. Saigon: La Nouvelle Revue Indochinoise, 1935.

Franchini, Philippe, ed. *Saigon 1925-1945 De la "Belle Colonie" à l'éclosion révolutionnaire ou la fin des dieux blancs.* Paris: Editions Autrement, 1992.

Fridenson, Patrick. *The French Home Front, 1914-1918.* Oxford: Berg, 1992.

Gaffarel, Paul. *L'Algérie et les colonies françaises: lectures géographiques et historiques.* Paris: Garnier, 1888.

Gantès de, Gilles. "La Population française au Tonkin entre 1931 et 1938." Mémoire de maîtrise, Paris, 1981.

————. "Coloniaux, gouverneurs et ministres. L'influence des Français du Viêt-Nam sur l'évolution du pays à l'époque coloniale 1902-1914." Dissertation, Paris VII, 1994.

Garane, Jeanne. "Cette Enfant Blanche de l'Asie: Orientalism, Colonialism, and Métissage in Marguerite Duras's *L'Amant.*" In *French Cultural Studies: Criticism at the Crossroads,* edited by Marie-Pierre Le Hir, 233-52. Albany, New York: State University of New York Press, 2000.

Genlis, Marcel. *Dans l'Incendie Tropicale: Angkor-Java-Burma-India (octobre 1912-mars 1913).* Paris: Librairie Plon, 1914.

Gfeller, Aurélie. "Communauté allogène européenne en Indochine française 1920-1939. Clivages et rapports de force." Mémoire de maîtrise, Lausanne, 2000.

Gillis, John, ed. *Commemorations: the Politics of National Identity.* Princeton: Princeton University Press, 1994.

Girardet, Raoul. *L'Idée coloniale en France.* Paris: La Table Ronde, 1972.

Goscha, Christopher. *Vietnam or Indochina? Contesting Concepts of Space in Vietnamese nationalism, 1887-1954.* Copenhagen: NIAS, 1995.

Graziano, Frank. *Alejandra Pizarnik: A Profile.* Durango, Co: Logbridge-Rhodes, 1987.

Groslier, Georges. *La Route du plus fort.* Paris: Emile-Paul Frères, 1925. Reprinted Paris/ Pondicherry: Editions Kailash, 1997.

————. *Le Retour à l'argile.* Paris: Emile-Paul Frères, 1929. Reprinted Paris/ Pondicherry: Editions Kailash, 1994.

Guillaume, Pierre. "Les Métis en Indochine." *Annales de Démographie historique* (1995): 185-95.

Guillemet, Eugène. *Sur les sentiers laotiens.* Hanoi-Haiphong: Imprimerie d'Extrême-Orient, 1921.

Ha, Marie-Paule. "Engendering French Colonial History: The Case of Indochina." *Historical Reflections/Réflexions historiques* 25, no. 1 (1999): 95-125.

————. "Durasie: Women, Natives, and Other." In *Revisioning Duras: Film, Race, Sex,* edited by James S. Williams, 95-111. Liverpool: University of Liverpool Press, 2000.

————. *Figuring the East: Segalen, Malraux, Duras, and Barthes.* New York: State University of New York Press, 2000.

————. "The Theme of Exile in Indochinese Return Narratives." *Mots Pluriels* (April 2001): http://www.arts.uwa.edu.au/MotsPluriels/MP1701index.html

————. "From 'nos ancetres les Gaulois' to 'leur culture ancestrale': Symbolic Violence and the Politics of Colonial Schooling in Indochina." *French Colonial History* 3 (2002): 101-18.

————. "Vietnamese Diaspora in France." *Contemporary French Civilization* 27, no. 2 (2003): 253-76.

————. "The Portrait of the Young Woman as a *Coloniale.*" In *Empire and Culture: the French Experience, 1830-1940,* edited by Martin Evans and Amanda Sackur, 161-80. London: Palgrave Macmillan, 2004.

224 SELECTED BIBLIOGRAPHY

Hargreaves, Alec G. "Ethnic difference in post-war France." In *Immigrant Narratives in Contemporary France*, edited by Susan Ireland and Patrice J. Proulx, 7-22. Westport, Conn./London: Greenwood Press, 2001.

Hayes, Jarrod. *Queer Nations: Marginal Sexualities in the Mahgreb*. Chicago: University of Chicago Press, 2000.

Heung, Marina. "The Family Romance of Orientalism: From *Madame Butterfly* to *Indochine*." In *Visions of the East: Orientalism in Film*, edited by Matthew Bernstein and Gaylyn Studlar, 158-83. New Brunswick: Rutgers University Press, 1997.

Holmlund, Christine. "Disrupting Limits of Difference." *Quarterly Review of Film and Video*, 13, nos. 1-3 (1991): 1-22.

Hougron, Jean. *Mort en fraude*. Paris: Domat, 1953. Reprinted Paris: Laffont, 1989. Translated as *The Fugitive*, by Mervyn Savill. London: Hurst & Blackett, 1955.

———. *Les Asiates*. Paris: Domat, 1954. Reprinted Paris: Laffont, 1989.

Hsieh, Yvonne Y. "L'évolution du discours (anti-)colonialiste dans *Un barrage contre le Pacifique*, *L'Amant* et *L'Amant de la Chine du Nord* de Marguerite Duras." *Dalhousie French Studies*, 35 (1996): 55-65.

Hùynh Kim Khánh. *Vietnamese Communism, 1925-1945*. Ithaca: Cornell University Press, 1982.

Jacnal, Jean. *Rêves d'Annam*. Paris: A. Challamel, 1913.

Jay, Madeleine and Antoine. *Notre Indochine 1936-1947*. Paris: Presses de Valmy, 1994.

Jeancolas, Jean-Pierre. "L'Odeur de la papaye verte: Un Viêt-nam mental." *Positif* (July-August 1993): 22-23.

Jennings, Eric. *Vichy in the Tropics: Pétain's National Revolution in Madagascar, Guadeloupe and Indochina, 1940-1944*. Stanford: Stanford University Press, 2002.

———. "From Indochine to Indochic: The Dalat Palace Hotel and French Colonial Leisure, Power and Culture." *Modern Asian Studies* 37, no. 1 (February 2003): 159-94.

———. "Conservative Confluences, 'Nativist' Synergy: Reinscribing Vichy's National Revolution in Indochina." *French Historical Studies* (June 2004), forthcoming.

———. "L'Indochine de l'Amiral Decoux." In *L'Empire de Vichy*, edited by Jacques Cantier and Eric Jennings. Paris: Odile Jacob, 2004, forthcoming.

Joyeux, André. *La Vie large des colonies*. Paris: Maurice Bauche, 1912.

Jung, Eugène. *La Vie européenne au Tonkin*. Paris: Flammarion, 1901.

Katz, Joseph, ed. *The Poems of Stephen Crane*. New York: Cooper Square Publishers, 1966.

Kennedy, Dane. *Islands of White: Settler Society and Culture in Kenya and Southern Rhodesia, 1890-1939*. Durham: Duke University Press, 1987.

———. *The Magic Mountains: Hill Stations and the British Raj*. Berkeley: University of California Press, 1996.

Knapman, Claudia. *White Women in Fiji 1835-1930: The Ruin of Empire?* Sydney: Allen & Unwin, 1986.

Knibiehler, Yvonne and Régine Goutalier. *La Femme aux temps des colonies*. Paris: Stock, 1985.

La Baume, Christian de. *La Fin de l'ère coloniale en Indochine: une vue politique, économique, sociale et culturelle*. Taulignan: Éditions du Regard, 1982.

Lê, Hữu Khoá. *La Part d'exil*. Provence: Publications de l'Université de Provence, 1995.

Lé, Lam. "La petite Cosette du delta du Mékong." *Libération*, June 9, 1993, 42-43.

Lê, Linda. *Un si tendre vampire*. Paris: Table Ronde, 1987.

———. *Fuir*. Paris: Table Ronde, 1988.

———. *Calomnies*. Paris: Christian Bourgois, 1993. Translated as *Slander* by Esther Allen. Lincoln: Nebraska University Press, 1995.

————. *Les Dits d'un idiot*. Paris: Christian Bourgois, 1995.

————. *Les Trois Parques*. Paris: Christian Bourgois, 1997.

————. *Tu écriras sur le bonheur*. Paris: Presses Universitaires, 1999.

————. *Kriss*. Paris: Christian Bourgois, 2004.

Lebovics, Herman. *True France: The Wars over Cultural Identity, 1900-1945*. Ithaca: Cornell University Press, 1992.

Le May, Reginald. *An Asian Arcady: The Land and Peoples of Northern Siam*. Bangkok: White Lotus Co., 1986.

Leuba, Jeanne. *L'Aile du feu*. Paris: Plon-Nourrit, 1926.

Lim-Hing, Sharon Julie. "Vietnamese Novels in French: Rewriting, Self, Gender and Nation." Ph.D. thesis, Harvard University, 1993.

Lionnet, Françoise. *Postcolonial Representations: Women, Literature, Identity*. Ithaca, NY: Cornell University Press, 1995.

Loti, Pierre. *Pêcheur d'Islande*. Paris: Calmann Levy, 1893. Reprinted Paris: Booking International/Classiques français, 1994.

————. *Un Pèlerin d'Angkor*. Paris: Calmann-Lévy, 1912. Reprinted Paris/Pondicherry: Kailash, 1994.

Maitam, Jean-Jacques. *A House Divided (Viet Nam)*. Greensboro: Tudor Books, 2002.

Malleret, Louis. *L'Exotisme indochinois dans la littérature française depuis 1860*. Paris: Larose, 1934.

Malraux, André. *La Voie royale*. Paris: Grasset, 1930. *The Royal Way*, translated by Stuart Gilbert. New York: Random House, 1955.

Mani. "En Indochine avec le ministre." *Le Monde colonial illustré*, 99 (November 1931): 245-46.

Marks, Laura U. *The Skin of the Film: Intercultural cinema, embodiment, and the Senses*. Durham, North Carolina: Duke University Press, 2000.

Marr, David. "The 1920s Women's Rights Debates in Vietnam." *Journal of Asian Studies*, 35, no. 3 (May 1976).

————. "A Passion for Modernity: Intellectuals and the Media." In *Postwar Vietnam: Dynamics of a Transforming So*ciety, edited by Hy Văn Lương, 257-95. Singapore: Rowman & Littlefield Publishers, 2003.

Maspéro, Georges, ed. *Un Empire Colonial Français: L'Indochine*. Paris: Les Editions G.Van Oest, 1930.

Mayne, Judith. "Paradoxes of Spectatorship." In *Viewing Positions: Ways of Seeing Film*, edited by Linda Williams, 155-83. New Brunswick: Rutgers University Press, 1995.

McClintock, Anne. *Imperial Leather: Race, Gender and Sexuality in the Colonial Context*. New York: Routledge, 1995.

McHale, Shawn. *Print and Power: Confucianism, Communism and Buddhism in the Making of Modern Vietnam*. Honolulu: University of Hawai'i Press, 2003.

McNab, Geoffrey. "Good Afternoon Vietnam." *Sight & Sound* 8 (2001): 27-28.

Memmi, Albert. *Portrait du colonisé précédé du portrait du colonisateur*. Paris: Buchet/Chastel, 1957. Translated by Howard Greenfeld as *The Colonizer and the Colonized*. Boston: Beacon Press, 1965.

Mouhot, Henri. *Travels in Siam, Cambodge and Laos 1858-1860*. Singapore: Oxford University Press, 1989.

Mulvey, Laura. *Visual and Other Pleasures*. Bloomington: Indiana University Press, 1989.

Naficy, Hamid. *An Accented Cinema: Exilic and Diasporic Filmmaking*. Princeton/ Oxford: Princeton University Press, 2001.

Nguyễn Văn Huy and Laurel Kendall, eds. *Vietnam: Journeys of Body, Mind, and Spirit*. Berkeley: University of California Press, 2003.

Nguyễn, Văn Ký. "La Société vietnamienne face à la Modernité: Le Tonkin de la fin du XIXe siècle à la seconde guerre mondiale," *Recherches asiatiques*, edited by Alain Forest, 193-228. Paris: Harmattan, 1995.

Nguyễn, Xuân Thu, ed. *Vietnamese Studies in a Multicultural World*. Melbourne: Vietnamese Language & Culture Publications, 1994.

Nicholson, Melanie. *Evil, Madness, and the Occult in Argentine Poetry*. Gainsville: University of Florida Press, 2002.

Ninh, Kim. *A World Transformed: The Politics of Culture in Revolutionary Vietnam, 1945-1965*. Ann Arbor, University of Michigan, 2002.

Norindr, Panivong. *Phantasmatic Indochina: French Colonial Ideology in Architecture, Film, and Literature*. Durham, NC: Duke University Press, 1996.

Ollier, Leakthina Chau-Pech. "Consuming Culture: Linda Lê's Autofiction." In *Of Vietnam: Identities in Dialogue*, edited by Jane Bradley Winston and Leakthina Chau-Pech Ollier, 241-50. New York: Palgrave, 2001.

Osborne, Milton. *From Conviction to Anxiety: Reassessing the French Self-Image in Viet-Nam*. Flinders: Flinders University Asian Studies Lectures, 1976.

———. *Fear and Fascination in the Tropics: A Reader's Guide to French Fiction on Indochina*. Madison: University of Wisconsin, 1986.

———. *The Mekong: Turbulent past, uncertain future*. Sydney: Allen and Unwin, 2000.

Pascal, Michel. "Cyclo Driver." *Le Point*, September 23, 1995.

Pégard, Mme. "La Société d'émigration des femmes 'une année d'existence.'" *La Quinzaine coloniale* (January, 1898): 40-44.

———. "Société française d'émigration des femmes." In *2ᵉ congrès international des œuvres et institutions féminines tenu au Palais des Congrès de l'Exposition Universelle de 1900. Compte rendu des travaux par Mme Pégard*, vol. II, 236-44. Paris: Imprimerie Typographique Charles Blot, 1902.

Persell, Stuart M. *The French Colonial Lobby, 1899-1914*. Dissertation, Stanford University, 1969. Ann Arbor: UMI, 1970.

———. "Joseph Chailley-Bert and the Importance of the *Union coloniale française*." *The Historical Journal* 17, no. 1 (1974): 176-84.

Peters, Erica. "Negotiating power through everyday practices in French Vietnam, 1880-1924." Ph.D. thesis, University of Chicago, 2000.

Peycam, Philippe. *Intellectuals and political commitment in Vietnam: the emergence of a public sphere in colonial Saigon (1916-1928)*. Ph.D. thesis, University of London, School of Oriental and African Studies, 1999.

Piolet, Jean-Baptiste. *La France hors de France*. Paris: Félix Alcan éditeurs, 1900.

Pratt, Marie Louise. *Imperial Eyes: Travel Writing and Transculturation* (New York: Routledge, 1992).

Quella-Villéger, Alain. *Indochine: Un rêve d'Asie*. Paris: Omnibus, 1995.

Raffin, Anne. "Easternization Meets Westernization: Patriotic Youth Organizations in French Indochina during World War II." *French Politics, Culture, and Society* 20, no. 2 (2002): 121-40.

———. "The Integration of Difference in French Indochina During World War Two: Organizations and Ideology Concerning Youth." *Theory and Society* 31, no. 3 (2002): 365-90.

Rondet-Saint,Maurice. *Choses de l'Indochine contemporaine*. Paris: Librarie Plon, 1916.

Rondet-Saint, Maurice. *Choses de l'Indochine contemporaine*. Paris: Plon, 1916.

Said, Edward. *Orientalism*. New York: Pantheon, 1978.

Sherman, Daniel. *The Construction of Memory in Interwar France.* Chicago: University of Chicago Press, 1999.

Sherzer, Dina. "Introduction." In *Cinema, Colonialism, Postcolonialism: Perspectives from the French and Francophone Worlds,* edited by Dina Sherzer, 1-19. Austin: University of Texas Press, 1996.

Spivak, Gayatri Chakravorty. "Can the Subaltern Speak?" In *Marxism and the Interpretation of Culture,* edited by Cary Nelson and Lawrence Grossberg, 271-313. Urbana: University of Illinois Press, 1988.

———. *In Other Worlds: Essays in Cultural Politics.* New York: Methuen, 1987.

———. "Practical Politics of the Open End." In *The Post-Colonial Critic: Interviews, Strategies, Dialogues,* 95-112. New York/London: Routledge, 1990.

Spurr, David. *The Rhetoric of Empire: Colonial Discourse in Journalism, Travel Writing and Imperial Administration.* Durham: Duke University Press, 1994.

Steinberg, David Joel, ed. *In Search of Southeast Asia: A Modern History.* Honolulu: University of Hawai'i Press, 1987 (first edition 1971).

Stilgoe, John R. *Metropolitan Corridor: Railroads and the American Scene* (New Haven/London: Yale University Press, 1983.

Stoler, Ann. *Carnal Knowledge and Imperial Power: Race and the Intimate in Colonial Rule.* Berkeley: University of California Press, 2002.

Strobel, Margaret. *European Women and the Second British Empire.* Bloomington: University of Indiana Press, 1991.

Stuart-Fox, Martin. *A History of Laos.* Cambridge: Cambridge University Press, 1997.

Suleri, Sara. *The Rhetoric of English India.* Chicago: University of Chicago Press, 1992.

Tai, Hue-Tam Ho. *Radicalism and the Origins of the Vietnamese Revolution.* Cambridge: Harvard University Press, 1992.

Thompson, Andrew O. "Vicious Cycle." *American Cinematographer* 77, no. 9 (September 1996): 62-68.

Tô, Ngọc Văn. *Chemins de fer de l'Indochine* (Hanoi: G. Taupin et Cie., 1928).

Trémolot, Laurence and Tran Anh Hung. *Cyclo.* Paris: Actes Sud, 1995.

Trương Bửu Lâm. *Colonialism Experienced: Vietnamese Writings on Colonialism, 1900-1931.* Ann Arbor: University of Michigan, 2000.

Vann, Michael. "Of Rats, Rice, and Race: The Great Hanoi Rat Massacre, an Episode in French Colonial History." *French Colonial History Society* 4 (May 2003): 191-203.

———. "The Good, the Bad, and The Ugly: Variation and Difference in French Racial Thinking in Colonial Vietnam." In *The Color of Liberty: The History of Race in France,* edited by Tyler Stovall and Sue Peabody, 187-205. Durham: Duke University Press, 2003.

———. "'All the World's a Stage', Especially in the Colonies: L'Exposition de Hanoi, 1902-1903." In *Culture and Empire: The French Experience,* edited by Martin Evans, 181-91. London: Macmillan, 2004.

Viện, Nguyễn Khắc. *Vietnam: A Long History.* Hanoi: Thế Giới Publishers, 1999.

Vincent, Thierry. *Pierre Dieulefils, photographe-éditeur de cartes postales d'Indochine.* Aix-en-Provence: T. Vincent, 1997.

Viollis, Andrée. *SOS Indochine.* Paris: Gallimard, 1935.

Walls, Jean Marie Turcotte. "Narrative and Representation in French colonial Indochina." Ph.D thesis, Louisiana State University, 1994.

Waters, Julia. "'La traversée du fleuve': Representations of the Mekong in Marguerite Duras's Post-colonial Works." *Bulletin of the Society of Francophone Postcolonial Studies* (Autumn-Winter 2002): 98-115.

————. "Marguerite Duras and Colonialist Discourse: An Intertextual Reading of *L'Empire français* and *Un barrage contre le Pacifique*." *Forum for Modern Language Studies* 39, no. 3 (July 2003): 254-66.

————. "Colonial Undercurrents: The Motif of the Mekong in Marguerite Duras's 'Indochinese' Texts." In *Francophone Postcolonial Studies: A Critical Introduction*, edited by Charles Forsdick and David Murphy, 253-62. London/New York: Arnold, 2003.

————. "Contextualising 'Métissage' in Duras's Indochinese Novels." *Francophone Postcolonial Studies* 2, no. 1 (Spring 2004): 79-82.

Winston, Jane Bradley. *Postcolonial Duras: Cultural Memory in Postwar France*. New York/Basingstoke: Palgrave, 2001.

————. *Of Vietnam: Identities in Dialogue*. New York/Basingstoke: Palgrave, 2001.

Wood, Jason, "A Quick Chat with Tran Anh Hung." <http://www.kamera.co.uk/interviews/trananhhung.html> (1 October 2004).

Yeager, Jack A. "'Préceptes de vie': Religious Syncretism in Vietnamese Francophone Literature." *Revue francophone de Louisiane* 1, no. 1 (Spring 1986): 36-49.

————. "Cultural Others in the Vietnamese Francophone Novel." *Notebooks in Cultural Analysis* 3 (1986): 134-67.

————. "Cultural Production in a Colonial Context: Vietnamese Literature in French." *The Vietnam Forum* 9 (Winter/Spring 1987): 92-110.

————. *The Vietnamese Novel in French: A Literary Response to Colonialism*. Hanover/London: University Press of New England, 1987.

————. "Bach Mai's Francophone Eurasian Voice: Remapping Margin and Center." *Québec Studies* 14 (Spring/Summer 1992): 49-64.

————. "Retour à la saison des pluies: Rediscovering the Landscapes of Childhood." *L'Esprit Créateur* 33, no. 2 (Summer 1993): 47-57.

————. "La Politique 'intimiste': la production romanesque des écrivaines vietnamiennes francophones." *Présence francophone* 43 (1993): 131-47.

————. "Blurring the Lines in Vietnamese Fiction in French: Kim Lefèvre's *Métisse blanche*," in *Post Colonial Subjects: Francophone Women Writers*, edited by Mary Jean Green, Karen Gould, Micheline Rice-Maximin, Keith L. Walker and Jack A. Yeager, 210-26. Minneapolis: University of Minnesota Press, 1996.

————. "Culture, Citizenship, Nation: The Narrative Texts of Linda Lê." In *Postcolonial Cultures in France*, edited by Alec G. Hargreaves and Mark McKinney, 255-67. New York: Routledge, 1997.

————. "Colonialism and Power in Marguerite Duras's *L'Amant*." In *Of Vietnam: Identities in Dialogue*, edited by Jane Bradley Winston and Leakthina Chau-Pech Ollier, 224-35. New York: Palgrave, 2001.

Yee, Jennifer. *Clichés de la femme exotique: un regard sur la littérature coloniale française entre 1871 et 1914*. Paris: L'Harmattan, 2000.

————. "Colonial Virility and the Femme fatale: Scenes from the Battle of the Sexes in French Indochina." *French Studies, A Quarterly Review* 54, no. 4 (October 2000): 469-78.

————. "'L'Indochine androgyne': the Curious Theme of Androgyny in Turn-of-the-century French Writing on 'Indochina.'" *Textual Practice* 15, no. 2 (Summer 2001): 269-82.

Zinoman, Peter. *The Colonial Bastille: a History of Imprisonment in Vietnam, 1862-1940*. Berkeley: University of California Press, 2001.

Name Index

Abbatucci, S, 104, 106n19
Ageron, Charles-Robert, 45n8,
107, 119n7
Ajalbert, Jean, 50, 84, 85, 93n11,
93n12, 93n13, 99, 106n13,
106n16
Aldrich, Robert, 44n4, 45n11, 61n3
Angladette, André, 41, 42, 43,
75n28
Annaud, Jean-Jacques, 9, 10, 154
Aragon, Isabelle, 33, 44n3, 45n14,
45n16, 45n17, 45n18, 45n19

Bahktin, Mikhail, 193, 194, 195,
205n12, 205n14, 205n15
Baille, Frédéric, 106n5, 106n9
Bảo Đại, 7
Barquissau, Raphaël, 6, 11n18
Bataille, Christophe, 3
Baudelaire, Charles, 52, 61n8
Bert, Paul, 98
Bhabha, Homi, 132, 138n36

Blanchard, Pascal, 11n19
Blanche, Charles and Gabriel, 20,
21, 22
Bodard, Lucien, 8, 11n21
Boissière, Jules, 5, 87, 93n22,
94n29, 98
Bonaparte, Roland (Prince), 16
Bonnetain, Paul, 5
Borel, Marius, 98, 106n12
Bouchareb, Rachid, 155
Boudarel, Georges, 8, 11n23
Bouilleveaux, Charles-Emile, 4
Bousquet, Gisèle, 217n4
Bredier, Sophie, 155
Britto, Karl Ashoka, 217n4
Brocheux, Pierre, 1, 2, 10n2, 10n3,
11n23, 11n26, 179, 189n3,
189n4, 190n12, 191n21
Bùi, Henriette, 127, 137n23,
137n24
Bùi, Madeleine, 127
Bùi Quang Chiêu, 127

Contributors' Details

Lily V. Chiu, Visiting Assistant Professor of Literature at Hampshire College, received her Ph.D. in Comparative Literature from the University of Michigan, Ann Arbor. Her research traces the trajectory of colonial, postcolonial and neo-colonial ideology in contemporary Francophone and Vietnamese literature and film, focusing on the figure of the native woman and questions of self-identification.

Nicola Cooper is Senior Lecturer (U.S. Associate Professor) in French at the University of Bristol. She has published extensively on French colonialism and Indochina and is the author of *France in Indochina: Colonial Encounters* (2001). She is currently producing a critical edition of Albert Sarraut's *Grandeur et servitude coloniales*, and is working on a new book about cultural representations of the French Foreign Legion.

David Del Testa is Assistant Professor of History at Bucknell University in Lewisburg, Pennsylvania. He has worked extensively with materials related to colonial Indochina at archives and libraries and from oral histories in Vietnam and France and he is preparing a book manuscript entitled *"Paint the Trains Red": Labor, Nationalism, and the Railroads in French Indochina, 1905-1945*.

Tess Do is Lecturer (U.S. Assistant Professor) in French at the University of Melbourne, Australia. Her doctoral dissertation focuses on the women laureates of the Prix Goncourt and the Prix Femina. Her current research centers on contemporary Vietnamese francophone authors and she has published articles on Linda Lê. She is currently working on a major research project on the Vietnamese diaspora and the representation of homeland in the works of Jean Vanmai, Anna Moï, Thu Vân Mai, Kim Lefèvre, Ly Thu Ho and Trần Anh Hùng.

Penny Edwards is a Research Fellow at the Centre for Cross-Cultural Research, Australian National University. She has published widely on questions of identity, gender and ethnicity in French Cambodia, British Burma, and Chinese diaspora. Her book *Cambodge: The Cultivation of a Nation, 1860-1945* is forthcoming with Hawai'i University Press, and she is currently researching a biography of the French Orientalist Suzanne Karpelès.

Marie-Paule Ha teaches in the History department at the University of Hong Kong, Pokfulam. She is the author of *Figuring the East: Segalen, Malraux, Duras, and Barthes* (2000), as well as numerous articles on Indochinese history, education and women in Indochina, the Vietnamese diaspora, Duras and Indochinese literature.

Judith Henchy is the Head of the Southeast Asia Section of the University of Washington Libraries. In this capacity she has a number of projects with Libraries in Vietnam. She is currently completing a Ph.D. in the University of Washington History Department focusing on the writings of Southern intellectuals Nguyễn An Ninh and Phan Văn Hùm in the 1920s and 1930s. She has published several articles on archival issues and preservation in Vietnam, as well as a history of the National Library of Vietnam.

Eric T. Jennings is Associate Professor of History at the University of Toronto. His publications concerning Indochina include a book: *Vichy in the Tropics: Pétain's National Revolution in Madagascar, Guadeloupe and Indochina, 1940-1944* (2001), as well as several articles and chapters on Indochina in the 1940s. He is currently working on a history of French colonial Dalat.

Christopher Robinson is Professor of European Literature at Christ Church, Oxford. His work is principally concerned with the interface between identity, marginalization and representation. His books include *Lucian and his Influence in Europe* (1979), *C.P. Cavafy* (1988), and *Scandal in the Ink: Male and Female Homosexuality in Twentieth-Century French Literature* (1995).

Kathryn Robson is Lecturer (U.S. tenured Assistant Professor) in French at the University of Newcastle, United Kingdom. She is the author of *Writing Wounds: The Inscription of Trauma in post-1968 French Women's Life-writing* (2004) and several articles on contemporary French women's writing, trauma and loss.

Carrie Tarr is a Research Fellow in the Faculty of Arts and Social Sciences, Kingston University, United Kingdom. She has written extensively on gender and ethnicity in French cinema. Her recent publications include *Cinema and the Second Sex: Women's Filmmaking in France in the 1980s and 1990s* (with B. Rollet, 2001), *Women, Immigration and Identities* (co-edited with J. Freedman, 2000) and *Reframing Difference: Beur and banlieue cinema in France* (2005).

Michael G. Vann earned his Ph.D. in History at the University of California and now teaches at Santa Clara University and the U.S. Naval Postgraduate School. He specializes in the history of Hanoi under French rule, but also works on wider issues of colonial history. He has published several articles on colonial history, the history of race, film and colonial history, colonialism in Hawai'i, and the French presence in colonial Indochina.

Julia Waters is Lecturer (U.S. tenured Assistant Professor) in French at the University of Bath. She is the author of *Intersexual Rivalry: a "Reading in Pairs" of Marguerite Duras and Alain Robbe-Grillet* (2000) and of numerous articles, particularly on Duras, francophone literature, and (post)colonialism. She is currently working on a book called *Duras and Indochina: Postcolonial Perspectives*, due out in 2005.

Jane Bradley Winston is an Associate Professor of French and Italian and Gender Studies at Northwestern University. She is the author of *Postcolonial Duras: Cultural Memory in Postwar France* (2001) and co-editor, *with* Leakthina Chau-Peck Ollier, of *Of Vietnam: Identities in Dialogue* (2001). She has also presented papers and published articles relevant to Indochina, including a forthcoming essay on its cultural circulation in the global era.

Jack A. Yeager is Professor of French Studies and Women's & Gender Studies at Louisiana State University in Baton Rouge. His publications include *The Vietnamese Novel in French: A Literary Response to Colonialism* (1987) and *Postcolonial Subjects: Francophone Women Writers* (co-editor, 1996) as well as several articles and book chapters on Francophone writers from Vietnam.

Jennifer Yee was Senior Lecturer (U.S. Associate Professor) in French at the University of Newcastle (United Kingdom) and is now a Fellow in Oxford (Christ Church). She is the author of *Clichés de la femme exotique: un regard sur la littérature coloniale française* (2000) and of several articles on colonial literature, including some on Indochina. She is currently writing a book on subversion in nineteenth-century exotic writing.